The Sociology of Criminal Law:
Evolution of Deviance in
Anglo-American Society

Robert M. Rich
Consulting Criminologist
Alexandria, Virginia

BUTTERWORTHS
Toronto

CANADA: BUTTERWORTH & CO. (CANADA) LTD.
                   TORONTO: 2265 Midland Avenue,
                             Scarborough, M1P 4S1

UNITED KINGDOM: BUTTERWORTH & CO. (Publishers) LTD.
                   LONDON: 88 KINGSWAY, WC2B 6AB

AUSTRALIA: BUTTERWORTH PTY. LTD.
                   SYDNEY: 586 Pacific Highway, Chatswood,
                             NSW 2067
                   MELBOURNE: 343 Little Collins Street,
                             3000
                   BRISBANE: 240 Queen Street, 4000

NEW ZEALAND: BUTTERWORTHS OF NEW ZEALAND
                   LTD.
                   WELLINGTON: 77-85 Custom House
                             Quay, 1

SOUTH AFRICA: BUTTERWORTH & CO. (SOUTH AFRICA)
                   (PTY.) LTD.
                   DURBAN: 152/154 Gale Street

Canadian Cataloguing in Publication Data

Rich, Robert M.
  The sociology of criminal law

ISBN 0-409-86220-7

1. Sociological jurisprudence. 2. Criminal law.
3. Deviant behaviour. I. Title.

K370.R53   340.1'15   C79-094701-3

Table of Contents

Acknowledgments

I would like to thank May Thompson for her patience and persistence at the task of typing the manuscript of this book.

Thanks also to Eileen Phillips, Diana Carswell, and Pam Caldarone for their work as proofreaders and content editors.

Preface

This text traces the evolution of criminal law theory and practice in Anglo-American society. Part I of the book deals with sociology of criminal law theory. It deals specifically with key theorists and their theories (i.e., structural-functional or consensus, conflict, the Chicago School of criminology, and the paradigmatic approach to criminological theory building).

Part II of the text examines the criminal law and societal deviance. Tracing the evolution of specific areas of societal deviance in both English and American societies (i.e., sexual, domestic, gambling, and drugs), this part of the book examines the origin of specific criminal laws, the modifications of the various statutes in both English and American societies, law enforcement policies, and problems caused by the overcriminalization and decriminalization of deviant behavior.

The text examines two major problems concerning the study of the evolution of criminal law in society. Firstly, the difficulty of developing an adequate paradigm to explain how society and its institutions function over time. Secondly, there is the difficulty of tracing the response of society to specific types of deviance over time and space. In particular, one must attempt to compare legislative action in a centralized society (i.e., England) with a decentralized society (i.e., the United States). This is made all the more difficult since each sovereign state in America has tended to have its own interpretation of the Common Law tradition.

Robert M. Rich

Part I

Sociology of Criminal Law Theory

Chapter 1

Structural-functional Theory

Introduction

The majority of sociology of criminal law theorists from the classical period of the late nineteenth century up until the early 1960s have been adherents to structural-functional theory.[1] Criminal law theorists believe that the law is a social norm and a form of social control. Human beings are perceived as manipulated by normative systems (i.e., value-attitudes) and social control agencies (i.e., police, courts, and mass media/ family influences). There is also agreement among structural-functional theorists that the source of control over the individual lies within the societal social structure and institutions which are coercive in nature.[2]

These theorists accept the conception that society consists of either individuals who willingly accept societal norms for the sake of societal stability or those who are pathological and/or anomic and collide with the structures and institutions of a stable society in an attempt to cause conflict and disorder. Thus structural-functionalists tend to have a conservative societal orientation (i.e., de-emphasize social change) and justify the status quo (i.e., that society is orderly and predictable over space and time).

Durkheim

Durkheim, in his book *Division of Labor in Society,* feels that crime is a necessary societal component and its presence allows for the evolution of criminal law. He maintains that the kind and degree of punishment and the rationale behind sanctions have varied according to societal organizational structure (i.e., homogeneous undifferentiated and advanced differentiated urban societal types).[3]

In the homogeneous undifferentiated type of society, punishment is meant to protect and preserve social solidarity. Punishment is a mechanical reaction to preserve social solidarity, and there is no concern with offender rehabilitation. The wrongdoer is punished as an example to the community that deviance will not be tolerated. In the advanced and differentiated urban type of society, punishment is focused upon the individual and deals with restitution and reparations (i.e., harm done to the victim). Crimes are thought of as acts which offend others and not the collective conscience of the community. Punishment is evaluated in terms of what is good and proper for the individual, and is therefore applied to the offender in order to reform him.[4]

Durkheim's concept of anomie is an attempt to explain crime in the advanced and differentiated urban society. Heterogeneity and increased division of labor weaken traditional societal norms and the resultant social changes loosen the social controls upon people allowing the development of a cult of materialism and individualism. This type of environment is conducive to producing crime and antisocial behavior on a large scale. Thus a society, where social cohesion has broken down and social isolation is great, loses its traditional social control mechanisms and eventually suffers from a high rate of crime.[5]

Luden and Gurvitch in separate essays concerning Durkheim's sociology of criminal law state that Durkheim is concerned with the relationship between forms of sociality (i.e., solidarity) and kinds of law found in societal types. Accordingly penal law corresponds to what Durkheim calls mechanical solidarity (i.e., Gemeinschaft-like society) while family, contractual, commercial, administrative, and constitutional law correspond to organic solidarity (i.e., Gesellschaft-like society). Law arising from mechanical solidarity is accompanied by repressive sanctions while law arising from organic solidarity is accompanied by restitutive sanctions.[6]

Equality, liberty, and justice as legal concepts evolved with the rise of organic solidarity according to Durkheim. The modern state is an equalitarian association of collaboration that favors contractual relations and affirms individual law. Durkheim also concerns himself with the relations between forms of sociality (i.e., solidarity) and kinds of law found in different legal systems. Thus he has studied different types of societies utilizing anthropological data and has attempted to correlate the development of a particular legal system with the development of a particular societal type.[7]

Hall

Hall has attempted to determine the relationship between legal changes and value changes in society through an analysis of the law of theft. He expresses four theories concerning sociology of criminal law: (1) the functioning of courts is related to accompanying cultural needs. This applies to both procedural and substantive law. (2) Legal change follows a definite order. First a lag occurs between the substantive law and the social needs of society followed by an attempt by judges, officials, and laymen to make adaptations (i.e., use of legal fictions). The last step in legal change is the enactment of new legislation to eliminate the lag. (3) Technicality and legal fiction function both to link the old law to the new and as indexes to solutions of societal legal problems between social orders. (4) Sociology of criminal law is represented by the "law process" of the norm-oriented and directed conduct of large sectors of a societal population.[8]

Allen

Allen feels that the concentration of interests on the nature and needs of the criminal law has resulted in an absence of concern with the nature of crime. The behavioral scientist has all but forgotten how to deal with the types of behavior that should be declared criminal.[9] Allen states there has been a systematic lack of attention to the substantive criminal law which is due to the Positivist bias against authoritative rules in any form and which even challenges the reality of such rules. Instead of considering the law as a set of rules or authoritative norms, Positivists have considered the law as a process according to Allen.[10] Interest has shifted from dealing with substantive law problems and definition of crime to dealing with procedural law and enforcement problems. Thus the systematic disconcern in the law of crimes has not stopped the enthusiastic enactment of penal laws which has created the problem of overcriminalization in our society. Allen refers to both offenses that affect or are believed to affect the security of the state as well as those crimes created by legislatures in large numbers to effect certain objectives of economic regulation or public welfare (i.e., regulatory offenses).[11]

Jeffery

Jeffery in his essay, "Criminal Justice and Social Change" states there is a basic dilemma between the Classical (i.e., legal reform) school and the Positive school (i.e., scientific criminal study) branches of criminology as the former school defines crime in legal terms and examines it as a legal entity while the latter school (which dominates American theory) rejects the legal definition of crime and examines it as a psychological entity. The Classical school defines crime within the strict limits of criminal law while the Positive school attacks the legal definition of crime and replaces it with sociological definitions of law.[12]

The rejection of the legal definition of crime has left sociologists with no agreement as to what is crime. Thus some sociologists believe that crime should be defined as antisocial behavior while a minority still adhere to a legal definition which has been resurrected by those theorists concerned with the sociology of criminal law. Most criminologists according to Jeffery are not interested in the sociology of criminal law since they are crime control oriented (i.e., have a reform orientation) and as positivists are concerned with the scientific solution of social problems (ala Comte), not with truly understanding social events (ala Weber).[13]

The Positive school seeks an explanation of crime in the criminal, not in the criminal law. Thus most criminologists seek a universal category of behavior that can be explained in terms of a theory of behavior and not in terms of legal definitions of crime. These theorists have developed an incomplete theory of criminal behavior which is not really a crime theory according to Jeffery. The Positive school is concerned with the doctrine of determinism, and the assumption is made that the criminal law holds the individual responsible for his conduct. Thus the Positive school stresses the importance of the criminal over the crime and consequently evaluates behavior solely as psychological while omitting completely the sociological determinants of behavior.[14]

Law is a measure of social rather than individual responsibility and assumes that individuals are responsible for their actions. Further the law evaluates behavior and establishes norms of conduct. The criminal is one who has been judged by the group to have violated the code of conduct and deserves to be punished. The Positive school in its psychiatric orientation is potentially in conflict with the criminal law since the psychiatrist is not interested in the meaning of crime and punishment, only in the criminal. Thus mental illness is not defined as a violation of codes of conduct.[15]

The Classical school punishes the man for the crime (i.e., a definite penalty for each crime) while the Positive school states that the punishment must fit the criminal (i.e., stresses individualized treatment and protection of society against the criminal). Positivists have ignored the criminal law and have abandoned the traditional legal safeguards (i.e., law protects society against the individual and simultaneously the individual against arbitrary actions of the state). The entry of positivism into criminal law theory has created an untenable position wherein the legal rights of juveniles, alcoholics, drug addicts, and the mentally ill are ignored in the name of treatment according to Jeffery. Positivists view punishment in the context of its meaning to the offender rather than its meaning to society (i.e., use of indeterminate sentence, parole, probation, suspended sentence, and good time laws).[16]

Positivistic criminology rejects the legal concept of crime and accepts the concept of individualized justice; rejects the concept of punishment and accepts the concept of treatment; and rejects the study of criminal law but accepts the study of the individual offender. Thus the Positive school studies the offender independent of the criminal law and with little concern for the legal process by which crimes are created. Positivists would like to ignore the deterrent aspect of the criminal law in favor of the rehabilitative aspect. Jeffery is an advocate of the Classical school and rejects the prevalent argument that criminology should be independent of the criminal law as, to his way of thinking, the latter must be a major part of criminology.[17]

In his essay, "The Historical Development of Criminology" Jeffery writes about the evolution of criminal law in society. Starting with anthropological data, Jeffery states that early anthropologists found it difficult to differentiate between law and custom in traditional societies. All law was either custom or no law existed in primitive society. These classical theorists believed that all primitive law was private law; that the kinship group enforced sanctions against the offender in the form of a blood feud; and only later was the feud replaced by payment of compensation. Only when traditional society evolved to the stage of urban-industrialism did private law change to public law. Jeffery utilizes Maine's classic, *Ancient Law,* to deal with legal evolution in ancient societies.[18]

Through the English historical example, Jeffery traces the development of the public law from its origins in private law (i.e., familial law to state law or kinship system based law to feudal law). First evolved the appeal which was settled by trial by battle. This type of legal self-help was followed by the indictment that was resolved either by trial by ordeal or by jury. During the Middle Ages as the commercial revolution progressed, the law of wrongs developed into the law of crimes and the law of torts. The criminal law in particular developed during this period as a means of meeting the problems created by the commercial-urban revolution (i.e., creation of laws of vagrancy, poverty, and theft).[19]

Criminal procedures slowly changed from arbitrary judge-made decisions to strict legal definitions of crimes as put forth in statutes passed by Parliament. The accusatorial (i.e., Anglo-American) and inquisitorial (i.e., Roman) criminal procedures systems evolved, the former system being a private matter while the latter is the concern of the state. Furthermore, the accusatorial system demands procedural safeguards for the offender while the inquisitorial system denies basic civil rights to the defendant.[20]

According to Jeffery, two basic theories of justice evolved in the last three centuries. These are the retributive theory whose purpose is to punish, not deter or rehabilitate; and the just punishment or deterrence theory whose purpose is to deter future criminal misconduct. The Positive school substitutes scientific categories of behavior for legal categories, substitutes treatment for punishment, and accepts punishment as retributive.[21]

The Positive school defines crime as undesirable anti-social behavior (i.e., accepts deviance as criminal rather than law breaking as criminal). The Positivists confuse crime and criminal behavior since they reject the legal definition of crime. Recent developments in Positivistic criminology have been the social welfare influence upon criminals and juvenile court practices and procedures and the psychiatric impact on the criminal law. The social welfare influence upon both criminal law and juvenile court procedures has resulted in denial of basic constitutional rights of the offender. Jeffery criticizes the psychiatric approach as providing no evidence that mental disease causes criminal behavior. According to Jeffery, Freudian theory (i.e., behavior determined by inner forces of psychic phenomena) is the one considered by the legal profession and the courts despite the fact that the Classical school argues that behavior is determined by its consequences (i.e., utilizing reinforcement theory).[22]

Akers

Akers in his article, "The Concept of Law" reviews some of the major concepts of law found in the literature. His purpose is to introduce some of the classic and recent formulations of law as a way of obtaining a perspective on important issues in the concept of law. The purpose is not to present a comprehensive review of the place definitions and theories of law have occupied in the history of sociology of criminal law.[23]

Law is initially considered as social control through legitimized coercion, and this is considered as the dominant concept. There is widespread agreement that law is part of society's control system; that the legal system is not coterminous with the whole system of social control; that law is just one type of social control; and that law is a normative system (i.e., a system of rules about the way people should behave and the attendant sanctions). The dominant theme is that legal norms are backed by some form of legitimized or authoritative coercion or force.[24]

Law is secondly seen as a system of rules made and enforced by the sovereign political community. The form which this legitimized force takes in definitions of law is that of the political community (i.e., sense of a governmental unit exercising control over a territory and recognizing no higher secular sovereignty). Such conceptions can be traced to the

Austinian philosophy of positive law. Ross, Sumner, Pound, Davis, Harvey, Chambliss, and Seidman hold this view of law.[25]

Thirdly, law is seen as the assumed basis for or predictions of authoritative decisions. The emphasis in sociological jurisprudence is on the law as it is actually carried out and enforced rather than law as a series of rules contained in statutes. Holmes and Cardozo's definitions of law typify this approach. Anthropologists such as Schapera and Pospisil also use authoritative decisions for the basis of law.[26]

Coercive definitions of law and the problem of stateless societies and international relations is the fourth category analyzed by Akers. Barkun believes that primitive societies and the world community represent cases of legal order without sanctions. Primitive societies and the international community do not lack means of coercion, rather they lack the ultimate monopolization of authorized force by a political entity. Further if the conceptual requirement be dropped that the use of legitimized force in support of norms be in the hands of a political state, then a definition of law can be devised which includes many stateless societies and the norms of international relationships. Such definitions have been devised by Llewellyn, Hoebel, Weber, and Gibbs.[27]

Noncoercive definitions view law as authoritative decision and procedure and constitute the fifth category of legal definitions. Some writers reject legitimized coercion (whether or not backed by the political state) as a defining characteristic of law. Coercive definitions restrict law to only that legitimized coercion which is applied in a regular and systematic way. Noncoercive definitions retain and elaborate on the criterion of authorization and proper procedure. They tend to stress the way in which rules are made and applied rather than the content of the sanctions enforcing conformity or settlement of disputes. Such definitions have been devised by Kantorowicz, Hart, Fuller, Selznick, Ehrlich, and Timasheff. Akers also examines law in private groups and associations as a part of noncoercion definitions.[28]

Akers states that all of the definitions of law (five categories) agree that law is a form of social control and consists of social norms. All definitions agree that a system of norms enacted and enforced by the coercive power of the modern political state is law, and that law can be distinguished in this way from other societal normative systems. There is some disagreement among definers about how law differs from other parts of the social control system in stateless societies and from other phenomena that are similar to law in many respects (i.e., internal order of private organizations). The dominant theme in making this distinction is the use or threat of coercion in a regularized way by authorized persons, whether or not these are agents of the political state.[29]

Those definitions that reject coercion as a criterion of law place emphasis on authoritative decisions that distinguish between primary and secondary norms (i.e., those that directly relate to personal conduct and those that specify how authorized persons who react to primary norm violations should behave).[30]

Coercive definitions include the requirement that sanctions be applied for norm violation or to enforce a dispute settlement in a systematic or socially approved (i.e., normative) way by socially approved agents. Coercive definitions identify primary norms which qualify as law by the requirement that their breach be met or decisions about them be made in a way and by persons who are authorized by secondary norms to do so.[31]

Akers concludes that every conception of law must recognize that both primary and secondary norms are involved. In no concept has the defining characteristic of law been located in the content of the primary norms of law as all refer to the secondary norms or the agents and actions governed by them. Lastly Akers defines law as social control exercised by the political community and ultimately backed by coercive sanctions.[32]

Schur

Schur, in his book *Our Criminal Society*, feels that criminal sanctions are not necessarily appropriate to every effort at social control. Attempts to employ criminal law to regulate morality ultimately face difficulties in society. Legal and sociological theorists have stated that criminal laws that do not have the support of the dominant societal social norms are limited in their effectiveness.[33]

American criminologists have focused on individual causation and have not concerned themselves with what the criminal law should be. This is in contrast to the findings of the British Governmental Committee on Homosexual Offenses and Prostitution which broke ground with its conception of the role that criminal law should play in society. The Committee places the burden of justifying applications of the law on those who seek to impose such control over the behavior of individuals.[34]

Sociologists are now beginning to look more directly at the socio-legal problems of societal reactions to deviance according to Schur. There is a growing recognition that the criminal law is the inappropriate means to deal with deviance. These crimes without victims are unenforceable laws that attempt to legally proscribe the willing exchange of socially disapproved but demanded goods or services (i.e., homosexuality, drug addiction, prostitution, gambling, etc.). These types of crimes involve a consensual transaction or exchange and no direct and clear harm is inflicted by one person against another so no complaint is lodged. Some criminal laws that deal with victimless crimes produce more social harm than good, cause a great deal of immorality, throw the legal system into disrepute, and allow organized crime to grow and prosper.[35]

According to Schur, we rely upon a criminal solution to all social problems and thus criminalize situations that do not concern the criminal justice system. There has been over-legislation in the area of deviance (i.e., sexual behavior, vice, and political white collar crimes). Political behavior should be designated a crime only if it constitutes a distinct threat to social order (i.e., Nixon era abuses). Schur also feels that many juvenile statutes and court procedures represent an over-extension of the crime defining process since they deal with behaviors which are noncriminal (i.e., ungovernability, waywardness, and incorrigibility) and violate due process of law guarantees of the Constitution.[36]

Gibbs

Gibbs in an essay, "Crime and the Sociology of Law" criticizes criminologists who tend to employ a statutory criterion of criminality (i.e., who accept the idea that crime is an act so designated by a statute). As inadequate as the statutory conception of crime is, alternative definitions of crime are not easily formulated largely because many of the attributes commonly ascribed to crimes are dubious. Gibbs examines some alternative solutions to statutory designations of crime such as violations of conduct norms, social evaluation of crime, and the analytical approach to crime.[37]

The proposal by Sellin that criminology abandon the concept of criminal law and study conduct norms is inadequate for the sociology of criminal law. The evaluation of acts which are distinguished by the character of public reaction to them as crime is difficult to deal with since crime definitions are neither right nor wrong. The analytic approach utilizes Sutherland's differentiae of crime which seeks a generic definition of crime from the common features of acts statutorily designated as crime. Sutherland defines crime as any conduct which is contrary to criminal law. Criminal law is defined from its essential characteristics—politicality, penal sanction, specificity, and uniformity. Gibbs finds fault with this definition when applied to other than American culture.[38]

Any definition should recognize that crimes are acts contrary to criminal law and not laws in general. Further Gibbs states that before one can formulate a definition of criminal law, one must define law in its generic sense. He selects Weber's definition of law. Law to Gibbs is an evaluation of conduct held by at least one person in a social unit; that these members of the social unit on their own initiative or at other's request, will use their special status to attempt by coercive or noncoercive means to revenge, rectify, or prevent behavior that is contrary to the evaluation with a low probability of retaliation by persons other than the individual(s) at whom the reaction is directed.[39]

Gibbs applies his legal definition to several traditional societies and concludes that his definition applies universally. He applies his definition to the criminal law where it is found not to provide a solution to the crime definition problem unless one distinguishes criminal law from tort and contract law.[40]

Notes

[1]Robert Rich, *The Sociology of Law: An Introduction to its Theorists and Theories,* Washington, D.C.: University Press of America, 1977, pp. 152-153.

[2]*Ibid.,* pp. 153-154.

[3]Emile Durkheim, *Division of Labor in Society*, New York: Free Press, 1964, pp. 68-80.

[4]*Ibid.,* pp. 81-110.

[5]*Ibid.,* pp. 1-132.

[6]Walter Lunden, Emile Durkheim, in *Pioneers in Criminology,* Hermann Mannheim (ed.), Montclair, New Jersey: Patterson Smith, 1972, pp. 390-393; Georges Gurvitch, *Sociology of Law*, London: Routledge & Kegan Paul, 1947, pp. 83-89.

[7]Walter Lunden, Emile Durkheim, in *Pioneers in Criminology*, Hermann Mannheim (ed.), Montclair, New Jersey: Patterson Smith, 1972, pp. 394-397; Georges Gurvitch, *Sociology of Law*, London: Routledge & Kegan Paul, 1947, pp. 90-96.

[8]Jerome Hall, *Theft, Law and Society*, Indianapolis: The Bobbs-Merrill Company Inc., 1952, pp. xii-xiii.

[9]Francis Allen, *The Borderland of Criminal Justice: Essays in Law and Criminology,* Chicago: University of Chicago Press, 1964, pp. 29 & 31.

[10]*Ibid.,* p. 125.

[11]*Ibid.,* pp. 126-130.

[12]C. Ray Jeffery, "Criminal Justice and Social Change," in *Society and the Law,* F. James Davis et al., New York: Free Press, 1962, pp. 264-270.

[13]*Ibid.,* pp. 271-276.

[14]*Ibid.,* pp. 277-281.

[15]*Ibid.,* pp. 282-287.

[16]*Ibid.,* pp. 282-287.

[17]*Ibid.,* pp. 296-304.

[18]C. Ray Jeffery, "The Historical Development of Criminology," in *Pioneers of Criminology,* Hermann Mannheim (ed.), Montclair, New Jersey: Patterson Smith, 1972, pp. 459-464.

[19]*Ibid.,* pp. 465-471.

[20]*Ibid.,* pp. 472-480.

[21]*Ibid.,* pp. 481-489.

[22]*Ibid.,* pp. 490-498.

[23]Ronald L. Akers, "The Concept of Law," in *Law and Control in Society,* Ronald Akers and Richard Hawkins (eds.), Englewood Cliffs, New Jersey: Prentice Hall, 1975, pp. 5-6.

[24]*Ibid.,* p. 7.

[25]*Ibid.,* p. 8.

[26]*Ibid.,* p. 9.

[27]*Ibid.,* p. 10.

[28]*Ibid.,* p. 11.

[29]*Ibid.,* p. 12.

[30]*Ibid.,* p. 13.

[31]*Ibid.,* p. 14.

[32]*Ibid.,* p. 15.

[33]Edwin M. Schur, *Our Criminal Society,* Englewood Cliffs, New Jersey: Prentice-Hall, 1969, pp. 191-194.

[34]*Ibid.,* pp. 195-201.

[35]*Ibid.,* pp. 219-223.

[36]*Ibid.,* pp. 224-227.

[37]Jack P. Gibbs, "Crime and the Sociology of Law," in *Crime, Criminology, and Contemporary Society,* Richard D. Knudten (ed.), Homewood, Illinois: The Dorsey Press, 1970, pp. 397-398.

[38]*Ibid.,* pp. 399-400.

[39]*Ibid.,* pp. 401-402.

[40]*Ibid.,* pp. 403-404.

Chapter 2

The Chicago School, its Heritage, and Criminological Theory

Deviance Definitions

Deviance is behavior that is contrary to the standards of conduct or social expectations of a given group, institution, community, or society. Deviance refers to the activities described in such terms as delinquency, crime, drug abuse, alcoholism, moral insanity, and sexual perversion. These concepts imply a departure by individuals from accepted standards of conduct of the group.

The use of the term deviance can be attributed to the statistical idea of atypical behavior as compared to that which is the norm. Both atypical and normal behavior are identified in relation to the standards of the group in which they take place. Deviant behavior is evaluated in terms of the degree to which it departs from these standards. It is typical for a person to deviate to some degree, but to oversubscribe to group norms is just as deviant as to deliberately violate standards of the group.[1]

Deviance As Social Pathology

The deviancy concept first appeared in the form of the theory of social pathology. According to Spencer and other biological sociologists social pathologies were reflected by maladjustments in social relationships (i.e., events were seen as deviant when they interfered with the normal functioning of some part of society just as a disease is seen as a problem because it disrupts a person's normal biochemical processes). These maladjustments developed as society progressed and some people and social groups were unable to keep up with the growth. This theory stated that one should create and protect healthy people and societies by eliminating social pathology which constitutes a violation of societal standards (i.e., morals, norms, and laws). Deviant behavior was seen as sick and pathological. Social pathology theory in its early form felt that the sickness resided within the individual while later views held that the environment was at fault. These social Darwinian views felt that the sick became useless or died out while the strong survived and multiplied. Thus deviant behavior was labeled as inherently defective, dependent, or delinquent/criminal.[2]

The theory of social pathology gradually declined due to its pronounced moral and naturalistic biases explicit in its structure. This theory is still found in the definitions of deviance that feel that the individual exhibits pathological traits or that deviant behavior is a manifestation of a sick society.[3]

Deviance As Social Disorganization

In the 1920's the social pathology theory (i.e., viewing people as injurious to society) was replaced by the social disorganization theory (i.e., examining learning theory to find out why some people learn to be deviant while others learn to conform). Social disorganization theory stated that there was a positive correlation between increasing social complexity of industrial society and higher rates of deviance especially in the large urban centers of the United States. Social disorganization theory is based on the assumption that social order and organization exists when there is a high degree of internal cohesion binding people and their institutions in a society closely together. This cohesion consists for the most part of consensus about the normative system (i.e., value-attitudes) that binds all groups and institutions in a common culture. When consensus concerning the normative system of society is upset and people no longer automatically apply common value-attitudes, conflict, social disorganization, and deviant behavior become increasingly common. Thus the basic premise of social disorganization theory is that conflict and disorganization increase when the status quo is disturbed (i.e., dysfunctioning in the social system) during periods of rapid technological change. Therefore as rapid socio-cultural change produces conflict and disorganization so the rate of deviant behavior escalates in society.[4]

Social disorganization theory especially deals with the disorganizing aspects of urban life and on the rates of deviant behavior within large urban areas. The city typified the social environment most conducive to social disorganization and the emergence of deviant behavior. The indicators of social disorganization developed by the Chicago School of Sociology were many (i.e., heterogeneity of population; normative conflicts between residential groups based on race, religion, and ethnicity; mobility of population—both socially and physically; lack of community organization; and physical deterioration of housing stock and recreational facilities). According to the theory, areas of a city which manifested most of these characteristics were viewed as disorganized and the high rates of deviance found validated the high degree of disorganization. This was especially true when comparing disorganization-deviance rates of suburban and rural areas with inner cities. Chicago School theorists concluded that only certain inner city neighborhoods were typical disorganized communities and these areas appeared to contain only lower class slum residents. Therefore social disorganization theory concluded that inner city slum lower class people tended to be deviant by nature.[5]

The Slum and Deviance

Urban slums of metropolitan areas have traditionally been noted for high rates of juvenile delinquency. The ecological analysis of urban areas began in 1916 with the work of Robert Park at the University of Chicago. This was followed by the research of his student, R.D. McKenzie, whose book, *The Neighborhood,* was the first important human ecology study. This work was followed by Park and Burgess' edited text *The City* in 1925 and the *Urban Community* edited by Burgess in 1926.[6] Both Park and Burgess who were admirers of Steffens applied the latter's muckraking approach to urban social problems. They decided to study the urban phenomena of organized crime and corruption but soon found out that most patterns of criminal behavior were learned during adolescence. Thus Park and Burgess through the research of their graduate students (i.e., Thrasher, Shaw, McKay) began the systematic analysis of juvenile delinquency in Chicago.[7]

Frederic Thrasher began his research on gangs in 1919 which initiated an exhaustive study of delinquency in Chicago that culminated in the 1927 publication of his text *The Gang.* He felt that gangs are found in the same slums that breed criminality, that gang membership was a natural response of adolescents living in such neighborhoods, and not all gang activity was deviant in nature. Last, Thrasher felt that gang formation and activity was in response to the breakdown of community institutions (i.e., family, school, church, and recreation).[8]

Clifford Shaw and Henry McKay at the Illinois Institute for Juvenile Research (Chicago) had worked closely with Burgess, Thrasher, and students at the University of Chicago since the early 1920's. The research at the Institute consisted of working on the verification of theories of delinquency causation. A major conclusion of this research was that most delinquency originates in the central slum areas of larger American cities and becomes successively less as one proceeds from each inner city zone to the suburbs (see Shaw and McKay—*Social Factors in Juvenile Delinquency,* 1931). Another important aspect of Institute research consisted of gathering life histories of male delinquents. The conclusion of this research (Shaw—*The Jack Roller*, 1930; *The Natural History of a Delinquent Career*, 1931; and *Brothers in Crime*, 1938) was that each male youth was introduced to delinquency by peers (i.e., experienced delinquents who comprised one's new peer group). Thus Shaw concluded that delinquency was not due to individual personality disorders but to conformity to peer expectations. Therefore delinquency was usually a group phenomena. These conclusions neatly applied to the inner city slum environment which was characterized by both political and social disorganization.[9]

In 1934 the Chicago Area Project originated at the Institute under the direction of Shaw in an attempt to test hypotheses dealing with neighborhood disorganization as the basic cause of delinquent behavior. The research of the Project concerns delinquency in Chicago neighborhoods. The research at the Institute led in part to the publication of *Juvenile Delinquency and Urban Areas* by Shaw and McKay in 1942. This book documents the social distribution, analyzes the subcultural origins, and traces the socialization processes leading to delinquency in slum areas of central cities. Although Shaw and McKay did not refer to Merton's anomie theory, their theoretical statements show they were aware of how anomie relates to delinquency. Shaw and McKay also did not conceptually utilize the concept of delinquent subcultures since they perceived delinquency as a normal aspect of lower class behavior systems in the neighborhoods under analysis. As Short states it was left to later theorists utilizing Shaw and McKay's data such as Cohen, Cloward and Ohlin, and Walter Miller to "isolate conceptually and empirically particular components of this process and mechanisms by which particular types of delinquency occur in groups and communities."[10]

In 1943, William Whyte published *Street Corner Society* which dealt with a slum in Boston. Delinquency and other forms of deviancy were present in this supposedly socially disorganized city neighborhood but the community in reality had a well organized social structure. Although Whyte's research did not add anything new conceptually to the work of earlier theorists, his systematic analysis of the social structures and processes of a classic slum made it apparent that there was middle class bias in what constituted social disorganization (i.e., slum dwellers were organized but ineffective in improving their low status in comparison with their middle class counterparts).[11]

The ecological studies have shown that there are differences in rates of delinquency from neighborhoods within one city, one metropolitan area, as well as between two or more metropolitan areas.[12] Shaw and McKay emphasized the importance of successful criminal role models in leading youth into delinquency in slum communities. They utilized Sutherland's theory of differential association to explain that delinquent behavior is learned through association with known delinquents.[13] The theory of differential association has been used in an attempt to explain variations in delinquency rates in different urban communities (i.e., native Americans, first or second generation ethnic, or nonwhite migrants). Sutherland and Cressey conclude that the higher rate of delinquency among second generation ethnics and recent nonwhite migrants in comparison to first generation ethnics and settled nonwhites is due to their assimilation of delinquency patterns already existing in American communities.[14]

On the other hand, Reckless attributes the higher rates of delinquency in second generation ethnic youth to conflict in values between the old world culture of the parents and the value-attitude system adopted by their Americanized children while Cloward and Ohlin perceive the lack of opportunity for legitimate advancement among slum dwelling lower class ethnic and nonwhite youth as the cause of their delinquency.[15]

Chilton in an attempt to relate anomie theory to the cause of urban distribution of delinquency analyzed similar work done by Lander in Baltimore and Bordua in Detroit with his own research in Indianapolis. He concluded that such factors as substandard and overcrowded housing, transciency, income, and education are related to high rates of delinquency. Chilton felt that these factors were not really indicators of anomie but just ecological findings.[16] Bordua perceives urban area delinquency as being due to both the normative and social structures of a community.[17] Thus such factors as degree of urbanization, transciency of population, racial and ethnic composition, lack of formal education and job skills, substandard and overcrowded housing stock, and low income are general characteristics of a high rate delinquency area.[18]

Social Class and Deviance

Most studies of delinquency causation have not been based on ecological theory but have centered on the stratification structure of the urban area in general and the low socioeconomic status of pre-adolescents and adolescents who become delinquent in particular. Social disadvantage theories of delinquency have been the most common explanations of this phenomena in recent decades.[19]

Lower Class Subculture

As Haskell and Yablonsky note, "sociologists tend to define social class as a stratum in society. They use an objective approach employing such criteria as education, income, occupation, and residence."[20] Most theorists have employed this objective approach in their research into lower class subcultures and its relationship to delinquency.

The lower class in American society is a stratum within our social structure comprising approximately sixty per cent of our total population. The lower class is usually divided by most stratification theorists into the lower lower class, and the upper lower class, the former comprising about twenty per cent of our population and the latter forty per cent.[21] Those comprising the lower class have been stigmatized since its members are supposedly at odds with our middle class cultural model in a normative sense. Thus as Centers has shown no individual wants to identify with the lowest stratum of society. Further it is common knowledge even to lower class people that it is advantageous to identify with higher status groups in society so many would rather refer to themselves as working class since it is a more positive term and less stigmatic than lower class.[22]

A survey of the literature shows that the lower lower class has been referred to as the "lower working class", "unskilled manual workers", or "those people who are apathetic". The first term describes the economic status of the individual while the second is indicative of both low economic status and educational attainment level. An apathetic lifestyle implies a socialization process characterized by a general disinterest in both vocational and intellectual pursuits. This is usually coupled with the knowledge that one is at the "bottom of the social pile". Some theorists have also used the term "lower class" to typify lack of power. Thus lower class becomes a term connoting the lowest status in the political, social, and economic hierarchies of society. The economic role performed by this individual is the most menial and his position in societal institutions reflects this. Further the individual and his family are usually negatively rewarded by society (i.e., socially and economically isolated by individuals of higher status).[23]

The upper lower class has been referred to as the "semi-skilled and skilled manual workers" or "those people who get by". The former term indicates that members of this social class possess specific economic skills that are achieved only after a specified amount of formal education and on the job training. The latter term is somewhat misleading since some semi-skilled and many skilled workers are quite "comfortable" in terms of usable wealth. Thus the "getting by" life-style refers to satisfaction with one's economic position which implies that one does not want to better one's educational or occupational status. The term upper working class as differentiated from lower working class is sometimes used as a way of stating that the upper lower class individual has superior job training and skills in relation to the workers below him. The term working class has also been used to differentiate the upper lower class from the lower lower class. Use of working class as applied only to upper lower class implies that lower lower class individuals are poor workers or do not want to work. This term also implies that there is a high proportion of people from the lower lower class traditionally on public assistance.[24]

Finally both lower class subcultures have been commonly referred to as "blue-collar workers". This concept implies that the manual laborer, no matter how much his monetary compensation, is inferior in status to the white collar worker who supposedly utilizes his intellectual abilities more than his physical and thereby is accorded higher status by members of society. In reality there are many exceptions to this view since skilled and technical workers are paid more than white collar employees who have far exceeded the societal demand for their services.[25]

Socialization Process

Upper lower and lower lower class socialization processes are quite similar. The father in the lower lower class generally is a weak role model for his children possibly due to the matriarchal structure of the family, but the upper lower class father also has a secondary socializing function. Consanguinal and affinal female relatives have a dominant role in the socialization of the upper lower class individual before and after marriage. This is especially true of the lower lower class maternal grandmother in her relations with her children and grandchildren.[26]

There appears to be relatively little parental planning and foresight regarding socialization of the children. Lower class parents also tend to be easy going when socializing their children. Langner states further:

> "Lower class parents exert irrational authority—respect for elders, 'do as I say, not as I do.' Social control is by shame, ridicule, or threat of punishment. The authority and control methods may lead to an externalized superego. Later abrupt responsibility is thrust on the child. Training is less consistent and more sporadic; discourage expression of hostility against parents; encourage or accept hostile expression or behavior outside the family and toward siblings. Training by teachers and others conflicts with parents values."[27]

There is relatively little identity training provided by lower class parents. Such items as scrapbooks, family albums, and birthday parties may not be a consistent part of lower class home life. Interchangeability of function is emphasized over a strong sense of self-identity. The unstable or low status job experiences of parents reinforce within the child that the individual is expendable. The child's concept of dominance may be weak which is reflective of low parental status in general. Parental sex roles tend to be distinct although children of both sexes usually identify with the mother or mother surrogate. Childhood concern with self-image may occur due to continuous subordination of the child to adults within the family setting. The basic lack of new or expensive toys, reliance upon handed down or poor quality clothes, and parental disinterest or rejection may cause the child to develop a weak sense of family ties as well as an inferiority complex.[28]

In the area of cognitive development, many lower class children develop a low self-concept, act immediately without thinking through consequences, and have a restricted range of cultural experiences. Further they have never developed a refined sense of auditory discrimination, have weak visual discrimination (i.e., are less able to deal with pictorial representations of objects and actions) and are limited in ability to conceptualize. Finally the lower class child is not prepared in skills highly related to academic achievement when he enters school, and has not been generally motivated for academic achievement above the most fundamental skill levels.[29]

Effect of the Family on Language and Cognitive Development

Language

There are very wide variations existing in the role language plays in family life. The home environment has the greatest influence on the language development of the child. This development seems to vary from social class to social class. Middle class parents generally spend more time using abstract words with their children who tend to develop sophisticated language patterns earlier than lower class children whose parents generally spend much time using street language in conversing with their offspring.[30]

The lower class home is not a verbally oriented environment. There is little opportunity for the lower class child to develop complex verbal skills because there is little time for discussion of important issues between parent and child nor opportunity for children to enter into conversation with parents especially if the family is authoritarian.

The culturally disadvantaged home is functional and lacks the large variety of educational preschool objects, toys, pictures, and other creative materials that require labeling and serve as referents for language acquisition. Thus the lower class child is restricted to his immediate environment which, if limited in amount and type of verbal communication, can cause language deficiencies.[31]

Compared to the middle class home, there is a relative absence of books, magazines, and newspapers in the lower class home. Furthermore adults usually spend little time reading for enjoyment so that the child cannot identify and emulate this type of behavior. Loud noises in and out of the home, the lack of privacy, and the use of television and radio as substitutes for reading also inhibit the child from fully developing and expanding his verbal skills at a normal rate.[32]

There are many language deficiencies attributable to the lower class family environment. The child from this subculture tends to have poor auditory discrimination and receives little corrective feedback regarding his enunciation, pronunciation, and grammar from parents or parental surrogate. The syntactical model provided the child by his parents is usually faulty; speech sequences seem to be very limited; and acquisition of more abstract and integrative language seems to be hampered by the home environment. Lower class youth also tend to have difficulty in structuring language and articulatory defects are also commonly present.[33]

Cognitive

The home environment is important for the intellectual growth of the child before he enters school and also during the elementary school years. Children from families of higher socioeconomic status are usually intellectually superior to peers who are from lower social class positions. Children whose parents value intellectual mastery will more frequently reward academic competence and proficiency at cognitive skills than those parents who are less concerned with this area of intellectual development.[34]

The home environment also makes an important contribution to the success of the child in school. The emotional atmosphere of the home is of great importance to the child's academic success. Children given emotional support at home tend to gain more rapidly in intellectual power than those who are only criticized.[35]

The lower class environment is generally characterized by limited parental formal education that is translated into low academic aspirations for their children. The negative orientation of many parents toward their own lack of achievement may influence their interaction with their children in everyday achievement experiences.[36]

IQ's generally increase with consistent positive parental emphasis on achievement in school. Intellectual curiosity is weakened by parents who have little interest in the value of education. Thus rewards for academic achievement are rare in homes where parents are unaware of the usefulness of formal education.[37]

Most lower class parents are interested in their children's education and are eager for them to succeed in school. Unfortunately many parents lack knowledge about the nature of gaining a formal education, lack basic skills in intellectually preparing their children for school, and lack the time to help their children develop their intellectual resources.[38]

The lack of interaction between parent and child in the disadvantaged environment hinders the child's normal development of intellectual and social skills and abilities. Most parents do not have the knowledge to satisfy the child's natural curiosity, cannot help him surmount academic difficulties, and cannot challenge his intellectual ingenuity since their formal education was so limited.[39]

The lack of intellectual stimulation and guidance by the typical parent is a major problem encountered by the lower class child. The home environment also may create deficiencies in perceptual skills that may lead to feelings of anti-intellectualism. Many parents socialize their children into a motoric style of conceptualization which usually results in poor reading ability.[40]

Social

Individuals from the lower socioeconomic strata have been handicapped because of the specific skills and work-habits acquired by the language and cognitive elements of lower class subculture. Each socioeconomic subculture in society fosters the development of a somewhat unique pattern of abilities.[41]

Lower and middle class environments differ in the opportunities afforded the individual for direct contact and interaction with the world at large and with the multitude of experiences represented by television, movies, records and tapes, books, travel, etc. Opportunities to solve problems, motivation to think about a variety of issues, and encouragement to solve problems generally differ between lower and middle classes. A socio-cultural environment that restricts these opportunities, which discourages intellectual curiosity, and which downgrades problem solving is likely to retard intellectual development.[42]

There are definite social class differences in abilities to learn and use basic mental skills. It is likely that environments that possess good models of language usage and which promote language development will stimulate general intelligence development while environments that possess poor language models and which discourage language development will retard general intelligence development.[43]

There is a correlation between social class differences and language behavior. Significantly higher scores are made in the upper rather than the lower socioeconomic groups on measured language skills. Children of different social class levels vary more in how they express themselves than how much they express themselves. Social class membership influences speech content as the range of oral vocabulary tends to be relatively independent of other language measures and shows a positive relationship to social class level.[44]

There are differences in educational value-attitudes and achievement motivation between social classes. Values and standards concerning education may conflict between social classes. Further there are social class differences in attitudes toward learning.[45]

Table 1

SOCIAL CLASS DIFFERENCES IN THE LANGUAGE AND COGNITIVE DEVELOPMENT OF SOCIALLY DISADVANTAGED CHILDREN

(L)—Language
(C)—Cognitive

Author	Disadvantaged (predominantly lower class youth)	Advantaged (predominantly middle & upper class youth)
Washington, B. B. (1964)	(L) they have difficulty in communicating. (C) they lack basic knowledge & information, are ignorant about themselves, and feel inferior about their mental capabilities.	
Reissman, F. (1965)	(C) their learning style is physical & visual.	
Duggins, J. H. (1965)	(L) lower class children have phonics trouble (vowels & consonants), dialect, no use of plurals, verb tenses & subject-predicate agreement, & lack of word meaning.	
Lighthall, F. F. (1963)	(L) lower class language tends to be characterized by semantic & syntactical short cuts.	(C) the middle class student is not disposed to jump at the first opportunity for gain but

Author	Disadvantaged (predominantly lower class youth)	Advantaged (predominantly middle & upper class youth)
	(C) the child tends to take immediate action on opportunities as they arise without thinking through the consequences.	delays action in favour of thinking through the consequences.
Sochet, M. A. (1964)	(C) lower class children feel unfavored in the home, community & school.	(C) middle & upper class children feel they are favored at at home, in the community, & the school.
Rosen, B. C. (1956)	(C) lower class children are less likely to be taught both the motives & the values that make achievement possible.	(C) middle class children are more likely to be taught both the motives & the values that make achievement possible.
Daniel, W. G. (1964)	(L) verbal environment is permeated with casual observances of standard English inflections, simple monosyllabic words, frequently mispronounced words, rare use of socially acceptable descriptive or qualifying terms, the simple sentence or sentence fragment, & a profuse use of slang & colloquialisms.	

Author	Disadvantaged (predominantly lower class youth)	Advantaged (predominantly middle & upper class youth)
	(C) their styles & modes of perceptual habituation do not complement the emphasis which are important to academic success; marked weakness in utilizing abstract congitive processes; favor concrete stimulus-bound learning situations; limited horizons function as a depressant to their motivation, aspirations, & achievement; do not like book-centered learning; & they suffer from sensory deprivation.	
Jackson, P. W., & Strattner, N. (1964)	(C) lower class students seem to learn better when reinforced by praise or tangible reward.	(C) middle class students secm to learn better when responding to intangible rewards.
Deutsch, M. et al. (1964)	(L) lower class students make functionally complete remarks & use of short sentences.	(L) middle & upper class children tend to make more complex & elaborated
	(C) performance in general in intellectual ability lags.	remarks. They are advanced in language skills in

Author	Disadvantaged (predominantly lower class youth)	Advantaged (predominantly middle & upper class youth)
		the areas of articulation of vowels, medical & final consonants, grammatical complexity, & recognition vocabulary.
Deutsch, M. (1964)	(C) lower class child is less likely to be prepared for school. School failure may be more final in terms of recovery of adequate school functioning.	(C) middle class child is more likely to be prepared for school.
McCarthy, D. (1930)	(L) lower socio-economic status children use a small percentage of adapted-information responses & ask few questions.	(L) upper socio-economic status children use a large percentage of adapted-information responses & ask many questions.
Deutsch, M. (1964)	(L) lower class students are deficient in the abstract & categorical use of language.	
Taba, H. (1964)	(L) they lack practice in developing the ability to convert objects & events to verbal symbols.	

Author	Disadvantaged (predominantly lower class youth)	Advantaged (predominantly middle & upper class youth)
	(C) they lack a systematic & ordered way of interpreting & mediating their environments, less opportunity to link experience with interpretation of it, less chance to explore causal relationships & form abstractions. The culturally deprived have a low self-concept, cling to the familiar, respond with trigger-like reactions, & have difficulty forming meaningful relation-ships.	
Havighurst, R. J. (1952)	(L) the lower class child learns that language usage is not the most important tool. (C) lower class children are not stimulated to high levels of develop-ment of mental skills in general past age 12.	(L) the middle class child is taught very early that language is important. (C) middle class children are stimulated to a high level of development of mental skills.
Vera, J. P. & Goldstein, L. S.	(L) children from the lower class speak in short sentences, are not too articulate &	(L) children from high socio-economic status groups speak in long

Author	Disadvantaged (predominantly lower class youth)	Advantaged (predominantly middle & upper class youth)
	have not too varied a vocabulary; language use is not flexible; & there is difficulty in acquiring words which appear in a number of different contexts.	sentences, are articulate, & have a varied vocabulary. Language use is flexible.
Farragher, M. (1964)	(L) words may be perceived as hostile in purpose, overwhelming in intensity, & something from which to flee in the pre-school lower class child. Passive-dependent ways of relating. (C) they have high impulsivity levels; failure to become autonomous; seeing & hearing are associated with environmental limitations; exploration remains fixed at a level of physical activity; exploration at the conceptual level fails to develop thoroughly; & development of theoretical	

Author	Disadvantaged (predominantly lower class youth)	Advantaged (predominantly middle & upper class youth)
	operations from concrete examples is rare & difficult.	
Bernstein, B. (1960)	(L) use of descriptive rather than abstract concepts & discouragement of use of verbally elaborating subjective intent. Limited types of stimuli to which the child learns to respond.	(L) use of a complex conceptual hierarchy for the organization of experience.
Bernstein, B. (1962)	(L) youths make selections from a relatively low level of the linguistic hierarcy.	(L) middle class youths make selections from a relatively high level of the linguistic hierarcy.
Bernstcin, B. (1962)	(L) working class youths use a long mean phrase length, spend less time pausing, & use a short word length.	(L) middle class youths usc a short mean phrase length, spend more time pausing and use a long word length.
Berstein, B. (1964)	(L) the normative system associated with some sections of the working class is	(L) the normative systems associated with middle class and associated

Author	Disadvantaged (predominantly lower class youth)	Advantaged (predominantly middle & upper class youth)
	likely to create individuals limited to a restricted code. Children socialized within some sections of the working class strata can be expected to be limited to a restricted code.	strata are likely to give rise to the modes of an elaborated code. Children socialized within middle class & associated strata can be expected to possess both an elaborated & a restricted code.
Bernstein, G. (1961)	(L) a linguistic environment limited to a public language is likely to produce deleterious effects both cognitive and verbal from an educational viewpoint. The disadvantaged youth is resistant to vocabulary extensions, word manipulation, construction of ordered sentences, new words & vocabulary order in middle class terms. Generalization is difficult; formal relationships are difficult to perceive; and these children are present-oriented.	

Author	Disadvantaged (predominantly lower class youth)	Advantaged (predominantly middle & upper class youth)
Bernstein, B. (1959)	(L) public language (restricted code): short, grammatically simple, often unfinished sentences, a poor syntactical construction with a verbal form stressing the active mood; simple & repetitive use of conjunctions; frequent use of short commands & questions; rigid & limited use of adjectives & adverbs; infrequent use of impersonal pronouns as subjects; statments formulated as implicit questions which set up a sympathetic circularity; the reason & conclusion of a statement are confounded to produce a categoric statement; individual selection from a group of idiomatic phrases will frequently be found; symbolism is of a low order of generality;	(L) formal language (elaborated code): accurate grammatical order & syntax regulate what is said; logical modifications & stress are modified through a grammatically complex sentence construction; frequent use of prepositions which indicate logical relationships as well as prepositions which indicate temporal & spatial contiguity; frequent use of impersonal pronouns; discriminative selection from a range of adjectives & adverbs; individual qualification is verbally explicit; expressive symbolism conditioned by this linguistic form distributes affectual support

Author	Disadvantaged (predominantly lower class youth)	Advantaged (predominantly middle & upper class youth)
	& the individual qualification is implicit in the sentence structure. Therefore, it is a language of implicit meaning. Curiosity is limited by the level of conceptualization which is fostered by this form of language use. Formal language will not be directly comprehensible but will be put into the public language. Where a translation can not be made, there is no communication. This language encourages an immediacy of interaction, a preference for the descriptive rather than the analytic.	rather than logical meaning to what is said; & a language use which points to the possibilities inherent in a complex conceptual hierarchy for the organizing of experience. An individual with a comprehension of formal language use can also understand public language. Subjective intent may be verbally elaborated & made explicit.
Deutsch, M. (1964)	(C) they are behind in skills highly related to academic achievement when they enter school. They are below the middle class child in intellectual and academic achievement. The child is	(C) they are generally prepared in skills highly related to academic achievement when they enter school. They are above the lower class child in intellectual & acadmic achieve-

Author	Disadvantaged (predominantly lower class youth)	Advantaged (predominantly middle & upper class youth)
	unable to cope with academic failures & generally has difficulty adjusting to school.	ment. The child is generally able to cope with academic failures & has little difficulty adjusting to school.
Newton, E. S. (1964)	(L) the lower class child's verbal environment is characterized by casual observances of standard English inflections, simple mono-syllabic words, frequently mispronounced words, rare use of "socially acceptable" descriptive or qualifying terms, the simple sentence or sentence fragment, & profuse use of regionalisms, slang & cant. (C) the child performs below grade level on verbal tests; his styles & modes of perceptual habituation limit academic success; weakness in utilizing abstract cognitive processes & favors concrete stimulus-bound learning situations;	

Author	Disadvantaged (predominantly lower class youth)	Advantaged (predominantly middle & upper class youth)
	limited academic motivation, aspirations, & achievement; general disenchantment with book-centered learning, & low self-concept.	
Goldberg, M. L. (1963)	(L) the expressive style is often motoric, concrete "thing-oriented", & non-verbal. (C) groups of pupils from lower class families score relatively low on cognitive measures. They are present-oriented, general lack of motivation toward academic achievement.	(L) the expressive style is often conceptual, abstract-symbolic, "idea-oriented", & verbal (C) groups of pupils from middle class families score relatively high on cognitive measures. They are future-oriented, definite positive motiva-tion toward academic achieve-ment.
Deutsch, M. (1963)	(L) lack adequate language training; identifying object with corrective feed-back; do not get a variety of verbal material to listen to; do not have the opportunity to observe much adult	(L) exposure to language training; identifying object with corrective feedback; listening to a variety of verbal material; observing adult language usage; variety of object

Author	Disadvantaged (predominantly lower class youth)	Advantaged (predominantly middle & upper class youth)
	language usage; & & lack a variety of objects to label & relate. Speech sequences are limited poorly structured syntactically; informal language usage; convey concrete needs, & immediate consequences.	labeling & object relation. High level of syntactical organization & subject continuity; formal language usage & emphasize the relating of concepts.
	(C) restricted range of experiences & lack of variety; lack of refined auditory discrimination; difficulty in handling items related to time judgments; & lack reward expectation for successful task completion.	(C) extensive range of experiences & variety; adequate auditory discrimination; little difficulty in handling items related to time judgments, & expect rewards for successful task completion.
Bloom, B. S. (1965)	(L) lower class children lack abstract language. They have difficulty with words for categories, class names, & non-concrete ideas. (C) they are weak in auditory discrimination & visual discrimination, generally lack	(L) middle class children possess adequate abstract language. (C) future-time orientation in motivation.

Author	Disadvantaged (predominantly lower class youth)	Advantaged (predominantly middle & upper class youth)
	motivation for academic achievement above fundamental levels, & present-time orientation motivation.	
Beilin, H. & Gotkin, L. G. (1964)	(C) lower class child has difficulty in making perceptual discriminations among physical objects, less able to deal with the pictorial representation of objects & actions, & limited in ability to conceptualize.	
Ausubel, D. P. (1965)	(L) lower class child responds more to the concrete, tangible, immediate & particularized properties of objects & situations. His speech is instigated by the objects & actions he sees & he makes more ancillary use of non-verbal forms of communication.	(L) middle class child responds more to abstract, categorical, & relational properties. Use of abstract ideas.
Whipple, G. (1962)	(L) use a smaller number & variety of words to express themselves; speak in shorter	

Author	Disadvantaged (predominantly lower class youth)	Advantaged (predominantly middle & upper class youth)
	sentences; use a large percentage of incomplete sentences; use a small proportion of mature sentences such as compound, complex & elaborate constructions; do not elaborate their ideas; errors with verbs & subjects not in agreement common; use of colloquialisms & slang; ommissions of auxiliaries; wrong word order; & misuse of prepositions.	
Reissman, F. (1962)	(L) lower class have definite lack of formal language skills but have high development of informal language & gestures. (C) physical & visual, content-centered, externally oriented, problem-centered, inductive, spatial, slow, careful, & persevering in areas of importance.	(L) middle class have definite formal language skills. (C) form centered, introspective, abstract centered, deductive, temporal, quick, facile, & flexible in areas of importance.
Fusco, G. C. (1964)	(L) the lower class child is deficient in the	

Author	Disadvantaged (predominantly lower class youth)	Advantaged (predominantly middle & upper class youth)
	ability to understand & use language. (C) they are unable to concentrate or listen beyond very short periods, deficient in cognitive powers & visual & auditory discrimination; unfamiliar with scheduling & order; apprehensive of formal education; & lacking in intrinsic or extrinsic motivation to succeed in academic achieve-ment.	

Table I lists the social class differences in the language and cognitive development of predominantly lower class children. In summary the most frequent occurring factors in the language and cognitive areas of disadvantaged youth due to social class are:

(language)

The lower class child uses short sentences and sentence fragments, uses short words, frequently mispronounces words, lacks variety of objects to label and relate, is present-oriented and conveys concrete needs and immediate consequences, lacks abstract language, and uses colloquialisms and slang.

(cognitive)

The lower class child has a low self-concept of himself, uses immediate action without thinking through consequences, has a restricted range of experiences, lacks refined auditory discrimination, has weak visual discrimination (i.e., perceptual discrimination among physical objects, less able to deal with pictorial representations of objects and actions), limited ability to conceptualize, is behind in skills highly related to academic achievement when he enters school, and generally lacks motivation for academic achievement above the fundamental level.

The Lower Class and Deviance

Miller explains delinquency on the basis of social class. He states that specific value-attitudes (i.e., "focal concerns") of the lower class individuals lead to behavior which by cultural standards of society is delinquent. There are two value-attitude systems within the lower class environment that are conducive to the development of delinquency according to Miller. These are the female-based household and the single-sex peer group. Miller lists his focal concerns as trouble, toughness, smartness, excitement, fate, and autonomy.[46]

These focal concerns are summarized by Bordua as follows: trouble is what life gets you into—especially trouble with the agents of the larger society. The central aspect of this focal concern is the distinction between law-abiding and law-violating behavior, and where an individual stands along the implied dimension either by behavior, reputation, or commitment is crucial in the evaluation of him by others. Toughness refers to physical prowess, skill, masculinity, fearlessness, bravery, daring. It includes an almost compulsive opposition to things seen as soft and feminine, including much middle class behavior, and is related, on the one hand, to sex-role identification problems which flow from the young boy's growing up in the female-based household and, on the other hand, to the occupational demands of the lower class world. Toughness, along with the emphasis on excitement and autonomy, is one of the ways one gets into trouble.

Smartness refers to the ability to "con", outwit, dupe (i.e., to manipulate things and people to one's own advantage with a minimum of conventional work). Excitement, both as an activity and as an ambivalently held goal, is best manifested in the patterned cycle of the weekend night-on-the-town complete with much drink and sexual escapades, thereby creating the risk of fighting and trouble. Between weekends, life is dull and passive. Fate refers to the perception of many lower class individuals that their lives are determined by events and forces over which they have little or no control. It manifests itself in widespread gambling and fantasies of "when things break for me". Gambling serves multiple functions in the areas of fate, toughness, smartness, and excitement.

The last focal concern described by Miller is that of autonomy—

concern over the amount, source, and serverity of control by others. Miller describes the carrier of lower class culture as being highly ambivalent about such control by others. Overtly he may protest bitterly about restraint and arbitrary interferences while covertly he tends to equate coercion with care and unconsciously to seek situations where strong controls will satisfy nurturance needs.[47]

The one-sex peer group is considered by Miller to be an important and common social group in the lower class community. He feels that the "prevalence and stability" of this peer group is due to the female-based household that is so common in lower class slum neighborhoods. Miller perceives the lower class subculture as composed of sets of age-graded one-sex groups which comprise the key psychic focus and reference group for late pre-adolescent and adolescent youth. Membership in the stable peer group provides the lower class youth with services not offered by the female-based household. The adolescent street corner group whether delinquent or not provides boys raised by female authority figures their first chance to learn the essentials of the male role with peers facing similar sex-role identification problems.[48]

The major concerns of these male adolescent corner groups stem from their psycho-social environment. Two key problems of these youth are "belonging" and "status". Each lower class youth wants to remain a member in good standing in his group. Thus there is a continuing concern of each peer group member that he demonstrate competence in and adherence to the group's normative system (i.e., "focal concerns") or else face exclusion from the group. Status is achieved and maintained by each corner group member through manifesting the value-attitudes of the lower class subculture (i.e., toughness, smartness, autonomy, etc.). Status is shown by street corner youth through demonstrated superiority in physical prowess in sports and fighting, outsmarting other gang members and outsiders, acting adult (i.e., drinking, smoking, sexual prowess, gambling), and being able to defend one's "turf" or stand up to authority figures such as teachers, police, and adults in general.[49]

It appears that Miller's stand on the existence of a uniquely lower class normative system which separates delinquent behavior is at odds with other delinquency theorists who perceive lower class deviancy from the perspective of middle class value-attitudes. Cohen states that lower class delinquents share middle class value-attitudes but their problems stem from an inability to achieve success utilizing this normative system with the result that middle class values are reversed.[50]

In particular Cohen feels that the crucial problem for the lower class youth who becomes delinquent is status deprivation. These adolescents live in an environment which stresses middle class goals but where the actual achievement of these goals in a legitimate manner is limited. According to Cohen, youth caught in this means-end dilemma band together and develop patterns of collective behavior that serve to relieve some of their frustrations and allow them to achieve status within the gang. In the process middle class norms are reversed and utilized as bases for determining the type of deviance that gang members should enter into. This collective delinquency represents what Cohen calls a shared "reaction formation" (i.e., the gang develops a means to overcome the status deprivation problems of each of its members).[51]

Cohen states that delinquent behavior is motivated and docs not simply result from the failure of the slum community or its institutions (i.e., school, family, recreation) to control its youthful inhabitants. Bordua feels that Cohen's emphasis on the internalization of middle class goals by lower class youth is too great. He also feels that Cohen has not placed enough emphasis on the role of the family in producing delinquent behavior among its members. Cohen feels that the major role of the family is its determination of the youth's social class position since this determines his socialization.[52]

Cloward and Ohlin state that youth whose means to culturally approved goals of success (i.e., wealth and power) are blocked by being lower class, non-white, or undereducated and who have access to deviant means (i.e., theft, robbery, etc.) of achieving success will become delinquent. Thus an adolescent will be prevented from becoming delinquent if he can find legitimate means of achieving success or if illegitimate means to success are blocked. According to Cloward and Ohlin the variations in illegitimate opportunity result in different delinquent subcultures and gang structures (i.e., opportunity for participation in rackets or theft results in the formation of a semi-professional theft or criminal gang; less opportunity for organized crime results in the formation of a conflict—oriented gang; and the complete failure of both legitimate and illegitimate opportunity results in the formation of a retreatist subculture).[53]

Irving Spergel in his book *Racketville, Slumtown, and Haulburg* found that each type of slum community in New York City analyzed had a different type of gang. Utilizing the opportunity structure theory of Cloward and Ohlin, he found a racket (i.e., criminal) subculture arising in the neighborhood where organized crime dominated, a conflict subculture existed in an organized slum neighborhood where some legitimate means to success existed. Spergel found no evidence of a retreatist subculture in the communities under study.[54]

Sykes and Matza state that lower class delinquents share middle class value-attitudes but have developed neutralization techniques that enable them to act in a deviant manner while rationalizing away this type of behavior. These neutralization techniques allow the delinquent to justify his behavior (i.e., projecting blame upon others or denying that there has been a victim as a result of his actions). Thus neutralization theory suggests that delinquents have extended the range of extenuating circumstances which excuse their social deviance while retaining middle class value-attitudes.[55] On the other hand, Rodman suggests that lower class delinquents have stretched their range of value-attitudes to include uniquely lower class values while keeping middle class values. He also perceives the lower class individual as possessing a minimal commitment to both lower and middle class value-attitudes. Thus lower class youth "stretch" their values and approve both lower and middle class norms. These delinquent youth hold a wide range of values but have minimal commitment to any particular value-attitudes. Thus lower class youth are more susceptible to behaving in ways that are viewed as delinquent by public authority figures in the community.[56]

Gordon et al. state that lower class youth value as high as middle class youth the cultural values of society. But delinquent youth place greater value upon strictly lower class norms in comparison to both lower class and middle class youth who are not delinquent. The results of this research appears to tie in with the "value stretch" theory proposed by Rodman.[57]

The Middle Class and Deviance

According to Vaz there are theoretical problems in explaining middle class delinquency since there are two groups of youth to analyze, the upwardly mobile lower class youth newly arrived to suburbia and the established, wholesome, respectable, fun-loving old line middle class adolescent. The former group may have problems in adjusting to new middle class surroundings while the latter group of youth may become delinquent through adherence to current fads or by imitation of lower class value-attitudes. There are also the typical adolescent peer pressures, the importance of status, the quest for masculinity and femininity, and the problems of adjusting to the transition from childhood to adulthood in middle class communities.[58]

Bohlke perceives delinquency as a function of the social marginality of the "nouvelle bourgeoisie" (i.e., recently arrived suburbanites whose families have the financial resources but who are socially unacceptable to old line middle class youth and their families). He also summarizes the position of several other theorists who state that middle class delinquency is due to "the diffusing working class values and behavior patterns to middle class youth", "the weakening of the deferred gratification pattern in middle class families", "the increasing difficulty that some sons have in trying to match the mobility of their fathers", and the lack of services and traditions in new or highly transient suburbs.[59]

Kvaraceus and Miller feel that lower class fads and value-attitudes influence some middle class youth through the process of diffusion. Thus a general weakening of the middle class normative system (i.e., achievement through directed work effort, deferment of immediate pleasures and gains for future goals, responsibility, ambition, maintenance of nuclear family solidarity, child rearing, accumulation of material goods and property maintenance, education, formal organization, and personal appearance) is hypothesized as leading to increased delinquency among middle class youth.[60]

Cohen sees middle class delinquency as a result of structural changes in society. Thus families considered to be middle class economically may not be middle class in terms of the way they socialize their children (i.e., upwardly mobile parents may transmit lower class value-attitudes to offspring). Cohen also notes that middle class youth tend to be raised by their mothers since their fathers are usually preoccupied by their careers. These youth may act in a deviant manner as a form of protest against so-called feminine dominated value-attitudes (i.e., mother stands for the moral order of the middle class). Finally Cohen perceives the prolonged dependence upon parents of middle class boys due to prolonged formal education as a basis for creating delinquent behavior.[61]

England sees the so-called youth culture as central to a theory of middle class delinquency. The normative system of this teen-age "culture" orients them toward activities that require leisure, spending money, and lack of responsibility. This youth culture has been referred to as immature and irresponsible hedonism by England. Thus adult middle class value-attitudes (i.e., hard work, thrift, and self-denial) tend to be rejected by this hedonistic youth culture. This normative system leads to delinquent behavior (i.e., abuse of rules of the road when driving; joyriding in stolen cars; vandalism and fighting as gangs; sex and love as ends in themselves; and drinking and drug use for thrill-seeking).[62]

Scott and Vaz attribute middle class delinquency to the need to conform to a youth culture. One can comprehend this "culture" through knowledge of the structure and content of the legitimate teen-age culture. Thus most middle class delinquency occurs in the course of typical nondelinquent activities and can be defined within the limits of adolescent value-attitudes. Scott and Vaz blame the permissive structure of both the middle class family and school for the vague normative system held by the typical adolescent. The peer group with its clear normative system replaces the ambiguous family and school value-attitude systems. Therefore youth can conform to peer norms which may deviate from value-attitudes of family and school because they have status and can easily and clearly realize group goals (i.e., joyriding, sex, drinking, and drug use).[63]

Notes

[1]The Dushkin Publishing Group, *Encyclopedia of Sociology,* Guilford, Connecticut: The Dushkin Publishing Group, 1974, p. 79.

[2]*Ibid.,* p. 79; Ritchie Lowry, *Social Problems: A Critical Analysis of Theories and Public Policy,* Lexington, Massachusetts: DC Heath and Company, 1974, pp. 81-82.

[3]Lowry, *op. cit.,* p. 82.

[4]Lowry, *op. cit.,* pp. 93-94; The Dushkin Publishing Group, *op. cit.,* p. 79; Stuart Traub and Craig Little (eds.), *Theories of Deviance,* Itasca, Illinois: F. E. Peacock Publishers, 1975, pp. 31-32.

[5]Traub and Little, *op. cit.,* pp. 33-34.

[6]Robert Faris, *Chicago Sociology,* Chicago: University of Chicago Press, 1970, pp. 44-46; 55.

[7]*Ibid.,* p. 72.

[8]*Ibid.,* pp. 73-74; Frederic Thrasher, *The Gang: A Study of 1313 Gangs in Chicago,* Chicago: University of Chicago Press, 1963.

[9]Faris, *op. cit.,* pp. 75-77; Clifford Shaw and Henry McKay, *Social Factors and Juvenile Delinquency,* Washington, D. C.: U. S. Government Printing Office, 1931; Clifford Shaw, *The Jack-Roller: A Delinquent Boy's Own Story,* Chicago: University of Chicago Press, 1930; Shaw, *The Natural History of a Delinquent Career,* Chicago: University of Chicago Press, 1931; Shaw, *Brothers in Crime,* Chicago: University of Chicago Press, 1938.

[10]Faris, *op. cit.,* p. 77; James Short, Introduction to Revised Edition, Clifford Shaw and Henry McKay, *Juvenile Delinquency and Urban Areas,* Chicago: University of Chicago Press, 1972, pp. xxxix-xiii.

[11]Short, *op. cit.,* p. xl.

[12]*Ibid.,* p. xxxv.

[13]Terrence Morris, *The Criminal Area,* London: Routledge and Kegan Paul, 1958; Sutherland and Cressey, *Criminology,* Philadelphia: Lippincott Co., 1970, pp. 180-197.

[14]Shaw and McKay, *Juvenile Delinquency and Urban Areas,* op. cit., pp. 170-189.

[15]Sutherland and Cressey, *op. cit.,* pp. 132-150.

[16]The President's Commission on Law Enforcement and Administration of Justice, *Task Force Report: Juvenile Delinquency and Youth Crime, op. cit.,* p. 189.

[17]Ronald Chilton, "Continuity in Delinquency Area Research: A Comparison of Studies for Baltimore, Detroit, and Indianapolis," *American Sociological Review,* 29 (1964), pp. 71-83.

[18]David Bordua, "Juvenile Delinquency and Anomie: An Attempt at Replication," *Social Problems,* 6 (1958), p. 237.

[19]Ruth Cavan (ed.), *Readings in Juvenile Delinquency,* Philadelphia: Lippincott, 1975; Rose Giallombardo (ed.), *Juvenile Delinquency,* New York: John Wiley, 1976; Knudten and Schafer (eds.), *Juvenile Delinquency: A Reader,* New York: Random House, 1970; Harwin Voss (ed.), *Society, Delinquency, and Delinquent Behavior,* Boston: Little, Brown and Co., 1970; James Short (ed.), *Gang Delinquency and Delinquent Subcultures,* New York: Harper and Row, 1968: Lewis Yablonsky, *The Violent Gang,* New York: Macmillan, 1963; Irving Spergel, *Racketville, Slumtown, and Haulburg,* Chicago: University of Chicago Press, 1964; Cloward and Ohlin, *Delinquency and Opportunity,* New York: Free Press, 1963; David Matza, *Delinquency and Drift,* New York: John Wiley, 1964; Albert Cohen, *Delinquent Boys,* New York: Free Press, 1955; Short and Strodtbeck, *Group Process and Gang Delinquency,* Chicago: University of Chicago Press, 1965; Malcolm Klein (ed.), *Juvenile Gangs in Context,* New Jersey: Prentice-Hall, 1967; Kvaraceus and Miller, *Delinquent Behavior,* Washington, D. C.: National Education Association, 1959; Herbert Gans, *The Urban Villagers,* New York: Free Press, 1962, pp. 64-73; 229-262.

[20]Haskell and Yablonsky, *Juvenile Delinquency,* Chicago: Rand McNally, 1974, p. 198.

[21]W. Lloyd Warner, *The Social Life of a Modern Community,* New Haven, Connecticut: Yale University Press, 1941, p. 82; Joseph Kahl, *The American Social Class Structure,* New York: Rinehart and Co., 1960; Harold Hodges, *Social Stratification,* Cambridge, Massachusetts: Schenkman Publishing Co., 1964; T. B. Bottomore, *Classes in Modern Society,* New York: Random House, 1966; Melvin Tumin, *Social Stratification,* New Jersey: Prentice-Hall, 1967.

[22]Richard Centers, *The Psychology of Social Classes,* Princeton, New Jersey: Princeton University Press, 1949, pp. 95-96.

[23]Joseph Kahl, *op. cit.*; Herbert Gans, *op. cit.*; Mirra Komarovsky, *Blue Collar Marriage,* New York: Random House, 1962; Jesse Bernard, *Marriage and Family Among Negroes,* New Jersey: Prentice-Hall, 1966; Queen and Habenstein, *The Family in Various Cultures,* Philadelphia: Lippincott, 1967; Bernard Farber, "Types of Family Organization: Child-Oriented, Home-Oriented, and Parent-Oriented," in Arnold Rose (ed.), *Human Behavior and Social Processes,* Boston: Houghton Mifflin, 1962, pp. 285-306; Lee Rainwater, "Social Class and Conjugal Role-Relationships," in Marvin Sussman (ed.), *Sourcebook in Marriage and the Family,* Boston: Houghton Mifflin Co., 1968, pp. 275-288; S. M. Miller, "The American Lower Classes: A Typological Approach," in Frank Riessman et. al., *Mental Health of the Poor,* New York: Free Press, 1964, pp. 139-154. Elizabeth Bott, *Family and Social Network,* London: Tavistock, 1957; Young and Willmott, *Family and Kinship in East London,* Baltimore: Penguin Books, 1957; Margaret Lassell, *Wellington Road,*

Baltimore: Penguin Books, 1962; Lee Rainwater et. al., *Workingman's Wife,* New York: McFadden-Bartell Corp., 1962.

[24]*Ibid.*

[25]*Ibid.*

[26]Havinghurst and Neugarten, *Society and Education,* Boston: Allyn and Bacon, 1967; Joan Roberts (ed.), *School Children in the Urban Slum,* New York: Free Press, 1967; Deutsch, Katz, and Jensen (eds.), *Social Class, Race, and Psychological Development,* New York: Holt, Rinehart, and Winston, 1968; Martin Deutsch, *The Disadvantaged Child,* New York: Basic Books, 1967; Allison Davis, *Social Class Influence Upon Learning,* Cambridge, Massachusetts: Harvard University Press, 1948.

[27]Thomas Langner, "Socioeconomic Status and Personality Characteristics," in Roberts, *School Children in the Urban Slum,* New York: Free Press, 1967, pp. 210-211.

[28]*Ibid.*

[29]Roberts, *op. cit.*; Deutsch, Katz, and Jensen, *op. cit.*; and Deutsch, *op. cit.*

[30]James Bossard, *The Sociology of Child Development,* New York: Harper and Row, 1954; Benjamin Bloom, *Stability and Change in Human Characteristics,* New York, John Wiley, 1964; Martin Deutsch, "Facilitating Development in the Pre-School Child: Social and Psychological Perspectives," *Merrill-Palmer Quarterly,* (1964), 249-263; Martin Deutsch, "Social and Psychological Perspectives on the Development of the Disadvantaged Learner," *The Journal of Negro Education,* (1964), 232-244; Martin Deutsch, "The Role of Social Class in Language Development and Cognition," Institute for Developmental Studies, New York City, 1964; Martin Deutsch, "Early Social Development: Its Influence on School Adaptation," in Daniel Schreiber (ed.), *The School Dropout,* Washington, D. C.: National Education Association, 1964, pp. 89-100; Esther Milner, "A Study of the Relationship Between Reading Readiness in Grade One School Children and Patterns of Parent-Child Interaction," *Child Development,* 1951, pp. 95-112.

[31]Martin Deutsch, "The Disadvantaged Child and the Learning Process," in Passow (ed.), *Education in Depressed Areas,* New York: Columbia University Press, 1963, pp. 163-180; Bloom, Davis, and Hess, *Compensatory Education for Cultural Deprivation,* New York: Holt, Rinehart, and Winston, 1965; Robert Havighurst, "Characteristics and Needs of Students that Affect Learning," in Robinson (ed.), *Meeting Individual Differences in Reading,* Chicago: University of Chicago Press, 1964, pp. 7-16; Havighurst, "Who Are the Socially Disadvantaged?," *The Journal of Negro Education,* 1964, pp. 210-217; Norma Redin and Constance Kamii, "The Child-Rearing Attitudes of Disadvantaged Negro Mothers and Some Educational Implications," *The Journal of Negro Education,* 1965, pp. 138-146; David Ausubel, "The Effects of Deprivation on Learning Patterns," *Audiovisual Instruction,* 1965, pp. 10-12; Bloom et. al., *op. cit.*

Gordon Little and Robert Rockwell, "The Role of Parents and Family Life," *Journal of Negro Education,* 1964, pp. 311-317; John Vera and Leo Goldstein, "The Social Context of Language Acquisition," *Merrill-Palmer Quarterly,* 1964, pp. 265-275.

[32]David Ausubel, *op. cit.*; Gordon and Rockwell, *op. cit.*; Havighurst, *op. cit.;* James Duggens, "Reading and Social Difference," *English Journal,* 1965, pp. 284-288.

[33]David Ausubel, *op. cit.*; Walter Daniel, "Educational Planning for Socially Disadvantaged Children and Youth," *The Journal of Negro Education,* 1964, pp. 203-209; Martin Deutsch, *op. cit.*; Robert Havighurst, *op. cit.*; John Vera, "The Intellectual Development of Slum Children: Some Preliminary Findings," *American Journal of Orthopsychiatry,* 1963, pp. 813-822; Kenneth Wood, "Parental Maladjustment and Functional Articulation Defects in Children," *Journal of Speech and Hearing Disorders,* 1946, pp. 255-275.

[34]Bloom, *op. cit.*; "Conrad and Jones, A Second Study of Familial Resemblances in Intelligence: Environments and Genetic Implications of Parent-Child and Sibling Correlations in the Total Sample," 39th *Yearbook of the National Society of the Study of Education,* part II, Chicago: University of Chicago Press, 1940, pp. 97-141; Jerome Kagan and Marion Freeman, "Relation of Childhood Intelligence, Maternal Behaviors, and Social Class to Behavior During Adolescence," *Child Development,* 1963, pp. 899-911.

[35]Baldwin, Kohloun, and Briese, "Patterns of Parent Behavior," *Psychological Monographs,* 1945; W. J. Campbell, "The Influence of Home Environment on the Educational Progress of Selective Secondary School Children," *British Journal of Educational Psychology,* 1952, pp. 89-100; John Blowquist, "Some Social Factors and School Failures," *International Review of Education,* pp. 163-173; W. B. Dockrell, "School Achievement and the Emotional Climate of the Home," *Canadian Education and Research Digest,* 1963, pp. 120-127; Drews and Teahan, "Parental Attitudes and Academic Achievement," *Journal of Clinical Psychology,* 1957, pp. 328-332; Morrow and Wilson, "Family Relations of Bright High-Achieving and Under-Achieving High School Boys," *Child Development,* 1961, pp. 510-610; Weiner and Murray, "Another Look at the Culturally Deprived and Their Levels of Aspiration," *Journal of Educational Sociology,* 1963, pp. 319-321.

[36]Walter Daniel, "Problems of Disadvantaged Youth Urban and Rural," *The Journal of Negro Education,* 1964, pp. 218-224; Otis Froe, "Educational Planning for Disadvantaged College Youth," *Journal of Negro Education,* 1964, pp. 290-303; Jacob Landers, "The Responsibilities of Teachers and School Administrators," *Journal of Negro Education,* 1964, pp. 318-332.

[37]Robert Havighurst, *op. cit.*; Martin Deutsch, *op. cit.*; Mary Farragher, "The Antisocial Child and the School," *The School Review,* 1964, pp. 472-479; G. O. Johnson, "Organizing Instruction and Curriculum Planning for the Socially Disadvantaged," *The Journal of Negro Education,* 1964, pp. 254-263; Moss and Kagan, "Maternal Influences on Early IQ Scores," *Psychological Reports,* 1958, pp. 655-661.

[38]Little and Rockwell, *op. cit.*; Deutsch, *op. cit.*; G. C. Fusco, "Preparing the City Child for His School," *School Life*, 1964, pp. 5-8.

[39]Bloom, *op. cit.*; Fusco, *op. cit.*; Johnson, *op. cit.;* Deutsch, 1964, *op. cit.*; Jackson and Strattner, "Meaningful Learning and Retention: Non-cognitive Variables," *Review of Educational Research*, 1964, pp. 513-529.

[40]Bloom, 1965, *op. cit.*; Deutsch, 1963, *op. cit.*; Duggins, *op. cit.*; Miriam Goldberg, "Factors Affecting Educational Attainment in Depressed Areas," in Passow (ed.), *Education in Depressed Areas,* New York: Columbia University Press, 1963, pp. 68-99; Frank Riessman, "The Overlooked Positives of Disadvantaged Groups," *The Journal of Negro Education*, 1964, pp. 225-231.

[41]Kenneth Eells et. al., *Intelligence and Cultural Differences*, Chicago: University of Chicago Press, 1951; Anne Anastasi, "Intelligence and Family Size," *Psychological Bulletin*, 1956, pp. 187-209.

[42]Bloom, 1964, *op. cit.*

[43]Basil Bernstein, "Language and Social Class," *The British Journal of Sociology*, 1960; Robert Havighurst, *Developmental Tasks and Education*, New York: David McKay and Co., 1952.

[44]Deutsch, 1964, *op. cit.*; Duggins, *op. cit.*; Vera and Goldstein, *op. cit.*; Jackson and Strattner, *op. cit.*

[45]Farragher, *op. cit.*; Bernard Rosen, "The Achievement Syndrome— A Psychological Dimension of Social Stratification," *American Sociological Review*, 1956, pp. 203-211.

[46]Walter Miller, "Lower Class Culture as a Generating Milieu of Gang Delinquency," *Journal of Social Issues*, 14 (1958), pp. 7-13.

[47]David Bordua, "Delinquent Subcultures: Sociological Interpretations of Gang Delinquency," *The Annals of the American Academy*, 38 (1961), pp. 128-129.

[48]Miller, *op. cit.*, pp. 13-15.

[49]*Ibid.*, pp. 15-17.

[50]The President's Commission on Law Enforcement and Administration of Justice, *Task Force Report: Juvenile Delinquency and Youth Crime, op. cit.*, p. 193.

[51]Cohen, *op. cit.*

[52]Bordua, *op. cit.*, 1961, and "Some Comments on Theories of Gang Delinquency," *Sociological Inquiry*, 32 (1962), pp. 245-260.

[53]Cloward and Ohlin, *op. cit.*, pp. 1-27.

[54]Spergel, *op. cit.*, pp. xv-xviii.

[55]Sykes and Matza, *op. cit.*, pp. 664-670.

[56]Hyman Rodman, "The Lower Class Value Stretch," *Social Forces*, 42 (1963), pp. 205-215.

[57]Robert Gordon et. al., "Values and Gang Delinquency: A Study of Street-Corner Groups," *American Journal of Sociology*, 69 (1963), pp. 109-128.

[58]Edmund Vaz (cd.), *Middle Class Juvenile Delinquency*, New York: Harper and Row, 1967, p. 201.

[59]Vaz, *op. cit.*, p. 202; Robert Bohlke, "Social Mobility, Stratification Inconsistency, and Middle Class Delinquency," *Social Problems*, 8 (1961), pp. 351-363.

[60]William Kvaraceus and Walter Miller, *Delinquent Behavior: Culture and the Individual*, Washington, D. C.: National Education Association, 1959, pp. 77-86.

[61]Cohen, *op. cit.*, pp. 88-102; 157-169.

[62]Ralph England, "A Theory of Middle-Class Juvenile Delinquency," *Journal of Criminal Law, Criminology, and Police Science*, 50 (1960), pp. 536-539.

[63]Joseph Scott and Edmund Vaz, "A Perspective on Middle Class Delinquency," *Canadian Journal of Economics and Political Science*, 29 (1963), pp. 324-330.

Chapter 3

Conflict Theory

Introduction

The sociology of criminal law is currently preoccupied with conflict theory. This is probably due to the fact that criminology has taken a radical or critical turn in theory building since the 1960s.[1] As Taylor et al. state criminology must concern itself with the abolition of inequalities of wealth and power, particularly inequalities in property and life-chances.[2] It must deal with people's relationship towards structures of power, domination, and authority and the ability of individuals to confront these structures in acts of crime, deviance, and dissent.[3] One must create a society in which human diversity (i.e., personal or social) is not subject to the power to criminalize.[4]

Conflict theory studies of the sociology of criminal law are characterized by a "conception of the complex interaction between developments in institutional and social structures and the consciousness of people living within such structures, not by a static conception of pathological and/or anomic individuals colliding with a simple and taken-for-granted set of institutional orders".[5] Conflict theorists conceive the criminal as pathological with the stress on the way in which individuals' criminal behavior and behavior in general are determined. They perceive a relatively simple relationship between power and interest. This view leads to an approach to crime in which action is simply a product of powerful interests or an unequal society and suggests that one can only be criminal when seen or described as criminal by powerful societal interests or when one is a member of a social minority.[6] Last, conflict oriented sociologists of criminal law do not directly address the more general propositions of

53

conflict sociologists such as Dahrendorf because the requisite links between the more general and the more specific concepts and propositions have not been made (i.e., theorists have failed to establish precise links between criminological propositions and the more general sociological concepts they generally reflect).[7]

Sociology of criminal law theorists who are conflict oriented are basically adherents to the social facts paradigm. This is due to their interest in the development of grand, abstract theory and their concern with social institutions, structures, and processes. These theorists are pre-occupied with debunking myths about society and trying to change what they regard as harmful social structures and processes that exist in today's post-industrial social order.

Hills

Law is not defined by Hills who accepts the conclusions of interest-group theorists that criminal laws change as the interest-power structure of society changes. Thus criminal law definitions change and adapt themselves to the changes in the societal social order.[8]

Hills states that there are two competing major theoretical perspectives to the sociology of criminal law: the value-consensus and interest-group theories. The value-consensus position states that criminal laws reflect those societal values which transcend the immediate, narrow interests of various individuals and groups, expressing the social consciousness of the whole society. The legal process thus regulates, harmonizes, and reconciles all conflicting claims to enhance the welfare of social order.[9]

The interest-group position states that criminal laws will change with modification in the interest-power structure of society. As societal social conditions change, the criminal law will adapt to these changes in the distribution of power of various interest groups. Interest-group theorists emphasize the ability of particular groups to shape the societal legal system to serve their needs and safeguard their interests.[10]

Turk

Turk attacks what he calls the "moral functionalist" (i.e., structural-functionalist) conception of law. This concept is defined as essentially a means for settling or precluding disputes by articulating the requirements of an idea of justice and retaining those whose actions are incompatable with such requirements.[11] A major weakness of the functional conception of law is its intellectual bias toward defining away the conflictual aspects of law. Thus the legal means of conflict management are peaceful and an assumption is made that consensual, non-coercive methods are the only effective means of conflict prevention or control. A second weakness of the functional approach is its tendency to equate legal with consensual means of conflict resolution, which is assumed to be more effective than coercive means. Law can be perceived here as an ideological tool to be utilized in the maintenance of social order by providing a constant means for channeling and limiting conflicts. Law is thus viewed as a normative system which is a weak and inconsistent conflict resolver. Third, the functional view assumes that theory should be based on the concept of natural law. Thus the theory of justice proposed by functionalism is based on faith, not upon empirical inquiry.[12]

A more value-neutral and empirical conception of law is offered by Turk based on the conception of law as a form of social power. Central to Turk's definition of law as the process of formally articulated normative expectations is the concept of conflict. The law appears to be a set of resources for which individuals contend and with which they are able to put forth their ideas and interests against others in order to work out and resolve conflictual situations (i.e., people use law as an instrument of power).[13]

Power is defined by Turk as the control of resources in an attempt to maximize the chance of acceptable solution of potential or actual conflict. Law can thus be considered as a form of power or resource control. There are several kinds of power contained in the legal concept: (1) police power (i.e., state sanctioned control of coercion)—police power means having the law on your side in conflictual situations with the implied use of coercion against one's adversaries if there is refusal to conform to legal agreement or a court order; (2) economic power (i.e., control of production, allocation, and use of resources)—economic power can enhance or erode an individual's life chances, economic changes can be facilitated by law but the law has difficulty in causing radical economic changes; (3) political power (i.e., control decision-making processes)—the law provides the format for articulating, interpreting, and implementing organizational norms and decisions, contributes to private as well as public order, and is the record of events and arbiter of rightness; (4) ideological power (i.e., control of knowledge and value-attitudes)—the law has authoritative force upon people's intellectual frames of reference: the concept of legality promotes adherence to the political order and gives prestige and approval to traditional conceptual frameworks while denying legitimacy to other conceptions through legal rejection or refusal of legal recognition; and (5) diversionary power (i.e., control of mass media and leisure)—preoccupation with the law as human interest or information diverts attention from potentially dangerous problems. This aspect of the law also reinforces the feeling that the law is all powerful, part of everyday life, and thus a constituent of social reality.[14]

Turk states that the conception of law as power is a more useful concept than law as conflict arbiter since the former concept utilizes conflict theory and is empirical while the latter concept is more deductive in nature and based on normative assumptions. Thus a structural-functional orientation to sociology of law creates ideological limitations since it does not question the motives of those who control and use legal power. The power orientation questions those who wield legal power and thus assumes that the law and the legal institution are not value-neutral but oriented to special interests. A particular advantage of the power approach to law is that it shows how laws become formally binding upon members of society who have neither created these laws nor been socialized into the acceptance of such laws (i.e., the power conception is more concerned with analysis of social processes rather than with social structures). Further the power approach to law is concerned with the human actions creating the legal/nonlegal distinction. Finally this conceptual approach of the law is concerned with the concept of social order, conflict, and change.[15]

Law is a source and means of conflict according to Turk. He has developed twelve propositions indicating the major ways that law promotes or facilitates conflict. The first proposition states that the availability of legal resources is an incentive to social conflict because potentially or actively conflicting parties cannot risk the possible costs of not having the law on their side (i.e., one must gain or increase control of legal resources in order to keep an opponent at a disadvantage).[16] The second proposition states that the individual with greater legal as well as nonlegal power may be able to increase his influence over less fortunate individuals who may ultimately be excluded from access to legal resources and thus unable to advance his interests through the courts (i.e., possession of nonlegal power can result in differential access to legal power).[17]

The next proposition states that legal power provides both the opportunity and the means to deny legal conflict-making abilities to those not having power. But where issues cannot be resolved legally, there is the problem of conflict resolution. It will occur at greater cost socially and economically due to the relative lack of status of nonlegal mechanisms for dispute settlement.[18] When power differences are less distinct between the parties, there is the likelihood of recourse to use of legal action since each party hopes to improve this position at the other's expense. On the other hand, where power differences are great between the parties, the less powerful may hope that a threat of legal action or actual action may be advantageous.[19] The fifth proposition states there is less likelihood of nonlegal dispute resolution when the parties have access to legal action (i.e., the availability of legal facilities decreases the possibility of conflict resolution through nonlegal means).[20]

Legalization of a conflict can create a climate making it more difficult for settlement of the dispute rather than transforming the disagreement into a form more readily solvable. Thus the formal legalizing of a dispute can harden existing social boundaries, cleavages, and inequities by making it difficult to live with, ignore, or alter them.[21] Legal procedures (i.e., normative) can be used to exclude or distort information that can be essential to adequate understanding of the conflict. Therefore procedural norms can prevent or slow down the resolution of a conflict.[22]

The eighth proposition states that legal formulae and processes emphasize the limitation and end of conflictual behavior (i.e., law is oriented toward regulation of conflict symptoms rather than eliminating the sources of conflict). Conflict legalization usually limits the means or confuses the issues. Thus those involved in the legal battle may eventually regard the legalization process as a means for out-maneuvering an opponent or as a tool for gaining time to plan a new strategy.[23] Legal settlement tactics can conflict with tactics needed to accomplish a real settlement (i.e., a formal concession obtained in court after protracted legal battle can create difficulties for one's opponent to accept defeat and can reduce the chances of future resolution outside of further legal action).[24]

Legal resolution of formal conflict may not actually resolve the conflict between the parties (i.e., formal court decisions may not be acceptable to either party in the litigation). Thus nonlegal means to conflict resolution may be resorted to and future recourse to formal legal action may be reduced as an unsatisfactory means to conflict resolution.[25] The law promotes cynicism, evasion, and defiance with respect to normative expectations and decisions due to the fact that bias is present among both court personnel and legal practitioners. In theory the law is value-neutral but in practice it is partial to those holding power or having access to power. Thus law believed to be biased may be as ineffectual as law that is biased to those who are powerless.[26] The last proposition states that legal changes that cause or ease nonlegal changes increase the likelihood of further conflicts (i.e., the short term effect of legally promoted changes contributes to increased conflicts).[27]

The use of the power conception of law as an empirical tool for the study of sociology of law is the basic contribution made by Turk. He correctly perceives the need for further historical and anthropological studies in an attempt to determine the origins and evolution of law in traditional and industrial societies. Second he feels that there is a need to have an objective conception of law which is not structural-functionally oriented. What is not wanted is the reifying of the legal/nonlegal distinction as is made by most functionalists according to Turk. He therefore proposes that the main research concern should be development of a useful comprehension of the control and mobilization of legal resources. Last Turk perceives law other than an essence, property, or function to be found in cultural and social institutions, structures, and processes but rather an "empirically specifiable set of objects of specific attention".[28] Turk is essentially examining both the concept of social norm as applied to the legal institution of society and the norm of reciprocity as applied to interpersonal and larger group relationships. He also wants to deal with the legal concept from the social psychological perspective. Thus his orientation to the sociology of law is similar to structural-functionalists but without the mystification of the legal institution in society.

Chambliss

Law is defined by Chambliss and Seidman as not merely a body of rules but as a dynamic process involving every aspect of state action, for this action involves either creation of a norm, adjudication about its content, adjudication that has been violated, or a sanctioning process. This set of processes comprises the law.[29]

In his writings, Chambliss refers to the consensus model or theoretical approach to law and society as the value-expression hypothesis and to the conflict model as the interest-group hypothesis.[30] In 1971, he renamed the two models of law and society value-concensus and value-antagonism.[31] In 1973 Chambliss refers to the models as positivist (i.e., functionalist) and conflict.[32] In 1975 he has updated his 1969 theoretical viewpoint and reutilizes the terms consensus and conflict models in reference to the legal system of society.[33] Here Chambliss refers specifically to both structural-functional and conflict perspectives.[34]

The sociology of criminal law is presently dipolar in theoretical orientation according to Chambliss. The functionalist view states that acts are defined as criminal because they offend the moral beliefs of society. Those who violate the criminal law are punished according to the prevailing mores of society. Individuals are labeled criminal because their behavior exceeds tolerance limits set by the community. The lower classes are more likely to be arrested because they commit more crimes. Criminal law becomes more restitutive rather than repressive (i.e., penal) as society becomes gesellschaft. The conflict view states that acts are defined as criminal because it is to the interest of the ruling class. Ruling class members are able to violate the laws while members of the subject classes will be punished. Individuals are labeled criminal because it is in the interest of the ruling class and regardless of community tolerance. The lower classes are labeled criminal more often because the bourgeoisie's control of the state protects them from stigmatization. As capitalist society becomes more gesellschaft and the gap between the bourgeoisie and proletariat widens, penal law will expand in an effort to coerce the proletariat into submission.[35]

With respect to the sociology of criminal law, the consensus and conflict models of society present quite different fundamental assumptions according to Chambliss. The consensus model emphasizes the shared interests of everyone in society and the consensus over fundamental values which this shared interest creates. The conflict model emphasizes the role of conflicts between social classes and interest groups as the moving force behind the creation and implementation of criminal law.[36]

Chambliss lists the theories derived from the consensus perspective. There are theories that see the law as a reflection of "perceived social needs" which all reasonable men agree must be met if society is to continue; theories that see the criminal law as an expression of what is in the "public interest"; theories that perceive the law as a reflection of the "moral indignation" of a particularly influential segment of society; and theories that see the law as an expression of the most fundamental values that are inherent in society.[37] Chambliss also lists the theories derived from the conflict perspective. There are theories that emphasize the role of "moral entrepreneurs" (i.e., groups that organize to achieve legal changes which they think are essential for societal well-being); theories that emphasize the importance of bureaucratic interests in the rationalization of problems that are inherent in society; theories that emphasize the conflicts that are inherent between interest groups competing for the favors of state power; and theories that emphasize the inherent conflicts between those who rule and those who are ruled and who perceive the criminal law as incorporating rules for enforcing the interests and ideologies of the ruling classes.[38]

The structural-functional perspective has dominated the sociology of criminal law for many years according to Chambliss. The basic assumption of this perspective is that the criminal law is a set of rules stipulated by legislatures and courts which reflect societal beliefs. This perspective also sees the criminal law as fulfilling certain basic societal needs. The problem with this perspective is its failure to specify whose interests, views, and needs are being satisfied by the societal legal system. The emergent perspective in sociology of criminal law is the one emphasizing social conflict as the moving force behind the criminal law in action. The social relations which are part of the class, labor, and productive systems of capitalist societies are viewed as more important in determining the content and functioning of the criminal law process than are societal values, norms, and beliefs.[39]

Quinney

In his book, *Crime and Justice in Society*, Quinney feels that the most significant developments in modern criminology have been the awareness of the criminal law and inquiries into its foundation, enforcement, and administration. This statement is based on the knowledge that criminal law only rarely is studied by criminologists despite the fact that Classical school theorists defined crime strictly in legal terms. This was due to the influence of the Positive school theorists who adopted a nonlegal conceptualization of crime. Only a small group of criminologists since the 1930's (i.e., Michael, Adler, Tappan, Vold, Jeffery, and Turk) have called for a sociological analysis of the criminal law. These theorists feel that crime should be studied within the framework of the criminal law.[40]

Quinney reviews the evolution of the criminal law in English society. The concept of criminal law emerged only when the custom of private vengeance was replaced by the principle of harm to the whole community when any member was injured. Criminal law developed only after the achievement of political unity which allowed the establishment of a centralized government that could administer the law universally. In turn the common law evolved as the king's power grew and criminal statutes evolved (i.e., laws of theft and vagrancy) in response to societal needs created by socioeconomic changes in society. American law developed from the common law traditions of England although tinged by a puritanical morality (i.e., Prohibition, sexual psychopath laws, and drug laws).[41]

Behind all law formulation are special interest groups who stand to benefit. Criminal laws are formulated to promote the interest of certain societal groups. Administration of the criminal law is political and extra-legal considerations are commonplace. Thus the criminal justice process is discretionary, caters to special interests, and is influenced by socio-economic considerations.[42]

Criminal law theory has not been developed despite considerable research on the topic over the years. Legal theory and sociological theory are as far apart today concerning the sociology of criminal law as they were in 1912. Quinney turns to Pound's theory of interests as a possible point of convergence for the legal theorists and sociological theorists to rally around. Despite Pound's theorizing, research on the role of interests in formulating and administering the law has been non-existent. Quinney feels that Pound's theory of interests is based on a consensus model of law that operates in a pluralistic society, and accordingly law adjusts and reconciles conflicting interests.[43]

A sociological theory of interests is presented by Quinney to provide a theoretical perspective for presenting and interpreting research in the sociology of criminal law. His theory postulates that law is created by interests, assumes a conflict-power model of society, and proposes a conceptual scheme for analyzing the relationship between law and interests. A number of propositions are put forth by Quinney in support of his interests theory. First, law consists of specialized rules that are created and interpreted in a politically organized society. Second, this type of society is based on an interest structure. Third, this interest structure is characterized by unequal distribution of power and by conflict. Last, the law is formulated and administered within the interest structure of politically organized society.[44]

Quinney, in *Criminal Justice in America*, takes up where he left off in his analysis of criminal law from previously published material. He states that since 1970, a body of empirical research has been developed on the sociology of criminal law but most of it has been positivistic and directed toward explaining how laws are formulated, enforced, and administered rather than devoted to questions about why law exists, whether law is necessary, or what constitutes a just and equitable legal system. Even Neoclassical (i.e., social constructionist) theorists avoid a critical analysis of the contemporary legal system, fail to analyze the legal order from a non-status quo perspective, and conform to the existing social order conception of the legal institution. Thus contemporary sociology of criminal law accepts and supports the existing legal order. It also analyzes the legal system in terms of the existing social order. Therefore there has been no critique of the legal order of advanced capitalist society in the sociology of the criminal law.[45]

A critical theory of criminal law that is based on a Marxist perspective and understanding of the legal order is advocated by Quinney. According to his critical theory, law in capitalist society gives political recognition to powerful social and economic interests. The legal system provides the mechanism for the forceful and violent control of the majority in society. The state and its accompanying legal system reflect and serve the needs of the ruling class. Awareness that the legal system does not serve society as a whole is Quinney's starting point for what he calls a critical understanding of law in capitalist society.[46]

The goal of a critical theory of criminal law is to demystify crime and justice in society. Quinney states his critical theory in a syllogistic fashion. His theory starts with the statement that the American state is based on an advanced capitalist economy organized to serve ruling class interests. Criminal law is an instrument of both the state and the ruling class who use it to maintain and perpetuate the existing social and economic order. The contradictions of advanced capitalism require that the subordinate classes remain oppressed, especially through the coercion and violence supplied by the legal system. Criminal law will be increasingly used in an attempt to maintain domestic order as capitalist society is increasingly threatened by oppressed people who are abused by the elitist oriented criminal law.[47]

Reasons

In his book, *The Criminologist: Crime and the Criminal*, Reasons states that the study of crime has been mostly of criminals, not the criminal law. He feels there is a need for studies dealing with the emergence of criminal laws within a socio-historical context. Further, criminologists have not been concerned with the sociological study of law but with crime control.[48]

The various schools of jurisprudence in general and the sociological jurisprudence of Pound in particular are discussed by Reasons. He deals with Quinney's social reality of crime theory, Quinney's sociological theory of interests, and Quinney's critical theory of criminal law. Reasons criticizes Quinney's theories by stating that all states whether capitalist or socialist have legal systems that serve some interests more than others. He faults Quinney further since the latter does not demonstrate that socialist society has a legal system that is equalitarian. Reasons does feel that Quinney demyths the American legal system on this particular issue.[49]

Finally Reasons examines the concepts of victimless crimes and of overcriminalization. He feels it is important to analyze the law and its agents as an independent variable in the creation and maintenance of criminal behavior. Crime may be viewed as phenomena created by special interests who wish their definition of rightness to triumph and become the laws of society.[50]

The Schwendingers

Sutherland's definition of crime as a violation of the criminal law is commonly accepted by most criminological theorists today. Thus most define crime and the criminal by referring to the definitions proposed by the state. Therefore criminological theory is indirectly determined by the legislative arm of the state because the definitions of specific crimes are formulated by the legislatures, county councils, and city councils of our society.[51]

There appears to be no single definition of crime acceptable to all criminologists (refer to Sellin, Sutherland, and Tappan). It appears that the types of activity or kinds of relationships examined by the criminologist determine his definition of crime. Four definitions of crime are analyzed by the Schwendingers: (1) operational (i.e., procedures for measuring crime); (2) analytic (i.e., meaning of categories such as crimes against the person or concepts such as anomie); (3) nominal (i.e., shortened forms of commonly understood meanings or use a property, relationship, or function); and (4) real (i.e., casual or what signifies the proper conditions for the existence of a phenomenon). Legal definitions of crime are of questionable value when used nominally or analytically, are invalid when used operationally, and are only descriptive when used in a causal framework. Therefore the Schwendingers question whether the legal definition of crime proposed by jurisprudents and most sociologists of law is the most scientific or should be standardized.[52]

Legal definitions assume certain political conditions (i.e., political power determines the precision of the definition). Most theorists believe that deviant behavior which is legally defined as crime existed in the community long before its legal definition was formulated (i.e., the law does not determine crime but crime determines the law). Theorists are continuously redefining the legal definition of crime, in part because once formed legally established sanctioning processes influence criminal behavior. There is the problem of differentiating between criminals who have been sanctioned by law and those deviants who have avoided sanctions but acted in a criminal manner and have not been tried and found guilty of any criminal statute violation.[53]

Theorists often use the concept of social sanction to define crime. They should organize their defining criteria with reference to a general theory of the political institution of society if they want to utilize real definitions of criminal justice institutions according to the Schwendingers. Thus the sanction concept is not necessary in constructing real definitions of the causes or control of crime. Therefore a definition that promotes crime as behavior which is state sanctioned is misleading.[54]

The idea that the sanction concept is necessary for any type of crime definition raises the question whether sanctions are generic to defining the crime concept. The sanction concept is not generic for defining crime according to the Schwendingers. Further, to state that crime must be defined in terms of sanction is to place the sanction concept as manditory for comprehension of crime causation, control, and prevention. The contention that sanctions are generic to the crime definition limits the definition of crime to those in political control of society. Thus power appears to make sanctions generic to the crime definition.[55]

Theorists have tended to avoid the use of standards which are useful in evaluating the moral justifications of legal codes. Explanation is needed of such ethical criteria as social injury, public wrong, and anti-social behavior if one is to replace the sanction criterion used by the state in the definition of crime. Theorists tend to ignore nonlegal definitions of crime as use of the legal norm in most definitions of crime persists in the form of conduct norms or normative conflict. Reference is made to the technocratic doctrines of society and their use of norms of established institutions as standards of behavior (i.e., creation and maintenance of normative consensus and minimization of conflict). All this is just a restatement of structural-functional theory (i.e., what Chambliss calls consensus theory) which emphasizes the social equilibrium concept approach to social systems.[56]

There is no attempt by the Schwendingers to propose a definitive alternative to the legal definition of crime. There should be an established moral criteria for defining crime. A value-free theory of crime is not possible since moral standards are always used in one form or another in defining crime. The Schwendingers feel that the historically determined rights of individuals are the only criteria which can define crime and thus reject the traditional structural-functional criterion (i.e., imperatives of social institutions). Egalitarianism and liberalism fail as concepts formulating a conception of human rights.[57]

Theorists must recognize the political limits of the ethical doctrine of equal intrinsic value when applied to people when formulating a human rights concept. Identification must be made of forms of individual and collective behavior which can be engaged in, in order to defend human rights. The crime definition using the human rights criterion will have to identify the violation of these rights and establish the priorities regarding different rights. Although portions of contemporary criminal law overlap with the human rights definition of crime, many forms of behavior would not be defined as crimes under this criterion (i.e., crimes without victims and crimes of consumption).[58]

Structural-functional theorists do not like social systems defined as criminal. Thus an analysis of social systems or social relationships alone is incomplete since one cannot limit research to only institutions that define, adjudicate, and sanction individual criminals. Structural-functionalists define crime in terms of the socially necessary and sufficient conditions for its existence (i.e., refer to the ways in which agents of the state react to criminal behavior). According to the Schwendingers, the existing social institutions and socio-economic relationships are criminal (i.e., social systems which can be regulated or eliminated in order to prevent or control crime). Further, the term crime as a label for social systems becomes the regulation or elimination of social relationships, properties of social systems, or social systems taken as a whole.[59]

When the human rights concept replaces the structural-functionalist (i.e., legally operative) definition of crime, then one can deal with violations of human rights as well as the rights of racial, economic, and sexual equality. Thus persons who deny these rights to others can be defined as criminal as well as social relationships and systems which cause the breach of these rights.[60]

The Schwendingers' basic purpose is to seek an alternative to the traditional structural-functionalist definition of crime. Their solution is to use the human rights doctrine. This doctrine is founded in conflict theory which challenges the basic tenets of consensus theory. Thus societal institutions, structures, and processes can and should be examined as possible causes of bias which perpetuate myths concerning what and who is criminal. The Schwendingers attack the majority of criminal theorists because they appear unable to perceive any other approach to criminology other than that proposed by traditional structural-functional theory.

Krisberg

Krisberg feels that traditional sociological theory and methodology (i.e., structural-functionalism) have little value to offer contemporary sociology of law theorists. It is felt that C. Wright Mills and his conception of the sociological imagination can provide a new perspective to sociological analysis. Krisberg utilizes five categories derived from Mills with which to define an alternative methodology for sociological research and theory development.[61] The first category is the relating of private troubles to public issues. Thus one wants to relate the personal problems of individuals with the societal social problems causal to individual problems. The methodology utilized by Mills was based on a study of individual value-attitudes within the sub-cultural and cultural environments. The researcher should analyze the personal interaction with societal social institutions. Krisberg advocates utilization of life histories, ethnographic and depth interviews. But he also advocates that the researcher be personally involved in the resolution of the social problem, not just aware of its existence.[62]

The second category is the use of the perspective and substance of the "new" history. This proposition is related to Mills' emphasis upon history as a vital part of social inquiry. Thus the theorist should approach history with skepticism and be prepared to demythify false conceptions of people, structures, processes, and institutions of society. Research should be guided by theoretical concerns, not by the availability of data. Thus abstract empiricism should be avoided at all costs since it makes the theorist into a "toolmaker" who attempts to apply natural science methodology to social science situations which are methodologically impossible to interpret accurately and precisely.[63]

The third category is the use of a compassionate as opposed to an appreciative mode in research. The sociological imagination is humanistic in orientation. The typical symbolic interaction theorist which Krisberg criticizes is able to appreciate the problems and suffering of those unfortunates observed in society but he lacks compassion. This theorist sees the world of the lower classes and can be a defender of these people but maintains his intellectual distance and retains his sense of superior status by not getting involved in "loser" causes. The sociological imagination approach demands that subject and theorist share their feelings, needs, rewards, and plans. There must be an empathetic tie and respect between researcher and subject. Thus the theorist must select a problem for analysis not for self-gratification but for the betterment of mankind.[64]

The fourth category is the relation of one's intellectual work to a change oriented practice and a refining of theory from the experience of that practice. The theorist must take ideological stances with respect to issues of political significance. Thus those theorists who are to closely approximate the sociological imagination have a history of praxis or are engaged in change directed practice. One must have political and moral commitments and avoid what Mills calls liberal practicality (i.e., the concept of value-neutrality).[65]

Mills is opposed to value-neutrality and advocates that one let his value-attitudes be felt but not totally destroy one's objectivity. Thus possibly value-neutrality is an intellectual device to deny any emotional involvement on a critical social issue. Liberal practicality also tends to support authority and to serve the interests of the status quo. It serves as a source of legitimation of those in power. Liberal practicality can also be indicted for lack of interest or concern with political and economic problems of society. Any concern with the redistribution of societal resources is rejected since this would destroy the status quo and threaten the elite who control society. Second those theorists who are adherents to liberal practicality tend to be unable to deal with political issues in proper perspective. There is no challenge of structural inequalities since this would destroy the status quo and expose both the elite with all their privileges and their system of exploitation of the majority of the members of society.[66]

Last the sociological imagination approach demands the careful selection of an audience with which to communicate. Thus theorists must reach people concerned with social change. This means that one's professional standing in the academic community should be subservient to the needs of the community. Therefore the theorist must become involved in grass roots organizations, protests, and use political pressure tactics which might place him in a delicate position regarding his academic career and standing in the intellectual community. To be an adherent of the sociological imagination approach commits the theorist to social change.[67]

The ideological position stated by Krisberg based on the writings of C. Wright Mills can only be pursued by those dedicated to the cause of eradication of social injustice who are willing to stake their personal reputation and professional careers in the cause of social change. It is potentially a dangerous position to take in today's uncertain academic social order.

The sociological imagination as applied to the sociology of law is generally a condemnation of structural-functionalism with its lack of comprehension of history and its myth perpetuating propensities. It is also a condemnation of Weber's action theory concept of *verstehen* with the implied notion of value-neutrality. Further it also rejects symbolic interaction theory ala Goffman and Becker since these theorists are relatively value-neutral. The sociological imagination approach is a combination of conflict theory with action theory that is value-biased.

The theorist should become involved in his research in order to change societal processes, structures, and institutions. He should also destroy societal myths in order to promote social change.

Thus the sociologist of law should reform or change the legal institution wherever needed and work for the reformation of both the criminal justice system and the criminal law where needed. The approach suggested by the sociological imagination would most admirably suit the radical approach to sociology of criminal law advocated by Chambliss, Turk, and Quinney but would meet with much opposition from theorists who are analysts in the subdivision of sociology of civil law, sociological jurisprudence, and anthropology of law where structural-functionalism still has control over most theorists' minds.

Notes

[1]Robert Rich, *The Sociology of Law: An Introduction to its Theorists and Theories,* Washington, DC: University Press of America, 1977; *Theory and Practice of Criminal Justice,* Washington, DC: University Press of America, 1977. Robert Rich, "Sociological Paradigms and the Sociology of Law: An Historical Analysis", in Reasons and Rich (eds.), *The Sociology of Law,* Scarborough, Canada: Butterworth and Company Ltd., 1978, pp. 1-40.

[2]Taylor, Walton, and Young, *The New Criminology: For a Social Theory of Deviance,* London: Routledge and Kegan Paul, 1973, p. 281.

[3]*Ibid.,* p. 268.

[4]*Ibid.,* p. 282.

[5]*Ibid.,* pp. 266-267.

[6]*Ibid.,* p. 268.

[7]Chiricos and Waldo, "Socioeconomic Status and Criminal Sentencing: an Empirical Assessment of a Conflict Proposition", *American Sociological Review* 40 (December, 1975), p. 770.

[8]Stuart Hills, *Crime, Power, and Morality: The Criminal-Law Process in the United States,* Scranton, Pennsylvania: Chandler Publishing Company, 1971, p. 5.

[9]*Ibid.,* pp. 3-4.

[10]*Ibid.,* pp. 4-5.

[11]Austin Turk, "Law as a Weapon in Social Conflict", *Social Problems* 23 (February, 1976), p. 276.

[12]*Ibid.,* pp. 277-279.

[13]*Ibid.*, pp. 276, 279-280.

[14]*Ibid.*, pp. 280-282.

[15]*Ibid.*, p. 282.

[16]*Ibid.*, pp. 283-284.

[17]*Ibid.*, p. 284.

[18]*Ibid.*, p. 284.

[19]*Ibid.*, pp. 284-285.

[20]*Ibid.*, p. 285.

[21]*Ibid.*, p. 285.

[22]*Ibid.*, p. 285.

[23]*Ibid.*, p. 286.

[24]*ibid.*, p. 286.

[25]*Ibid.*, pp. 286-287.

[26]*Ibid.*, p. 287.

[27]*Ibid.*, p. 287.

[28]*Ibid.*, p. 283.

[29]William Chambliss & Robert Seidman, *Law, Order, and Power,* Reading, Massachusetts: Addison-Wesley Publishing Company, 1971, p. 9.

[30]William Chambliss (ed.), *Crime and the Legal Process,* New York: McGraw-Hill Book Company, 1969, pp. 8 & 10.

[31]William Chambliss & Robert Seidman, *Law, Order, and Power,* Reading, Massachusetts: Addison-Wesley Publishing Company, 1971, pp. 17, 40, 45-46, 53-54.

[32]William Chambliss, "Functional and Conflict Theories of Crime," New York, MAA Modular Publications, *Module* 17, 1973, pp. 1-23.

[33]William Chambliss (ed.), *Criminal Law In Action*, Santa Barbara, California: Hamilton Publishing Company, 1975, pp. 5-6.

[34]*Ibid.*, pp. 476-477.

[35]William Chambliss, "Functional and Conflict Theories of Crime," New York: MSS Modular Publications, 1973, *Module* 17, pp. 1-23.

[36]William Chambliss (ed.), *Criminal Law In Action*, Santa Barbara, California: Hamilton Publishing Company, 1975, p. 5.

[37]*Ibid.*, p. 6.

[38]*Ibid.*, p. 6.

[39]*Ibid.*, pp. 476-477.

[40]Richard Quinney, *Crime and Justice in Society*, Boston: Little, Brown and Company, 1969, pp. 1-9.

[41]*Ibid.*, pp. 10-16.

[42]*Ibid.*, pp. 17-21.

[43]*Ibid.*, pp. 22-26.

[44]*Ibid.*, pp. 27-30.

[45]Richard Quinney, *Criminal Justice in America*, Boston: Little, Brown and Company, 1974, pp. 8-16.

[46]*Ibid.*, pp. 17-21.

[47]*Ibid.*, pp. 22-25.

[48]Charles E. Reasons, *The Criminologist: Crime and the Criminal*, Pacific Palisades, California: Goodyear Publishing Co., 1974, pp. 99-100.

[49]*Ibid.*, pp. 101-102.

[50]*Ibid.*, pp. 103-104.

[51]Herman and Julia Schwendinger, "Defenders of Order or Guardians of Human Rights?", *Issues in Criminology* 5 (Summer, 1970), pp. 128-129.

[52]*Ibid.*, pp. 129-132.

[53]*Ibid.*, pp. 133-134.

[54]*Ibid.*, pp. 134-135.

[55]*Ibid.*, pp. 135-136.

[56]*Ibid.*, pp. 136-142.

[57]*Ibid.*, pp. 143-145.

[58]*Ibid.*, p. 146.

[59]*Ibid.*, pp. 146-148.

[60]*Ibid.*, pp. 148-149.

[61]Barry Krisberg, "The Sociological Imagination Revisited", *The Canadian Journal of Criminology and Corrections* 16 (April, 1974), pp. 146-148.

[62]*Ibid.*, pp. 148-150.

[63]*Ibid.*, pp. 150-152.

[64]*Ibid.*, pp. 153-154.

[65]*Ibid.*, pp. 154-155.

[66]*Ibid.*, pp. 155-158.

[67]*Ibid.*, pp. 158-160.

Chapter 4

The Paradigmatic Approach

Non-Marxian Models

Paradigm Definitions

A paradigm is defined as a collection of the major assumptions, concepts, and propositions in a substantive area. Paradigms serve to orient theorizing in an intellectual discipline and resemble models. A conceptual model is a picture of social reality. It is a set of assumptions that are accepted as true and that influence one's perception of the working of society. A model only reflects limited aspects of the totality of social reality and is thus biased to all reality. A model is not a theory since it is more general. Thus models cannot be proved wrong but consist of generally more than one related theory of specific phenomena that can be tested in reality.[1]

Thomas Kuhn's research on paradigms in the early 1960's was modified in the early 1970's to apply to the field of sociology. The initial application of this approach to sociology was made by Friedrich followed by further analyses by Lakatos and Musgrave, Lodahl and Gordon, Phillips, Effrat, and Ritzer. It was not until 1973 that the paradigmatic approach was applied to the field of criminology by Chambliss followed by Reasons. Finally it was not until 1976 that this perspective was applied to sociology of criminal law theory by Rich.[2]

The Paradigms of Ritzer

According to Ritzer, there are currently only three basic paradigms in sociology. These are the social facts paradigm, social definition paradigm, and social behavior paradigm.[3] A paradigm is defined as:

> "a fundamental image of the subject matter within a science. It serves to define what should be studied, what questions should be asked, and what rules should be followed in interpreting the answers obtained. The paradigm is the broadest unit of consensus within a science and serves to differentiate one scientific community or subcommunity from another. It subsumes, defines, and interrelates the exemplars, theories, and methods/tools that exist within it."[4]

Criminology and its subdivision, sociology of law should fit into one or more of these paradigms. We will begin the analysis of Ritzer's work by first defining the various applicable paradigms and describing their theories.

Social Facts Paradigm

The social facts paradigm is composed of two theories, structual-functional and conflict theory. Structural-functionalists feel that structures and institutions can contribute to the maintenance of other social facts and can also have negative consequences for them (i.e., utilize the concepts of function and dysfunction). Followers of this theory justify the status quo and tend to have a conservative societal orientation (i.e., emphasize order in society and de-emphasize conflict and change).[5] In particular structural-functionalists are oriented toward the analysis of social structures and institutions. Concern is with relationships between structures, between institutions, and between structures and institutions. The individual is largely controlled by social facts that are external and coercive. Functionalists view society as static or in a state of moving equilibrium. They strongly emphasize the fact that society is orderly; that every societal element contributes to stability; and that society is kept together informally by norms, values, and a common morality.[6]

Conflict theory for the most part is simply a series of positions directly antithetical to structural-functionalist ideas according to Ritzer. Thus conflict theorists are oriented toward the study of social structures and institutions like functionalists but perceive society as based on conflict and consensus emphasizing the role of power in maintaining societal order.[7] In particular, conflict theorists see every structure and institution of society subject to change, conflict-ridden, and riddled by dissension. Whatever order there is in society stems from the coercion of the powerless by those in authority. Differential authority is an attribute of various societal positions. Authority does not reside in individuals but in these positions. Thus the individual is concerned with societal positions and the differential distribution of power among these positions. Hence the structural origin of conflicts must be sought in the arrangement of social roles endowed with expectations of domination or subjection (i.e., authority implies both superordination and subordination). Finally, the identification of various authority roles within society is the primary focus of conflict theorists.[8]

Social Definition Paradigm

The social definition paradigm is composed of three theories: action, symbolic interaction and phenomenology. Action theorists (ala Weber) view the individual as possessing a dynamic, creative, voluntaristic mind. They see Weber's *verstehen* concept as a method for gathering data on social institutions and social structures, not as a method for understanding the mental process. The action theorist attempts to put himself in the place of the actor, not in order to comprehend the person but to understand the cultural and societal milieu in which the actor exists.[9] Social action theorists examine the problem solving process through the minds of the actors under study. They examine the actor's means to ends whether both are valued in the same manner or differently utilizing the *verstehen* concept (i.e., empathy and reliving the experiences of the actor). The feelings, emotions, and habits of the actor are sometimes receptive to analysis using this concept (i.e., interpretive understanding).[10]

Symbolic interaction theory deals with covert aspects of behavior. Theorists view behavior as a process of interpretation inserted between the environmental stimulus and response of the actor. Social facts are not viewed as things controlling or coercing the individual but only as the framework within which symbolic interaction takes place. Individuals fit their actions to those of others through a process of interpretation. Through this process actors form groups, the action of the group serving as the action of all actors within it. The world of the actor is found in the process of interpretation or orientation of himself vis-a-vis the group. The mind is a process in which the individual interacts with himself and others through symbol utilization.[11]

Phenomenological theory is more philosophical than sociological. These theorists state that man constitutes and reconstitutes what is real (i.e., objective social reality is not independent of the individual). Thus to define a situation as real makes it real. Phenomenologists try to comprehend the meaning that the actor's behavior has for him by both studying the process through which social facts are created by the actor rather than the social facts themselves and by examining the ongoing process of reality construction in society as social facts do not possess an objective existence. By uncovering the processes through which social order emerges from the negotiative behaviors of everyday life, phenomenologists hope to learn how people engage in the process of creating the social facts that are coercive on them. Order and meaning cannot have an objective existence since people impose order and meaning on themselves through manipulation and molding of norms. Reality is what one makes of it. Thus order and social reality have a tenuous existence according to this theory.[12]

Social Behavior Paradigm

Sociology of criminal law theorists tend not to be oriented toward the social behavior paradigm by definition if one goes according to Sutherland. He states that this division of criminology "is an attempt at systematic analysis of the conditions under which criminal laws develop."[13] The crime causation and crime control divisions of criminology appear to be primarily concerned with the social behaviorist paradigm as they tend to be individual oriented. On the other hand, the sociology of criminal law is theoretically both group and individual-group oriented since it deals with people on the basis of laws and legal institutions, not on the basis of individual behavior patterns. Thus sociology of criminal law theorists would tend to either fit into the social facts or social definition paradigms. Therefore one will not deal with the theories of the social behavior paradigm in this text (see Ritzer, *Sociology: A Multiple Paradigm Science,* Allyn & Bacon, 1975).

The Paradigms of Reasons

Reasons creates what he calls three major paradigms for the field of criminology. The *kinds of people* paradigm asserts that the cause of criminality is in the characteristics of the criminal (i.e., positivistic view).[14] The *kinds of environments* paradigm asserts that crime is a product of the social system (i.e., social deterministic view).[15] Both these paradigms accept a legalistic definition of crime (i.e., behavior violating criminal laws) according to Reasons.[16] The third paradigm, *power/conflict* recognizes the importance of power, politics, and people in creating, sustaining, and shaping conditions conducive to criminality.[17]

The three paradigms proposed by Reasons "fit" into the three paradigms proposed by Ritzer which has been expounded upon in a previous section of this book. Reasons' kinds of people paradigm can be placed in part in both the social behavior and social definition paradigms. His kinds of environments and power/conflict paradigms can both be placed in the social facts paradigm. It is possible that if Reasons knew of the work of Ritzer before creating his paradigms he would have utilized the concise system devised by the latter rather than the vague descriptions he uses that in actuality overlap with two of Ritzer's paradigms or are part of the same paradigm.

Sociology of law theorists should look at behavior patterns which violate other norms which transcend the political state (i.e., basic concepts of humanity and justice) rather than a continuation of analyzing those behaviors which are officially prohibited by state laws according to Reasons.[18]

To comprehend the law, power/conflict theorists want to demystify the misconceptions concerning the nature and function of the law. The law must be understood in the context of power, politics, and people.[19] Legal system personnel hold values, attitudes, and orientations which influence their intellectual atmosphere. The law is an instrument of those in power who use it to maintain their positions of high status and privilege in society through utilization of interest groups whose function is to put pressure on legal system personnel.[20]

The power/conflict paradigm demystifies the traditional conception of the criminal and non-criminal which pervades contemporary criminological thought. By focusing on the political nature of criminal definitions, their application, and enforcement, the power/conflict perspective asserts that crime is a product of current power differentials and conflicting world views. Crime is a definition of behavior made by officials of the state and is not inherent in an act. Those behaviors which are offensive to the establishment will be made crimes. Rather than focusing on the crimes of the common criminal, this paradigm places emphasis on the lawless behavior of the state and those in power positions. When attending to common crimes and criminals, paradigmatic emphasis is placed on the oppressive, arbitrary, and self-serving nature of the criminal justice system and its injustices from the offender's perspective.[21]

Marxian Models

The Paradigms of Chambliss

Chambliss states that there are two dominant paradigms within the field of criminology: functional and conflict.[22] Ritzer and Rich both feel that the structural-functional and conflict approaches to sociology are theoretical, not paradigmatic. Thus there is initial disagreement as to the definition of paradigm. One has no disagreement with Chambliss as to the importance of both the functional and conflict theories in the field of criminology, only to elevating these two theories to the stature of paradigm or model. It is the contention of both Ritzer and Rich that both functional and conflict theory are a part of the "social facts" paradigm. Both theories tend to be holistic (i.e., look at society as composed of inter-related parts with an interest in the interrelationship between the parts); both theories ignore each other (i.e., one emphasizes societal integration while the other emphasizes societal conflict); both share an evolutionary view of social class; and both are basically equilibrium theories.[23]

The functional "paradigm" of Chambliss underscores the importance of socialization into criminality, of ascribed status characteristics, and societal reaction to the causation of criminal behavior with Durkheim as exemplar while the conflict "paradigm" stresses interest group competition as the main source of societal conflict, utilizes the concept of social power, and is oriented toward the methodology of dialectic materialism with Marx as exemplar. Further functionalism assumes value-consensus as the starting point for comprehension of criminality while the conflict view begins with the Marxian orientation toward historical materialism.[24]

Durkheim states that crime is behavior which occurs when an institution or structure of society does not properly socialize its members with the customs of the culture. The criminal law is a reflection of societal value-attitudes. Criminality and criminal law have their basis in the culture of society. Durkheim feels that only an act punishable by law is a crime, the act must be offensive and opposed by the total community, and the act must be clearly understood by all. Thus crime serves as an establisher and preserver of community value-attitudes.[25]

Marx states that customs are only a reflection of the status of the economic institution of society. Criminality and criminal law are products of a particular type of society in a particular social order (i.e., capitalist society where there are owners of property and those who work for these owners). The criminal law evolves as a result of the struggle between the class that rules and the class that is ruled. The state serves the interests of the rulers and creates laws that preserve the status quo (i.e., prevent those who are ruled from overthrowing those who rule). Thus criminality and the criminal law are the result of the socio-economic order of capitalist society (i.e., the rulers exploit the labor of the ruled for their self-betterment). Therefore as capitalism evolves more and more frequent conflict will occur between the ruling class and the exploited class which will result in more behavior of the latter group being defined as criminal.[26]

Functional theory is ahistorical, that is it perceives society as a reality which is unconnected to a particular social order with its peculiar social needs and problems. On the other hand, conflict theory states that society is connected with a particular social order (i.e., reflection of the needs, characteristics, and problems at a particular point in time in that society's history). Structural-functional theory accepts the social order as given while conflict theory stresses the need to change the social order. The functionalist tests the logical structure or fit of data to existing societal institutions while conflict theorists use theory to bring about change in societal institutions. With respect to criminality, functional theory states that criminal behavior can be comprehended by asking why some individuals adopt value-attitude systems (i.e., norms) conducive to criminal behavior while most people accept the value-attitude systems of the culture of society. Second the criminal law is commonly accepted as a body of rules which reflect societal social consensus. Conflict theorists do not accept value consensus as the dominating factor in theory building and see it as a reflection of elitist control of both the economic and educational institutions (i.e., value-attitudes) of society. Finally the elites create a myth about the value-attitude system of society which allows oppression of the masses so that they will more easily serve the elites.[27]

Chambliss has clearly demonstrated that there are differences between the two perspectives. Functional theory perceives the criminal law as representing societal value-attitudes that are fundamental to social order (i.e., a standard reflecting societal social consensus); the law upholds the normative system which protects the public interest; the legal system is value-free; the law represents the neutral state which through the law mediates disputes between competing interest groups; criminal behavior is a violation of key community customs; criminal behavior is due to improper socialization practices; and criminal behavior reinforces the sacred nature of community standards.[28]

Conflict theory sees the criminal law as a set of rules created by the state in the interest of the elite, not as a reflection of community normative systems; the criminal law is the result of class struggle in capitalist social orders; criminal law is problematic, not a standard reflecting societal social consensus; some criminal behavior is rebellion against rules imposed by the state as agent of the ruling class in order to economically exploit those ruled; criminal behavior is the result of either alienation from the myths put forth by the establishment or from competition for control of societal institutions with the elite; criminal behavior is the end product of the capitalist economic and political systems.[29]

The functionalist premise that criminal law is a body of rules reflective of societal morality (i.e., normative systems) is false since the elite of society are truly the major power in the creation of criminal laws (i.e., those who own or control societal resources or occupy authority positions in political bureaucracies). Further societal class structure conflicts are an important force in legal change (i.e., struggles of idealists and moralists, riots, rebellions, and revolutions all force new criminal law enactments).[30]

Both functional and conflict theories suggest different expectations for the sociology of criminal law according to Chambliss. Functional theory states that responses to deviance move toward reliance on restitution rather than repression as society evolves from a gemeinschaft to gesellschaft social order. Conflict theory suggests the opposite (i.e., gesellschaft societies will use the criminal law increasingly as a means to keep the lower classes in their place as technology changes society).

Chambliss feels that the criminal law in capitalist societies has shown no trend toward dependence on restitutive law rather than repressive law as Durkheim predicted. In fact there appears to be a greater use of the criminal law to resolve disputes including areas of morality (i.e., crimes without victims). Further traditional societies show a reliance on restitutive rather than repressive law as Durkheim hypothesized.[31] Thus functionalist theory apparently does not stand the test of empirical analysis according to Chambliss. This assumes that contemporary functionalism strictly adheres to the thoughts of only Durkheim.

The statement that criminal acts are more often committed by the lower classes is rejected by Chambliss who feels that criminal acts (i.e., acts which violate the criminal law) are widely distributed throughout the stratification structure of capitalist societies. What apparent class differences exist are really differences in type of criminal act, not in the prevalence of criminality. Thus both functional theory, which perceives crime as a result of the lower class life-style, and conflict theory, which sees crime as a result of the elite's coercion of the masses to its ideas of conformity, are wrong.[32]

It can be concluded that Chambliss is clearly an adherent to the conflict perspective. He feels a criminality that serves the interests of the elite will be sanctioned while acts that do not coincide with elitist interests will be punished. Further criminal activity in capitalist society is a reflection of one's position in the class structure. Chambliss criticizes the conflict approach for its conceptual shortcomings. First, there is the assumption that the elite would control white collar crime and crimes without victims since it is in their interest. Second, conflict theory has not realized that the elite accept legislation that may appear to be in the public interest but which actually does little harm to elitist interests. Last conflict theory has not recognized that there are disagreements between governmental bureaucratic elites and corporate managerial elites (i.e., accept a monolithic rather than pluralistic theory of elites).[33]

One would have to concur with Chambliss that conflict theory is the emerging perspective in the analysis of sociology of criminal law. It is true that several contemporary theorists have shifted their attention from the deviant person to the societal social structures and institutions which are defined as deviant. One would disagree with Chambliss that Marxian conflict theory is adhered to by most theorists since the majority of those oriented toward the conflict perspective are non-Marxian in their analyses. Last it would be more precise to state that there is a shift in theory rather than paradigm as Chambliss states since both functional and conflict theories are part of the social facts paradigm.

The Paradigms of Quinney

A radical approach to the Western concept of law is proposed by

Quinney who is convinced that our traditional view of the inevitability of law is a myth which is perpetuated and perpetrated by those in power. A radical social theory of law will aid in the revision of our notions concerning law and order, natural law, civil liberties, civil disobedience, and morality.[34]

The actual role of law in society is quite different from what we have been traditionally told. The structural-functional or consensus model perceives law as a special form of social control that exerts pressure upon each person so as to make him be a model citizen whose conduct conforms to societal norms. Thus law can be assumed to possess several characteristics: it is a societal product that reflects societal consciousness; it reflects the needs of society; it serves those interests that are for societal good; and it settles individual and group disputes in the name of social order. This mythical view of law regards it as an instrument of society that controls diversity and change in the name of social order and consistency. Thus law is used for the good of the whole society.[35]

Social theorists have traditionally believed that laws protect all citizens and bring order, progress, and civilization to humanity. This idea of law is based on the traditional (i.e., structural-functional) assumption that humanity must be controlled and regulated for the good of both the individual and the society. Quinney believes that traditional structural-functional theorists (i.e., consensus) perpetuate the myth of law and order through use of the concept of rule of law (i.e., to obey the law is a good, a moral absolute). This conception of law as a tool for the maintenance of the status quo is abhorrent to Quinney since this is an ideological weapon used to maintain the dominance of the upper classes over the rest of society. In reality the law of the people is the law of the elite used to promote and protect its own interests.[36]

The concept of natural law plays an important role in Quinney's radical view of law. Radical theory perceives natural law as a tool protecting the rights of each member of society as well as the rights of social groups within society. Only man and collectivities of men have rights as society and its institutions do not possess these inalienable rights. Government is only a tool of the people and can be valued only as long as it serves the people. It has no moral value if it serves only the elite and their representatives.[37] Legal positivism and its structural-functional adherents hold a view of natural law which Quinney opposes since it minimizes individual freedom and the right of revolution (i.e., the good of society rather than the good of the individual is stressed so that societal demands rather than individual rights are met).[38]

Individual freedom is a right guaranteed by the concept of natural law but is more a theoretical concept than a practical application according to Quinney. Civil liberties are abstractly guaranteed and are the province of the ruling class which controls the government and economy. Only when the government is controlled by the people can civil liberties and the greater issue of human rights be secured.[39]

The related concept of civil disobedience faces the same problem in application as the concept of individual freedom (i.e., it is more for the protection of the elite and their authority structure than for the right of citizens to express their dissatisfaction with the functioning of contemporary government). Civil disobedience does not coincide with the elitist position that it is more important to preserve law and order than it is to allow a fair and equitable life for the average member of society. Civil disobedience may be a moral right but the legal system of society must be obeyed no matter how unjust it is in reality. Verbal expression of opinion differences may be tolerated but refusal to obey governmental commands cannot be tolerated unless the majority of the people challenge the government.[40]

From the conflict perspective of Quinney, the structural-functionalist interpretation of the role of civil disobedience in society is false. The individual who breaks the law in the name of civil disobedience is not bound by the rules of the system since to obey the system is to preserve it. If the law is immoral, then violation of it is not to be considered immoral according to Quinney. Thus violations of laws which reflect an oppressive government or governmental policy are justified in the name of human rights.[41]

Civil disobedience can never succeed in society since the elite control police opinion, the government, and the law. Thus the true will of the majority can never be expressed unless the law is changed.[42] But the legal system of society is controlled by the government which is under the grip of the elite. This aspect of Quinney's argument is quite inconsistent since only an overthrow of the elite will bring about the ultimate changes required to create a new legal system that will lead to a new society. To say that the conscience of people is the only valid law in society is to lead to anarchy followed by dictatorship.

To have a societal legal system or not is a debatable point to Quinney. Most theorists assume that a legal system stripped of its moralistic overtones would be a more just system. For instance the criminal law could abolish all crimes without victims (i.e., drunkenness, prostitution, gambling, etc.) and thus eliminate moral bias. Quinney believes that the criminal is inherently moralistic. Thus legal reform or revolution cannot be accomplished by eliminating morality from the law since one form of morality or another determines the form and function of criminal law (i.e., egalitarian, totalitarian, etc.).[43]

Quinney's solution to the problem of bringing about change in the societal legal system is a faith in a natural law of human rights. One must be educated to the fact that the law exists to protect the status quo and is utilized to prevent the changes that will make all citizens free. The law and order doctrine as a positive absolute value is spread by the elite in order to control the masses and stifle dissent. Thus the elitist authority structure uses the law not only to control the masses but to further its own purposes.[44]

Specific alternative solutions to the problem of an elitist criminal law system are advocated by Quinney. The criminal law could be abolished since it does not prevent or control crime anyway. Second the criminal law statutes could be kept as symbols of how people should behave but never enforced. A more realistic solution to the law problem is to decentralize it since one criminal code can not deal with the realities of a pluralistic society. Quinney believes that the problem with the criminal law has been the acceptance of a centralized system of control. He feels that a decentralized government would provide the basis for a democratic criminal law which would stress subcultural differences rather than legal substance. Law outside the culture area (i.e., regional, rural-urban, etc., subcultures) would only provide for the regulation of needed services such as health, transportation, and welfare. This decentralized legal system would ultimately create a life for all free of oppression and allow people to become truly liberated.[45] This solution of decentralization of the criminal law is no solution at all since the fifty sovereign states were set up originally to cater to subcultural needs. This state autonomy has worked to the detriment of human rights in several areas which is why in the late 1950s the Supreme Court and Congress began centralizing the criminal codes to make them all begin to conform and offer more basic rights to all citizens. Thus Quinney would have us go backward to a utopian idea founded in a gemeinschaft social order which increasingly has failed in our gesellschaft reality.

The radical approach employed by Quinney is self-evident from his attack upon what he calls the liberal consensus theorists. The argument he puts forward concerning elite control of the state and its political and legal systems is a clear example of exposing the myths of contemporary society. Quinney's analysis of the shortcomings of the legal system points up his theoretical shifts as a theorist since 1969 when he began to seriously question the structural-functional approach. By 1972 he had switched to a conflict perspective which was evident by his concern with exposing the myths of a criminal justice system and his theoretical attempt to find a better legal system for society. By 1977 Quinney's intellectual position shifted from a non-Marxian conflict perspective to a Marxian perspective. His search for a theory proposing a legal system free from control by elites utilizing a non-Marxian approach had obviously failed him intellectually. Thus in *Class, State, and Crime* he proposes a socialist theory despite the fact that some theorists think it inapplicable to the resolution of the problems of the criminal justice system.[46]

Notes

[1] *Encyclopedia of Sociology,* Guilford, Connecticut: The Dushkin Publishing Group, 1974, pp. 189, 203.

[2] Thomas Kuhn, *The Structure of Social Revolutions,* Chicago: University

of Chicago Press, 1962; Robert Friedrich, *A Sociology of Sociology,* New York: Free Press, 1970; Lakatos and Musgrave, *Criticism and the Growth of Knowledge,* Cambridge: Cambridge University Press, 1970; Lodahl and Gordon, "The Structure of Scientific Fields and the Functioning of University Graduate Departments", *American Sociological Review* 37 (1972), pp. 57-72; Derek Phillips, "Paradigms, Falsifications, and Sociology", *Acta Sociologica* 16 (1973), pp. 13-31; Andrew Effrat, "Power to the Paradigms: an Editorial Introduction", *Sociological Inquiry* 42 (1972), pp. 3-33; George Ritzer, *Sociology: A Multiple Paradigm Science,* Boston: Allyn and Bacon, 1975; Charles Reasons, "Social Thought and Social Structure: Competing Paradigms in Criminology", *Criminology* 13 (November, 1975), pp. 336-349; Robert Rich, "The Sociology of Law: Toward a Paradigmatic Perspective", paper presented to the American Sociological Association, August, 1976; Rich, "The Sociology of Criminal Law: Toward a Paradigmatic Perspective", paper presented to the American Society of Criminology, November, 1976; Rich, "Toward a Sociology of Law Paradigm", in Rich, *Essays on the Theory and Practice of Criminal Justice,* Washington, DC: University Press of America, 1977, pp. 1-40; Rich, *The Sociology of Law: An Introduction to its Theorists and Theories,* Washington, DC: University Press of America, 1977; Rich, "Sociological Paradigms and the Sociology of Law: An Historical Analysis", in Reasons and Rich, *Sociology of Law,* Scarborough, Canada: Butterworth and Company, 1978.

[3]George Ritzer, *Sociology: A Multiple Paradigm Science*, Boston: Allyn and Bacon, 1975, p. 24.

[4]*Ibid.*, p. 189.

[5]*Ibid.*, pp. 48-57.

[6]George Ritzer, "Sociology: A Multiple Paradigm Science," *The American Sociologist* 10 (August, 1975), pp. 159-160.

[7]George Ritzer, *Sociology: A Multiple Paradigm Science,* Boston: Allyn and Bacon, 1975, pp. 57-67.

[8]George Ritzer, "Sociology: A Multiple Paradigm Science," *The American Sociologist* 10 (August, 1975), p. 160.

[9]George Ritzer, "Sociology: A Multiple Paradigm Science," *The American Sociologist* 10 (August, 1975), pp. 161-162.

[10]George Ritzer, *Sociology: A Multiple Paradigm Science,* Boston: Allyn and Bacon, 1975, pp. 86-87; George Ritzer, "Sociology: A Multiple Paradigm Science," *The American Sociologist* 10 (August, 1975), p. 162.

[11]George Ritzer, *Sociology: A Multiple Paradigm Science,* Boston: Allyn and Bacon, 1975, pp. 96-115; George Ritzer, "Sociology: A Multiple Paradigm Science," *The American Sociologist* 10 (August, 1975), p. 162.

[12]George Ritzer, *Sociology: A Multiple Paradigm Science,* Boston: Allyn and Bacon, 1975, pp. 96-115; George Ritzer, "Sociology: A Multiple Paradigm Science," *The American Sociologist* 10 (August, 1975), p. 162.

[13]E. H. Sutherland and D. R. Cressey, *Criminology*, Philadelphia: J. B. Lippincott Company, 1970, p. 3.

[14]Charles Reasons, "Social Thought and Social Structure: Competing Paradigms in Criminology," *Criminology*, 13, no. 3, November, 1975, pp. 336-337.

[15]*Ibid.*, pp. 337-339.

[16]*Ibid.*, p. 342.

[17]*Ibid.*, pp. 342-343.

[18]*Ibid.*, p. 344.

[19]*Ibid.*, p. 346.

[20]*Ibid.*, pp. 346-347.

[21]*Ibid.*, pp. 348-349.

[22]William Chambliss, "Functional and Conflict Theories of Crime", New York: MSS Modular Publications, 1973 (identical to Chambliss and Mankoff (eds.), *Whose Law, What Order: A Conflict Approach to Criminology*, New York: John Wiley, 1976, p. 1).

[23]George Ritzer, *Sociology: A Multiple Paradigm Science,* Boston: Allyn and Bacon, 1975, pp. 86-87; Ritzer, "Sociology: A Multiple Paradigm Science", *The American Sociologist* 10 (August, 1975), p. 162.

[24]Chambliss, *op. cit.*, pp. 1-2.

[25]*Ibid.*, pp. 4-5.

[26]*Ibid.*, p. 5.

[27]*Ibid.*, pp. 2-3.

[28]*Ibid.*, pp. 4-6.

[29]*Ibid.*, pp. 6-7.

[30]*Ibid.*, pp. 9-11.

[31]*Ibid.*, pp. 16-17.

[32]*Ibid.*, p. 24.

[33]*Ibid.*, pp. 24-25.

[34]Richard Quinney, "The Ideology of Law: Notes for a Radical Alternative to Legal Oppression", *Issues in Criminology* 7 (Winter, 1972), pp. 1-2.

[35]*Ibid.*, pp. 3-4.

[36] *Ibid.*, pp. 4-7.

[37] *Ibid.*, pp. 8, 13.

[38] *Ibid.*, p. 12.

[39] *Ibid.*, pp. 13-16.

[40] *Ibid.*, pp. 16-21.

[41] *Ibid.*, pp. 20-21.

[42] *Ibid.*, pp. 22-23.

[43] *Ibid.*, pp. 24-25.

[44] *Ibid.*, pp. 27-30.

[45] *Ibid.*, pp. 25-27.

[46] Richard Quinney, *Crime and Justice in Society,* Boston: Little, Brown and Company, 1969, pp. 1-30; Quinney, "The Ideology of Law: Notes for a Radical Alternative to Legal Oppression," *op. cit.,* pp. 1-35; Quinney, *Class, State and Crime: On the Theory and Practice of Criminal Justice,* New York: David McKay Company, 1977; Taylor, Walton, and Young, *The New Criminology,* New York: Harper and Row, 1973, pp. 252-267; Piers Beirne, "Marxism and the Sociology of Law; Theory or Practice", *British Journal of Law and Society* 2 (Summer, 1975), pp. 78-81.

Part II

The Criminal Law and Societal Deviance

Chapter 5

Sexual Deviance

Pornography and Obscenity

Legal History

The Curl case in 1797 (i.e., Curl was prosecuted for publishing a book entitled *Venus in the Cloister or the Nun in her Smock*) set the common law crime of obscenity in England and subsequently in the United States. *Fanny Hill* was the first book prosecuted under the Curl ruling. The publisher was found guilty of obscenity in an 1821 English court. In the United States, Vermont was the first state to legislate against obscenity followed by Massachusetts in 1835 which initiated the so-called obscenity test (i.e., a book or writing which corrupts youthful morality). New York passed a statute in 1868 banning obscene literature.[1]

The first federal legislation called the Comstock law (i.e., banning the sale and distribution of obscene materials through the mail) was passed by Congress in 1873. The first Federal court case was the novel, *Ulysses,* by Joyce. The Court of Appeals rejected the Massachusetts test and established a new test of obscenity. This test stated that obscenity must be examined on the basis of its effect on the average individual, not on its effects upon certain types of individuals (i.e., adolescents).[2]

A number of cases were adjudicated based on this test between 1933 and 1957 when the U.S. Supreme Court examined the obscenity issue. Most notable cases were *Thornhill v. Alabama* (1940), *Prince v. Massachusetts* (1944), *Kovacs v. Cooper* (1949), *Breard v. Alexandria*

(1951), *Joseph Burstyn Inc. v. Wilson* (1952), and *Butler v. Michigan* (1957). The Supreme Court in 1957 heard *Roth v. United States* in order to examine the relationship between obscenity and the guarantees of the First and Fourteenth Amendments of the Constitution (i.e., freedom of speech and due process respectively). The Court reaffirmed the *Ulysses* decision (i.e., average individual test) and added two more tests (i.e., whether the dominant theme of the material appeals to prurient interests and whether the material is without redeeming social importance). The Court also ruled that obscenity was not protected by First Amendment guarantees.[3]

Manual Enterprises v. Day in 1961 resulted in the expansion of the tests of obscenity as determined in *Roth* to include the concept of patent offensiveness of the material.[4] *Jocobellis v. Ohio* decided the issue of whether obscenity can be determined by national or community standards. The Court decided that national standards should determine whether a work is obscene or not.[5]

In 1966 the Supreme Court heard three cases: *Ginzberg v. United States, Mishkin v. New York,* and *Memoirs v. Massachusetts.* These cases moved away from the *Roth* decision. The new test of obscenity was that the dominant theme of the material taken as a whole appeals to a prurient interest in sex; the material is patently offensive because it affronts contemporary community standards relating to the description or representation of sexual matters; and the material is utterly without redeeming social value. This new test of obscenity called on the prosecution to prove something that is almost impossible to do (i.e., a work has no redeeming social value). Thus the Court at this point in time was unable to agree on a standard to determine what constituted in a clear manner obscene/pornographic material that was subject to regulation under each state's police power.[6]

A whole series of cases rapidly followed *Ginzberg, Mishkin,* and *Memoirs.* There was *Redrup v. New York* (1967); *Interstate Circuit Inc. v. Dallas* (1968); *Stanley v. Georgia* (1969). *Stanley* was convicted for owning at home some pornographic films. The Supreme Court held that it is not criminal to privately own obscene material (i.e., read or view this type of material in the privacy of one's home): *U.S. v. Thirty-Seven Photographs* (1971). In 1971 the Court also ruled that postal authorities can not prohibit the mailing of obscene materials since consenting adults have the right to choose their own moral standards as long as they do not directly offend other members of the community: *Kois v. Wisconsin; U.S. v. Reidel; Rabe v. Washington; Paris Adult Theatre v. Slaton* (1973); *U.S. v. 12-200 Foot Reels Film* (1973); and *Miller v. California* (1973).[7]

Miller reaffirms *Roth* in that obscene material is not protected by the First Amendment. It also rejects the test of utterly without redeeming social value that was stated in *Memoirs. Miller v. California* states that a work may be subject to state regulation where that work, taken as a whole, appeals to the prurient interest in sex; portrays, in a patently offensive way, sexual conduct specifically defined by the applicable state law; and taken as a whole, does not have serious literary, artistic, political, or scientific value. The basic guidelines are whether the average person, applying *contemporary community standards* would find that the work, taken as a whole, appeals to the prurient interest, etc.[8] Thus the Court has apparently given up on a national standard for obscenity and returned the decision of what constitutes obscenity to the local communities. The Court does make the attempt to offer brief guidelines but the issue today is quite confused to say the least as to the legal standard of obscenity in America.

Legal Definitions

Webster defines obscene as disgusting to the senses; grossly repugnant to the generally accepted notions of what is appropriate; offensive or revolting as countering or violating some ideal or principle. The Oxford English Dictionary defines obscene as offensive to the senses, or to taste or refinement; disgusting, repulsive, filthy, foul, abominable, loathsome.[9] Black defines obscene as offensive to chastity of mind or to modesty, expressing or presenting to the mind or view something that delicacy, purity, and decency forbids to be exposed; calculated to corrupt, deprave, and debauch the morals of the people, and promote violation of law; licentious and libidinous and tending to excite feelings of an impure or unchaste character; tending to stir the sex impulses or to lead to sexually impure and lustful thoughts; tending to corrupt the morals of youth or to lower the standards as to sexual relations.[10]

Webster defines pornography as a written depiction of licentiousness or lewdness; a portrayal of erotic behavior designed to cause sexual excitement. Black defines pornographic as that which is of or pertaining to obscene literature.[11] Thus the two terms obscenity and pornography are used interchangeably in the criminal law and are synonymous in popular usage.

Obscenity Statute and Enforcement Policy

The D.C. code (i.e., section 22-2001) is a typical example of the statute enacted against the crime of obscenity in the United States. The obscenity statute states that it is unlawful to sell, deliver, distribute, or provide any obscene, indecent, or filthy writing, picture, sound recording, or other article or representation. It is unlawful to present, direct, act in, or otherwise participate in the preparation or presentation of any obscene, indecent, or filthy play, dance, motion picture, or other performance. It is unlawful to pose for, model for, print, record, compose, edit, write, publish, or otherwise participate in preparing for publication, exhibition, or sale, any obscene, indecent, or filthy writing, picture, sound recording, or other article or representation. It is unlawful to sell, deliver, distribute, or provide, or offer or agree to sell, deliver, distribute, or provide any article, thing, or device which is intended for or represented as being for indecent or immoral use. It is unlawful to create, buy, procure, or possess any matter so described with intent to disseminate such matter. It is unlawful to advertise or otherwise promote the sale of any matter so described. It is unlawful to advertise or otherwise promote the sale of material represented or held out by such person to be obscene.[12]

The D.C. Code defines the various terms described. Nudity includes the showing of the human male or female genitals, pubic area or buttocks with less than a full opaque covering, or the showing of the female breast with less than a full opaque covering of any portion thereof below the top of the nipple, or the depiction of covered male genitals in a discernibly turgid state. Sexual conduct includes acts of sodomy, masturbation, homosexuality, sexual intercourse, or physical contact with a person's clothed or unclothed genitals, pubic area, buttocks, or if such person be a female, breasts. Sexual excitement is the condition of human male or female genitals when in a state of sexual stimulation or arousal. Sado-masochistic abuse includes flagellation or torture by or upon a person clad in undergarments or a mask or bizarre costume, or the condition of being fettered, bound, or otherwise physically restrained on the part of one so clothed.[13]

It is a valid defense to the charge of obscenity, according to the D.C. Code, if the violation of the code was for scientific, educational reasons or there is other special justification for the possession of such material by a person or institution. A person convicted of obscene behavior as a first offender shall be fined not more than $3000.00 or imprisoned not more than one year, or both. An individual convicted a second time or more shall be fined not less than $1000.00 nor more than $5000.00 or imprisoned not less than six months or more than three years, or both.[14]

The Obscenity Squad of the Morals Division of the Metropolitan Police Department (Washington, D.C.) is assigned the task of enforcing the obscenity statute described. The squad is composed of a sergeant and four detectives. Their task is to watch the many bookstores, movie theatres, topless and bottomless dancer establishments, and burlesque houses. In addition all complaints concerning obscene material and/or performances are investigated as well as routine checks of all night clubs, restaurants, and movie theatres that do not normally feature X-rated movies and/or performances.[15]

The law enforcement process consists of the continuous systematic checking of various theatres, bookstores, nightclubs, and bars to see that the obscenity statute is not violated. Taking the X-rated movie theatres and adult bookstores as an example, members of the obscenity squad regularly check the theatres and bookstores viewing the new films and books. After each check a resume of the contents of the book or film is made by the officer. In the case of indecent publications only those portraying sadistic sex scenes or those featuring juveniles in explicit sex scenes are recorded. In the case of X-rated films, only those displaying sex scenes between humans and animals (i.e., bestiality), homosexuality, urination, defacation, sodomy, sadism, the use of juveniles in sexual activity are written up by the officer.

Each case is reviewed by the sergeant and then given to a special United States Attorney of the United States Department of Justice to review. If the U.S. Attorney feels the material is unacceptable in terms of the obscenity statute, a search warrant is issued for the seizure of the material. In some situations films and books are purchased by the detective and presented with the resume to the U.S. Attorney. In these cases an arrest warrant is issued for the person selling the material. After the warrant is served and the person arrested or material seized, the evidence and testimony of the detective are presented to a grand jury which determines whether or not to indict the person responsible for selling or showing the material. Then follows a trial where the detective again must testify followed by an acquittal or conviction in the case.[16]

Description of Pornography and Obscenity

There appears to be a historical concern with what one might call erotica from ancient Greece and Rome to present-day traditional societies.[17] The League of Nations in 1929 established the International Convention for the Suppression of the Circulation and Traffic in Obscene Publications which was concerned with suppression of obscene material. The United States Congress established a Commission on Noxious Printed and Pictured Material in 1960. In 1967 Congress established the President's Commission on Pornography and Obscenity which reported its findings in 1970.[18]

The Commission report stated that the pornography industry has estimated sales in excess of two billion dollars a year (i.e., sales of films, books, journals, tapes, records, photos, and assorted equipment). Also reported by the Commission were the facts that eighty-five percent of adult men and seventy percent of adult women have been exposed to such material on a voluntary basis. Depictions of nudity with exposed sex organs and of heterosexual intercourse are quite common while homosexual activites and oral sex are less common but increasing in interest. The Commission estimates that 20-25 percent of males have regular experiences with such materials although only 10-12 percent actually purchase the materials on a regular basis. First experience with such erotica usually occurs during adolescence as eighty percent of adolescent males and seventy percent of adolescent females reported seeing visual or textual descriptions of sexual intercourse by the time they reached eighteen. Last, the Commission reported that the typical customer of adult bookstores and X-rated theatres were usually middle class, middle aged, white married men.[19]

A number of studies have been conducted by social scientists for the Commission to determine the effects of exposure to sexually explicit (i.e., erotic) materials. The Commission concluded that exposure to sexually explicit material does produce sexual arousal in many men and women although the extent of sexual excitement depends upon the particular characteristics of those viewing and the type of material. Younger individuals are more readily aroused than older people; college educated, non-religious, and sexually active individuals are more likely to become sexually excited than less educated, religiously active persons, and those who think sex is "dirty". Erotic materials generally cause an increase of heterosexual rather than homosexual activity. Viewers of sexual intercourse are more excited than viewers of oral sex. Finally older, less educated, puritanical, and sexually confused individuals label erotic material as obscene more often than more educated, sexually active, and liberal individuals.[20]

Commission research showed that most individuals exposed to erotic material had no change in their sexual behavior although some people did report short term increase in masturbation and frequency of sexual relations. This increase of sexual activity usually occurred with available sex partners who were known to the individual. Couples who viewed erotic materials noted an increase in sexual intercourse for a 24-hour period after seeing X-rated films. This sample also reported an increase of erotic dreams and conversations about sex after seeing such films. Most importantly the Commission research concluded that exposure to sexually explicit material has little or no effect on established value-attitudes concerning sexuality or sexual standards (i.e., those with liberal value-attitudes towards sex are more tolerant of erotic materials while those who are negative toward sex are repulsed; those who are unfamiliar with erotic materials are usually confused emotionally).[21]

Sexually explicit material has often been cited by theorists and social critics as a contributing factor towards the creation of social deviance (i.e., criminal and delinquent behavior). Commission studies state that there is no evidence that erotic material plays a major role in the causation of delinquent or criminal behavior. Delinquent and non-delinquent adolescents state similar experiences with erotic material. In fact most youth have had widespread exposure to such material despite the criminal laws. Thus the age of first exposure, the type of material seen, the quantity and circumstances of exposure to materials are about equal for both delinquents and nondelinquents when social class and community are held constant. Peer pressures do play an important part in an adolescent's exposure to erotic materials.[22]

The Commission states that pornographic and obscene material is not associated as a cause of sex offenses. Studies in the United States show that during periods of increased availability of erotic material, some specific rates of arrest for sex crimes have increased (i.e., forceable rape) while others have declined (i.e., juvenile arrests for sex crimes). A Danish study of sexual assaults against females shows that there has been a substantial decline in certain offenses since pornographic material was legalized and available to the public (i.e., exhibitionism declined 58 percent; voyeurism declined 80 percent; exposure to women 56 percent; child molesting 69 percent). Part of the decline in sex crimes is explained by more public tolerance (i.e., less reporting to police) and more police tolerance (i.e., less arrests for offenses).[23]

A study of typical community members and those convicted of sex offenses (i.e., rapists, child molesters, homosexuals, trans-sexuals, and those convicted under obscenity laws) was undertaken by Goldstein and Kant. The typical community members were exposed to explicit acts of sexual intercourse during adolescence while the sex offenders were not. The offenders felt more guilty when thinking about sex or exposed to erotic material when growing up. The research concluded that abnormal development of sexuality can lead to either an absence or excessive interest in pornographic material by sex offenders. Finally the study reported that pornography does not tend to incite deviant behavior (i.e., delinquent or criminal) in most cases.[24]

Prostitution

Legal History

Prostitution was not regarded as a criminal offense in England but as a vice that was under the jurisdiction of the ecclesiastical court. The English common law does not mention prostitution until after 1640 and it was regarded as a tort rather than a crime.[25] The New England colonies that were under Puritan rule passed statutes against nightwalkers and bawdyhouses as early as 1648.[26] This type of statute was in force in England in 1707 as it refers to the *Ann Dekins* case where she was detained on suspicion of solicitation for prostitution as a nightwalker.[27] According to Holmes, many early state statutes contained statements concerning prostitutes or nightwalkers who loitered on the street or in a public place for the purpose of prostitution.[28]

Taking New York state as an example, prostitution was legal, unregulated, and operating openly even to the extent of advertising in the newspapers. Thus the New York Penal Law of the period 1864-1881 did not make prostitution per se a crime. But the New York State Supreme Court in 1893 did rule that the profession of prostitution is a deplorable vice productive of disorder and disease even though the prostitute is not committing a crime.[29]

By the early twentieth century many state criminal codes allowed for the arrest of prostitutes, not on charges of prostitution, but for disorderly conduct. This led to the creation of so-called red light districts in the larger metropolitan areas where prostitutes and their employers were segregated from the rest of the community. Thus houses of prostitution were tolerated under the watchful eyes of the police but streetwalkers were arrested under the disorderly conduct statute.[30]

Just prior to World War I the problem of white slavery (i.e., girls kidnapped and used for prostitution) became a public issue. During and after World War I it was commonly thought that the prostitute was a victim of a white slaver who induced young women into the life. In 1919 the American Social Health Association drafted a model statute which later became incorporated into both federal and state legislation that was opposed to prostitution (i.e., customers as well as prostitutes were considered as criminals in nineteen states). Laws were also passed prohibiting the establishment or maintenance of houses of prostitution in every state during the 1920s.[31] On the federal level the White-Slave-Traffic Act (i.e., Mann Act) made it illegal to transport women across the state lines for the purpose of prostitution or other immoral acts. In the 1930s no significant anti-prostitution laws were enacted. In the 1950s efforts were made to break up organized prostitution, especially that linked to organized crime.[32]

The final report of the Committee on Homosexual Offenses and Prostitution (i.e., the Wolfenden Committee) in England in 1957 favored removal of the criminal statutes on prostitution per se but wanted stiff penalties for repeated street prostitution, rental of premises for purposes of prostitution, and living off the earnings of prostitutes. The Committee recommendations were enacted in the Street Offenses Act of 1959. The result was that the prostitutes became more mobile so that they would not be charged with a second infraction in the same police district and cars and vans were used in place of apartment rentals. Thus the law was circumvented.[33]

By 1970 prostitution and related crimes were totally illegal in the United States. The particular wording of the statutes vary as twenty-seven states do not specifically mention prostitution but legally place such behavior under their vagrancy laws. Most states have statutes governing such individuals as procurers, pimps, and madams. Only eight states make it a crime to be a prostitute's customer or participate in sexual intercourse with a prostitute.[34] Today only five states still have prostitution statutes that only apply to women since male prostitutes are now a recognized phenomenon (i.e., both heterosexual and homosexual prostitutes).[35] Nevada in 1971 allowed the legalization of prostitution on a county basis. There is legalized prostitution in thirteen of Nevada's seventeen counties today. Other than the state of Nevada, prostitution is prohibited and prostitutes are considered criminals.[36]

The 1970s have witnessed a challenge to the laws governing prostitution. The Woman's Liberation movement has looked upon prostitution as a form of sex discrimination. A number of suits have been filed in federal court dealing with the solicitation statutes under the First Amendment of the Constitution (i.e., freedom of speech). There has been concern that women's rights to privacy have been violated by the wording of the various prostitution laws. The prostitution statutes have been attacked as sexist. The statutes have also been attacked as not allowing the prostitute to control her bodily functions without unreasonable interference from the state.[37]

The Supreme Court held in *Cherry v. Maryland* and *United States v. Moses* that solicitation can be declared criminal by the states since it is a commercial proposal. Solicitation to commit a crime had already been established as a criminal act at common law. In the case of *United States v. Ceasar* and *Whitt v. United States,* the Court stated that immoral conduct includes not only prostitution but also sodomy, fornication, adultery, and related crimes. Prostitutes are sometimes charged under these adultery, fornication, or sodomy statutes. This was upheld in *Doe v. Commonwealth of Virginia.*[38]

Legal Definitions

According to Black, prostitution is defined as common lewdness of a woman for gain; whoredom; the act or practice of a woman who permits any man who will pay her price to have sexual intercourse with her. A prostitute is a woman who indiscriminately consorts with men for hire.[39] A pimp is defined as an individual who provides for others the means of gratifying lust; a procurer, a panderer; one who solicits trade for a prostitute. A procurer is one who procures the seduction or prostitution of young women. A madam is one who operates a house of prostitution and who may or may not herself be a prostitute.[40]

Prostitution Statutes and Enforcement Policies

District of Columbia Criminal Code defines prostitution as the unlawful process of inviting, enticing, persuading, or addressing for the purpose of inviting, enticing, or persuading any person or persons sixteen years of age or over for the purpose of prostitution, or any other immoral act or lewd purpose and attaches the penalty of not more than 250 dollars or imprisonment for not more than ninety days, or both.[41] Virginia Code states that any person who for money or its equivalent, commits adultery or fornication and thereafter does any substantial act in futherance thereof, shall be guilty of being a prostitute, or prostitution, which shall be punishable as a class one misdeameanor.[42]

The D.C. Code defines pandering as any person who shall place or cause, induce, procure, or compel the placing of any female in the charge or custody of any other person, or in a house of prostitution, with intent that she shall engage in prostitution, or who shall compel, induce, entice, or procure or attempt to compel, induce, entice, or procure any female to reside with any other person for immoral purposes or for the purpose of prostitution, or who shall compel, induce, entice, or procure or attempt to compel, induce, entice, or procure any such female to reside or continue to reside in a house of prostitution, or compel, induce, entice, or procure, or attempt to compel, induce, entice, or procure her to engage in prostitution, or who takes or detains a female against her will, with intent to compel her by force, threats, menace, or duress to marry him or to marry any other person; or any parent, guardian, or other person having legal custody of the person of a female who consents to her taking or detention by any such person, for the purpose of prostitution or sexual intercourse. Such person or persons shall be guilty of a felony and upon conviction shall be punished by imprisonment for not more than five years and by a fine of not more than one thousand dollars.[43]

A procurer is any person who shall receive any money or other valuable thing for or on account of arranging for or causing any female to have sexual intercourse with any other person or to engage in prostitution, debauchery, or any other immoral act, and shall be guilty of a felony and upon conviction shall be punished by imprisonment for not more than five years and a fine of not more than a thousand dollars.[44] A procurer for a house of prostitution is any person who shall pay or receive any money or other valuable thing for or on account of the procuring for, or placing in, a house of prostitution, for purposes of sexual intercourse, prostitution, debauchery, or other immoral act, any female and shall be guilty of a felony and punished by imprisonment of not more than five years and a fine of not more than one thousand dollars.[45] A procurer for a third person is any person who shall receive any money or other valuable thing for or on account of procuring and placing in the charge or custody of another person for sexual intercourse, prostitution, debauchery, or other immoral purposes any female and shall be guilty of a felony and shall be punished by imprisonment for not more than five years and by a fine of not more than a thousand dollars.[46]

An individual who runs a house of prostitution is one who knowingly accepts, receives, levies, or appropriates any money or other valuable thing, without consideration other than the furnishing of a place for prostitution or the servicing of a place for prostitution from the proceeds or earnings of any female engaged in prostitution and shall be guilty of a felony and shall be punished by imprisonment for not more than five years and by a fine of not more than one thousand dollars.[47] Whoever is convicted of keeping a bawdy or disorderly house shall be fined not more than five hundred dollars or imprisoned not more than one year, or both.[48]

Any person who for purposes of prostitution persuades, entices, or forcibly abducts, from her home or usual abode, or from the custody or control of her parents or guardian, any female under sixteen years of age shall be punished by imprisonment for not less than two nor more than twenty years; and whoever knowingly secretes or harbors any such female so persuaded, enticed, or abducted shall suffer imprisonment for not more than eight years.[49] Any person who by threats of duress, detains any female against her will, for the purpose of prostitution or sexual intercourse, or any person who shall compel any female against her will to reside with him or with any other person for the purpose of prostitution or sexual intercourse will be guilty of a felony and shall be punished by imprisonment for not more than five years and a fine of not more than one thousand dollars.[50] Any person who by force, fraud, intimidation, or threats, places or leaves, or procures any other person or persons to place or leave, his wife in a house of prostitution, or to lead a life of prostitution shall be guilty of a felony and shall be imprisoned not less than one nor more than ten years.[51] Any person or persons who attempt to detain any girl or woman in a disorderly house or a house of prostitution because of any debt or debts she has contracted, or is said to have contracted while living in said house of prostitution or disorderly house shall be guilty of a felony, and be imprisoned for a term not less than one nor more than five years.[52]

Some states such as New York make it a crime to participate in a sexual act with a prostitute or to solicit a prostitute for her services.[53] Georgia and Hawaii require the forfeiture of an individual's driver's license if convicted of soliciting for the purpose of prostitution. Wisconsin has a statute that provides a penalty of one hundred dollars fine and/or a three months jail term if a male enters a house of prostitution for the purposes of engaging in nonmarital sex.[54]

The Mann Act (i.e., White-Slave-Traffic-Act) deals with the interstate transportation of females for purposes of prostitution. The United States Code states that whoever knowingly transports in interstate or foreign commerce, or in the District of Columbia, any girl or woman for the purpose of prostitution or debauchery, or for any other immoral purpose, or with the intent and purpose to induce, entice, or compel such girl or woman to become a prostitute or to give herself up to debauchery, or to engage in any other immoral practice, shall be fined not more than five thousand dollars or imprisoned not more than five years, or both.[55]

The Metropolitan Police Department of D.C. (i.e., MPD) has two units which handle solicitation violations, the Prostitution Enforcement Detail and the Youth Division Prostitution and Perversion Squad. All pandering and procuring violations are handled by the Vice Squad.[56]

Prostitution arrests usually come under one of three headings: (1) solicitation, (2) disorderly conduct or vagrancy, or (3) violation of jurisdictional health regulations. Depending on the political pressures applied by elected officials, mass media coverage, and citizen's complaints, the police enforce the laws against prostitution in a somewhat inconsistent fashion. Enforcement policy also depends on whether the prostitute is a streetwalker, bar-girl, massage parlor girl, or call girl (i.e., the more visible the deviant behavior, the more likely an arrest will be made). Most prostitutes who are arrested tend to be either juveniles, those who are drunk, or high on drugs. The police department has to be careful concerning the relationships between police and prostitutes as graft and free access to services become a problem for every large police department.[57]

There is also the ever present problem of entrapment. Entrapment is the persuasion or influence of a person who otherwise would not have committed the criminal act by a law enforcement officer. Metropolitan Police Departments utilize police women as decoys so that they can arrest potential male customers on charges of solicitation. Sometimes officers will knowingly use entrapment of a prostitute so that she will become an informer on her pimp, keeper or a bawdy house, or give information on other criminal types such as narcotics pushers and other street criminals.[58]

Street prostitution presents the most common problems for police officers. The most common and most dangerous crime committed by prostitutes is robbery. For example a customer met a prostitute and they agreed upon a price. The prostitute led him to a room in a vacant building where her accomplice hit the customer over the head and then beat him up. The prostitute and her accomplice proceeded to steal the man's wallet and watch and left him. Larceny is another common crime committed against customers. In this case a customer will be trusting enough to leave his wallet where the woman can get access to its contents during or after sexual relations when the client is preoccupied.

A third common offense is being pickpocketed. This usually involves two or more prostitutes who are dealing with a potential client. They usually approach the victim and one prostitute will proposition him and fondle him to divert his attention from the other girl who will take his wallet. Assault and assault and battery are another common type of crime. This may occur when a customer becomes angered with the prostitute about the service rendered; the customer may be the type that can only obtain sexual gratification if he beats the woman; two prostitutes fight over a customer; or the prostitute's pimp assaults her for a variety of reasons. Murder of a prostitute or client is not very common but does occur. Prostitutes have been murdered by insane customers so many will refuse to perform certain types of sexual requests since previous experience indicates trouble may occur. There was one incident in Washington, D.C. where a client was murdered by a pimp after the customer had severely beaten the prostitute.

A prostitute may claim she is a rape victim especially if the customer refuses to pay or when he forces her to perform some act that she is totally opposed to. The police have a difficult time handling such cases since the prostitute only wants to harass her client and knows that the police will not arrest the customer on the charge of rape since they can easily arrest both parties on a variety of other charges.

There are also several crimes that are not related directly to prostitution but are secondary crimes considered to be part of the illicit sex problem. The most common crime is a con game known as "the Murphy Game". In this game, the con man frequents the same area as the prostitutes. He usually approaches his victim and tells him that he can take him to a place where there are prostitutes. He takes the person to a hotel lobby and then informs him that it would be best to leave his extra money with him while the customer looks for a suitable woman. While the customer is looking for the woman or a room number, the con man leaves with the remainder of the victim's money and/or watch. A variation of this con game ends with the victim arriving at the hotel and going into a room where several of the con man's associates rob him and flee.

Finally there is normal street crime associated with the influx of potential clients for prostitutes in a neighborhood who park their cars outside of motels and hotels where prostitutes are known to frequent. In these cases the cars are often broken into and wallets, c.b. radios, spare tires, tape decks, etc., are taken at will.[59]

Massage parlor crimes are less common than those connected with street prostitution. Many times investigating officers with warrants will find juveniles working in a parlor with falsified work papers or ID's. Sometimes routine checks of employees would reveal that they were wanted for prostitution in another jurisdiction. Massage parlors also have been noted as places that sell or give away a variety of drugs to clients or are used by the girls. The police then arrest the users or suppliers on drug charges but not on prostitution charges. Two types of crimes that are associated with massage parlors are bilking and blackmail. Bilking occurs when the customer pays for services rendered by use of a credit card. The girls would either use his card for filling out two copies or raise the cost after he signed the statement. Obviously when the customer receives two bills or a higher charge he is not going to call the police for that would admit that he was engaged in criminal activity and/or ruin his standing with family and community. Some wealthy clients write out personal checks with which to pay the girls and leave themselves wide open to blackmail. Sometimes the girls will inform on other prostitutes or other massage parlors so as to eliminate their personal or business competition. This is especially true when a girl or parlor cuts prices below the agreed on rates for all parlors.[60]

The largest problem in dealing with crimes associated with prostitution is deliberate non-reporting of the crime by the victim. This in itself can be a criminal offense. Usually crimes that involve violence are reported by prostitute and client alike. Robberies involving threat of force or use of force are also often reported. Theft of money or wallet is not usually reported because of the circumstances under which the theft occurred since the victim does not want the adverse publicity. Several United States Congressmen have been victims of secondary crimes associated with prostitution on the streets of Washington, D.C. but have been able to keep the information out of the press in recent years.[61]

Unfortunately the attitude of some law enforcement officers, prosecuting attorneys, judges, and jury members have been negative toward the victims of secondary crime associated with prostitution. These members of the criminal justice system along with the mass media feel that the customer is acting in a deviant manner and they deserve what happens to them at the hands of prostitutes and other criminals. The typical prostitute usually gets her case thrown out by the judge or magistrate, is fined under fifty dollars for a first offense, or given less than fifteen days in a municipal or county jail. Thus rehabilitation is not the goal of the criminal court but keeping the girls off the streets as long as possible.[62]

Description of Prostitution

It is estimated that prostitution is a billion dollar industry and involves as many as 500 thousand full and part-time women in the United States with the exception of the counties in Nevada where the profession is legal and taxed by both state and federal agencies.[63] In 1976, out of 58,000 arrested for prostitution and commercialized vice, 71 percent were women and 29 percent were men. But only 22 percent of women were arrested for vagrancy and only 16 percent of women were arrested for disorderly conduct.[64] Since 1976 in the District of Columbia, twenty-four hundred cases of prostitution have been handled. This figure breaks down to 1507 females (1212 blacks and 295 whites) and 1821 males (928 blacks and 893 whites) arrested for soliciting prostitution. There have also been 167 juvenile prostitution cases involving mostly females from the ages between ten and seventeen.[65]

There are several types of prostitutes, both female and male in society today. There are the streetwalkers, bar-girls, massage parlor girls, women working in houses of prostitution, call girls, and call service/escort service girls. Male prostitutes are not very numerous. Some specialize in female clientele while the majority deal with homosexual clients.

The common prostitute or streetwalker gets her trade on the streets or at public places such as bars, hotel lobbies, and other places of recreation although she does not work in such places. Streetwalkers usually do not have direct connections with organized crime but usually have to pay protection to members of organized crime and/or corrupt police officers to save themselves from robbery or arrest. Bar girls, strippers, and other women associated with commercial night life are legitimately employed but may select clients and split the fees with their employer. These prostitutes are safer from the influence of organized criminals and corrupt police officers. Prostitutes who work in houses of prostitution are fairly rare in the United States except in the State of Nevada. House girls are supervised by a manager or madam who provides protection from the police and unruly patrons, offers room and board for the girls, and pays for police protection. Most often the house of prostitution either is run by organized crime or pays it for the privilege of existence.[66]

The call girl is becoming quite common today since she is safer from the dangers and expenses of organized criminals, pimps, madams, the police, and health officials. This type of prostitute may operate from her own apartment or go to meet a client. She usually has an answering service and may work loosely in conjunction with other call girls who give each other their extra clients for a split of the fee for services rendered. The call girl may work for a large corporation and cater to special clients of the firm, be a housewife, a model, or any number of legitimate occupations. She usually is protected by the secrecy of her approach to prostitution although if she works conventions, she may become known to hotel detectives or the manager of the residential hotel she uses for her work. In these cases she may have to split fees with hotel staff or the police for protection.[67]

The massage parlor is a recent innovation as far as a haven for prostitutes. A customer can get a legitimate massage from a masseuse or for a substantial fee obtain a number of sexual services (i.e., masturbation, normal sexual intercourse, anal intercourse, fellatio). He can also receive special services (i.e., flagellation, voyeurism, exhibitionism, triolism, koprolognia, urolagnia, transvestism). One must be a steady customer to receive special services from a massage parlor girl since the owners want to make sure that their clients are not undercover police officers. Thus the masseuse will only provide a massage unless the client requests some sexual service. In this way she can use the defense of entrapment if the client turns out to be a law enforcement officer and the massage parlor operator can claim the client was at fault since his establishment is legitimate.

Massage parlors have become fashionable since they do offer legitimate services as well as cater to those wanting to endulge in acts of sexual deviance. Most massage parlors that are fronts for prostitution are operated by organized crime or those who pay it for protection against the police and politicians who might legislate the parlor out of existence. The typical massage parlor has a manager and a male bouncer to keep abusive or dissatisfied customers from bothering the girls. Since this is a "legitimate" business operation, the police must also respond if a customer tries to assault a girl. Girls must notify the manager if a customer wants sexual services and fraternization with customers outside the parlor is grounds for firing since the management would not get its share of the profits.[68]

The massage parlor masseuse is much safer than the streetwalker or house girl since she is legitimately employed and protected by both the management and the police from abusive clients. She can set her own hours of work, refuse certain kinds of sexual services, and earn a steady income with no fear of robbery or lack of medical insurance. On the other hand the streetwalker has to worry about being robbed, beaten up by clients or her pimp, has to work long hours to support herself and her pimp or pay protection to organized crime, is harrassed by the police and vulnerable to arrest or bribery, and has to pay her own doctor's bills for checkups. Only the call girl has a safer and securer vocation and income than the massage parlor girl.

The massage parlor business has recently moved into the call service/ escort service business in response to legislation closing down some operations or making licensing of masseuses required. The customer in this case places a call from an advertisement. The masseuse calls the number back to check its legitimacy (i.e., hotel, motel, or private residence). The girl or girls are transported to the location by the bouncer who talks to the prospective client (i.e., quotes price, amount of time allowed for the service, and takes payment). Then the girl(s) go in and perform their service. The bouncer serves as protection and makes sure that the girl(s) do not stay longer than the agreed time. This is similar to the call girl but protection is provided against a potentially difficult client or one who demands services not agreed upon.[69]

Male prostitutes usually service homosexual clients and frequent homosexual bars, theatres, and public baths. Some statutes requiring that massage parlors employ only same sex employees have resulted in an increase of male prostitution rather than the elimination of prostitution altogether. Male prostitutes who cater to female clientele are quite rare and are found at resort locations, bars, and residential hotels catering to wealthier middle class women who are usually middle-aged and looking for paid male companions.[70]

Characteristics of Prostitutes, Clients, and Pimps

Most prostitutes are between the ages of seventeen and twenty-four although girls have been picked up as young as ten. Juvenile prostitution is becoming an increasingly troublesome problem since runaway girls and some boys turn to prostitution (i.e., heterosexual and homosexual respectively) as the only way of support. This area of prostitution is hard to deal with since most police department youth divisions do not have the staff to handle such cases. Further, those who procure, harbor, and request the services of juveniles are open to harsh penalties so are particularly careful as to the public exposure of the girl or boy. Finally since the juvenile is a runaway who does not want to either return home or be taken to a juvenile justice facility, she is unlikely to be cooperative with the police or social services personnel about her contacts and associates.[71]

Bell states four basic reasons why men seek out prostitutes: (1) avoid competition (i.e., those who are emotionally insecure, physically or mentally limited, ugly, or old); (2) impersonal sex (i.e., those who want sexual release with no commitment); (3) sexual deviance or peculiarities (i.e., those who want to take part in sadomasochistic or other fetishes, or kinds of sexual activities in which wives or girl friends would not normally want to take part); and (4) uncomplicated sex (i.e., no worries about one's partner, freedom to choose any woman for sexual variety without dating, need for companionship and intimacy without obligation to sexual partner).[72]

The pimp is a man who lives off the earnings of the prostitutes who work for him. He is particularly susceptible to arrest since the procuring of women for prostitution or the solicitation of customers for prostitutes is a felony while prostitutes who solicit clients directly are charged only with a misdemeanor. Thus most pimps do not procure or pander but attract vulnerable young women by overtures of love and protection in return for their prostituting themselves for money which the pimp takes for their mutual benefit. According to Goode the pimp provides the prostitute with protection against clients and police; takes his girls to expensive restaurants, resorts, and other places in order to attract better clientele; gives her expensive clothes and a sumptuous place to live; provides her with psychological support and a father figure; manages her finances and daily routine; and paints a picture of future security, both financial and emotional for himself and his girl(s).[73]

Heterosexual Deviance

Legal History

According to the Common Law, all acts of heterosexual deviance, with the exception of adultery, were torts. Adultery was specially handled by ecclesiastical law in England. The various forms of sexual deviance were considered in general to be wrongs directed against community norms or standards of conduct rather than crimes for centuries. Colonial America, especially Puritan New England, accepted the various sexual restrictions placed on adult behavior as passed down from the English Common Law intact.[74] After independence the various states made all forms of sexual behavior within the marital context criminal offenses. Thus the United States had the most moralistic criminal law in recent history.[75] For example, Connecticut passed statutes which prohibited kissing in public, adultery, fornication, and lascivious carriage (i.e., conduct that is wanton, lewd, or lustful and tends to arouse sexual emotions).[76] These statutes were challenged in the federal courts and since 1970, all sexual behavior between two consenting adults is now legal in that state.[77]

Bigamy was not a crime until it was made a felony at the time of King James I.[78] Adultery was handled by the ecclesiastical court in England under the Common Law. Sodomy, whether buggery or bestiality, was considered a crime under the Common Law. Seduction was made a criminal offense under the reign of William and Mary.[79] Illicit cohabitation was not a crime under the Common Law. Fornication that was practiced in private was not a crime at the Common Law. On the other hand indecent public exposure and notorious lewdness were crimes at the Common Law.[80] The United States accepted and strengthened the criminal law concerning premarital, marital, and extramarital sexual relations after 1776 so that until very recently most states had statutes governing sexual behavior.[81]

Legal Definitions

There are three categories of heterosexual deviance which are defined by legal authorities: premarital, extramarital, and comarital. Some forms of sexual deviance are not criminal offenses while others are classified as crimes. There is also overlap between some forms of sexual deviance which can be classified as premarital and marital deviance or premarital and extramarital deviance, while other forms of sexual deviance are strictly premarital or extramarital.

Premarital heterosexual deviance consists of statutory rape, sodomy (i.e., also known as "crimes against nature" or bestiality and buggery), seduction, fornication, and cohabitation. Statutory rape is the unlawful carnal knowledge of a female under statutory age with or without the consent of the girl.[82] Sodomy is a carnal copulation by human beings with each other against nature or with an animal. The terms are often referred to in criminal statutes as "crimes against nature".[83] According to Black, sodomy is the sexual act as performed by a male upon the person of a female by penetration of the anus.[84] Buggery is a rarely used term that is equivalent to sodomy. Bestiality is the carnal copulation of a human with an animal of the opposite sex. The term according to Black is not identical with sodomy but is confused with it in some criminal codes.[85] Fellatio or fellation (i.e., the offense of placing the male sex organ in the mouth of a female human being) is not a form of sodomy but is also confused by statute with it.[86] Finally cunnilingus is an act committed with the mouth of the male in contact with the female sex organ but is not identical with sodomy.[87]

Seduction is defined as the act of a male enticing a female to have unlawful sexual intercourse with him by means of persuasion, solicitation, promises, bribes, or any other means that does not imply the use of force.[88] Cohabitation is the living together of a couple as man and wife in a state of fornication or adultery (i.e., living together as husband and wife for the purpose of sexual relations).[89] Fornication is illegal sexual intercourse between two unmarried individuals. If one of the couple is married that party is guilty of adultery while the unmarried party is guilty of fornication. Some jurisdictions consider the act adultery on the part of both parties if only the woman is married.[90]

Extramarital deviance consists of adultery and bigamy although a married party can also be guilty of statutory rape, sodomy and related crimes, seduction, and cohabitation. Adultery is defined as voluntary sexual intercourse of a married individual with a person other than the offender's spouse.[91] Adultery can be open and notorious where it is common knowledge to members of the community or it can be secretive. Bigamy is the crime of deliberately and knowingly taking a second spouse through marriage or going through the form of second marriage while knowing that the first marriage still is in legal existence.[92]

Comarital sex relations (i.e., also known as swinging, group sex, mate swapping, or wife swapping) consists of sexual relations involving two couples or single individuals in a threesome. In both situations (i.e., among married couples and singles in threesomes) the spouses or partners are exchanged. Thus swinging is in reality a mass form of adultery and fornication.[93]

There are also a number of other sexually deviant behavior patterns that are found in the criminal codes of various jurisdictions. A sexual psychopath is one who is not insane but who by a course of repeated misconduct in sexual matters has evidenced such lack of power to control his sexual impulses as to be dangerous to other persons because he is likely to attack or otherwise inflict injury, loss, pain, or other evil on a member of the opposite sex.[94]

Lewd and lascivious behavior is gross and wanton indecency in sexual relations. The term includes both illicit sexual intercourse and irregular indulgences of lust, whether public or private.[95] Within the term can be found the sexual social deviance known as exhibitionism and voyeurism. Exhibitionism or indecent exposure is exposure to sight of the sex organs in a lewd or indecent manner in a public place.[96] Voyeurism is the act of watching persons who are nude, in the act of sexual intercourse, or in the act of other sexual deviance.[97] This includes sadomasochism, koprolagnia (i.e., sexual excitement watching a person defecate), and urolagnia (i.e., sexual excitement produced by watching a person urinate).[98]

Sadism is sexual deviance in which satisfaction is derived from the infliction of cruelty upon another. This may be in the form of anal erotism or oral erotism.[99] Masochism is a form of sexual deviance in which cruel treatment gives sexual gratification to the individual.[100] Sadomasochism is a combination of being sexually aroused by the fantasies of being beaten, tortured, flogged, etc., by a member of the opposite sex. A person who obtains sexual gratification from an object of unnatural adoration is a fetishist.[101] Transvestism is the overwhelming desire to wear the clothing, shoes, etc., of the opposite sex which brings about sexual excitement.[102]

Heterosexual Deviance Statutes and Enforcement Policy

Statutory rape is the carnal knowledge of a female child under sixteen years of age and the perpetrator of this crime shall be imprisoned for any term of years and for life.[103] A person is guilty of sodomy if one takes into his or her mouth or anus the sexual organ of any other person or animal, or who shall place his or her sexual organ in the mouth or anus of any other person or animal, or who shall have carnal copulation in an opening of the body except sexual parts with another person. Said person shall be fined not more than one thousand dollars or be imprisoned for a period not exceeding ten years. Any person committing such act with a person under the age of sixteen years shall be fined not more than one thousand dollars or be imprisoned for a period not exceeding twenty years. In any indictment for the commission of any of the acts declared to be offenses, it shall not be necessary to set forth the particular unnatural or perverted sexual practice with the commission of which the defendant may be charged, nor to set forth the particular manner in which said unnatural or perverted sexual practice was committed, but it shall be sufficient if the indictment set forth that the defendant committed a certain unnatural and perverted sexual practice with a person or animal, as the case may be. Any penetration however slight is sufficient to complete the crime specified and proof of emission is not necessary.[104]

If any person shall seduce and carnally know any female of previous chaste character, between the ages of sixteen and twenty-one years, out of wedlock, such seduction and carnal knowledge shall be deemed a misdemeanor and the offender being convicted shall be punished by imprisonment for a term not exceeding three years, or fined not exceeding two hundred dollars, or both fined and imprisoned.[105] If any unmarried man or woman commits fornication, each shall be fined not more than three hundred dollars or imprisoned not more than six months, or both.[106] Any person or persons who make any obscene or indecent exposure of his or her person, or make any lewd, obscene, or indecent sexual proposal, or commit any other lewd, obscene, or indecent act may suffer penalty of not more than three hundred dollar fine, or imprisonment of not more than ninety days, or both, for each and every such offense. Any person or persons who commit an offense of lewd, indecent, or obscene acts knowingly in the presence of a child under the age of sixteen years shall be punished by imprisonment of not more than one year, or fined in an amount not to exceed one thousand dollars, or both for each and every such offense.[107]

Any person who shall take or attempt to take any immoral, improper, or indecent liberties with any child of either sex, under the age of sixteen years with the intent of arousing, appealing to, or gratifying the lust or passions or sexual desires, either of said person or of such child, or of both such person and such child, or who shall commit or attempt to commit, any lewd or lascivious act upon or with the body, or any part or member thereof, of such child, with the intent of arousing, appealing to, gratifying the lust or passions or sexual desires, either of such person or of such child, or of both such person and such child shall be imprisoned in a penitentiary not more than ten years. Any person who takes any such child or shall entice, allure, or persuade any such child, to any place whatever for the purpose either of taking any such immoral, improper, or indecent liberties with such child, with said intent or of committing any such lewd, or lascivious act upon or with the body, or any part or member thereof, of such child with said intent, shall be imprisoned not more than five years.[108]

Whoever commits adultery shall on conviction be punished by a fine not exceeding five hundred dollars, or by imprisonment not exceeding one year, or both; and when the act is committed between a married woman and unmarried man, both parties to such act shall be found guilty of adultery; and when such act is committed between a married man and an unmarried woman, the man only shall be guilty of adultery.[109] A person who has a living husband or wife and who marries another shall be guilty of bigamy, and on conviction shall be imprisoned for not less than two nor more than seven years. This statute shall not apply to any person whose spouse has been continually absent for five successive years next before such marriage without being known to such person to be living within that time, or whose marriage to said living spouse shall have been dissolved by a valid decree of a competent court, or shall have been pronounced void by a valid decree of a competent court on the ground of the nullity of the marriage contract.[110]

The police and other members of the criminal justice system have a difficult time in dealing with heterosexual deviance in most instances.

This is due to the fact that the police have a difficult time getting at the deviant behavior since most of it is conducted in private. Further the public tends to be rather indifferent to the enforcement of the statutes unless the behavior is open and notorious.[111] In general the public is tolerant of cohabitation, fornication, adultery, swinging, and bigamy. It is much less tolerant of statutory rape, seduction, sodomy, and lewd and indecent behavior. The public has mixed feelings about voyeurism, transvestism, and fetishism while generally disapproving sadomasochism. The sexual psychopath laws especially the sections dealing with sexual abuse of children are strongly supported by public opinion.[112]

Less than one percent of the arrests made by the police are for sex offenses, excluding forcible rape and prostitution. Just what percentage of this figure constitutes heterosexual sex offense is impossible to know by the police reports.[113] A study of the disposition of persons formally charged by the police with such sex offenses shows that nearly half of those arrested plead guilty to the original charge against them, five percent plead guilty to a lesser offense, twenty-eight percent were either acquitted or had the charges dropped against them, and seventeen percent were referred to juvenile court.[114] From the official statistics, one can see that the police rarely enforce the statutes against heterosexual deviance which creates the problems of arbitrary police and prosecutorial discretion. This is due to the fact that there is extreme difficulty in detecting sexual deviance by normal police practices. Thus many law enforcement officers overlook many acts that come to their attention via third parties; many prosecutors will not process a great number of cases; many judges will dismiss the charges if brought before them or refer the defendants to private community agencies for treatment, and juries will readily acquit persons charged with some heterosexual offenses out of a feeling that the crime does not merit punishment of any sort.[115]

Description of Heterosexual Deviance

It appears that premarital, extramarital, and comarital deviance are becoming more and more common in American society with each passing year.[116] Previous studies have shown that heterosexual deviance varied with race, ethnicity, religion, region, social class, and inner city-suburb-rural areas.[117]

Premarital sexuality is becoming the norm in American society although Reiss feels that it is still deviant.[118] Premarital sexual behavior of all types is becoming increasingly the standard for high school students to the elderly in our society.[119] The sexual revolution has, along with the women's liberation movement, created an atmosphere where both sexes are increasingly engaging in sexual expression of all sorts outside the marital context for the pleasure of indulging in sexual behaviors.[120]

Individuals who engage in premarital deviance come from all age groups, but it appears that those becoming sexually active since the 1960s have the most varied of sexual experiences, both males and females. Premarital sexuality tends to center around both physical attraction and emotional attachment. More individuals appear to feel less guilty about sexual experimentation every year regardless of religion or social class. The age of first sexual experience has been steadily declining so that it is not uncommon to see junior high school aged youth engaged in all sorts of sexual activities. Thus many critics of sex laws are calling for the lowering of the age for statutory rape from sixteen to fourteen.[121]

Premarital sexual deviance covers quite a collection of sexual practices (i.e., crimes against nature, seducers, rapists, exhibitionists, voyeurs, transvestites, sadomasochists, and fornicators). The general public and criminal justice system consider all of these forms of sexual deviance clearly criminal when a juvenile is involved with an adult. On the other hand there is a great deal of confusion on the part of the public and those involved in the criminal justice system when only consenting adults of the opposite sex are involved in these practices.[122]

The statutory rapist is a male who knowingly or unknowingly has consensual relations with a girl under the age set by the statute of the particular jursidiction. Most studies show that this male is not the same type of individual as the rapist of adult women who uses force or threat of force.[123] It appears that the young men convicted of statutory rape for the most part are the least deviant of all categories of sex offenders.[124]

Crimes against nature and sodomy generally come under the sexual psychopath statutes in many jurisdictions yet the behavior of these heterosexual individuals is not usually dangerous to the other party engaged in these deviant activities. Sutherland states that the sexual psychopath laws are impossible to enforce because it is virtually impossible to identify such an individual.[125] Yet all kinds of overtly normal people engage in such activities as fellatio, anal intercourse, voyeurism (i.e., triolism, koprolagnia, urolagnia), transvestism, and sadomasochism. It appears that only those who are exhibitionists and indulge in bestiality are dealt with negatively by both the public and criminal justice system. Court cases have even found husbands guilty of soliciting their wives to commit sodomy with them. Even Kinsey was opposed to sodomy laws as they related to voluntary behavior among adult heterosexual couples.[126]

Voyeurism constitutes a criminal act that comes under lewd and indecent behavior. There are all types of voyeurs, some of whom cannot be prosecuted for their behavior is not deemed illegal. The classic peeping tom type can be dealt with by the criminal justice system but this type of offender is usually a teenager or young but immature adult. This activity is usually considered as a public nuisance in this particular instance.[127] On the other hand those individuals who take and get sexual pleasure from seeing individuals engaged in sexual intercourse, triolism, koprolagnia, and urolagnia are usually prosecuted on charges of lewd conduct or related statutes.[128] Another form of voyeurism is nudism. Unfortunately many nudists find that their right to display their bodies absent of clothes with no sexual purpose is often considered to be criminal even if done in the privacy of one's roof garden or back yard.[129] Finally going to see a striptease act, topless or bottomless dancers at a bar or restaurant is an obvious form of legitimate voyeurism although the female peformers are viewed as deviant in this social situation.[130]

Exhibitionists are usually considered as relatively harmless individuals, usually male. They are usually charged with lewd and indecent behavior but the general public and members of the criminal justice system usually regard this form of social deviance as relatively harmless. Exhibitionists are usually young adults; very timid, and very conscientious persons who no one would expect to behave in such deviant manner.[131]

Extramarital sexual deviance consists of adultery and its offshoot, swinging, and bigamy. Adultery is a crime in all jurisdictions but is very rarely enforced. In the past in jurisdictions with strict divorce laws (i.e., New York) adultery was very common grounds given for divorce yet almost no one admitting to it was tried and found guilty of a crime. It is estimated that both husbands and wives engage in this type of sexual deviance in almost equal numbers.[132] Various reasons are given for spouses engaging in adultery (i.e., variation in partners, retaliation against spouse, rebellion against spouse, emotional attachment with another person, encouragement of spouse, fear of losing one's youth, and pleasure from a variety of sexual partners).[133]

Swinging is a variation of adultery but in this case both husband and wife exchange sexual partners in the presence of each other and with mutual approval. This group sex is conducted in private with contacts made through magazines, word of mouth, and attendance of so-called swingers bars. Comarital sex allows both spouses to endulge in partner encouraged adultery, sodomy, fellatio, triolism, and homosexuality in a truly voyeuristic atmosphere with supposedly no guilt toward one's spouse who is also engaged in the same practices. In fact this allows each spouse to see just how popular and expert his or her spouse is with other individuals. It appears that most swingers are metropolitan area residents, young to middle aged, and usually upper middle class.[134]

Homosexuality

Legal History

According to Bailey, the origin of ecclesiastical laws dealing with homosexuality date back to Jewish laws that were eventually incorporated into Christian Church rulings. The Code of Justinian (538 AD) punished homosexuals with the death penalty.[135] English ecclesiastical courts dealt with homosexuals through the use of torture or the death penalty. The Common Law defined homosexuality as a crime, an obvious reflection of the early Church's influence. Under Henry VIII in 1553, the English parliament made homosexuality (i.e., buggery) a secular offense punishable by death.[136]

Historically both the ecclesiastical and criminal laws have applied to male homosexuals, not females.[137] From 1696 until 1952, there was not a single conviction of a female in the United States for homosexual practices.[138] Most of the states do not have laws against lesbians, and in the states that do prosecute women for homosexual practices, most receive minor punishments (i.e., misdemeanor charges with fines, short jail sentences, suspended sentences, or probation).[139]

It was not until 1861 in England that the Offenses Against the Person Act of Parliament reduced the penalty for homosexuality from death to life imprisonment. This act remained in effect until 1956 and dealt with sodomy between two adult males as well as between husband and wife. An act of parliament in 1956 stated that sodomy with a child or juvenile was a crime punishable by life imprisonment but the prison sentence for acts of sodomy between adults was reduced. Certain types of homosexual behaviors in public were considered misdemeanor offenses in this statute.[140]

The Wolfenden Report (i.e., Report of the Committee on Homosexual Offenses and Prostitution) stated that homosexuality was a moral issue and not a criminal law matter when adults who consent engage in these practices. The committee concluded that it found no facts supporting the common view that homosexuality led to the decline of society. Parliament acting on the recommendations of the committee passed the Sexual Offenses Act of 1967 which removed the criminal penalties for homosexual practices between consenting adults in private. The Act retains the penalty of life imprisonment for homosexual offenses against males under age sixteen; retains acts of gross indecency against juveniles (i.e., ages 16-21) as a criminal offense with a five year sentence; and public homosexual acts that are indecent are punishable by a two year sentence in prison.[141]

The history of criminal sanctions against homosexual behavior in the United States closely follows the English Common Law and British criminal law practices. For example in an Illinois case of 1897, the defendant was convicted of crimes against nature. The Court defined various acts (i.e., fellation, anal intercourse, bestiality) as sinful and applied the statute to the homosexual act of the defendant.[142] In 1961 the Illinois legislature accepting the suggestions of the Model Penal Code revised its crimes against nature statute. The new statute followed the recommendations made by the Wolfenden Report. The Illinois statute defines deviant sexual conduct as any act of sexual gratification involving the sex organs of one person in the mouth or anus of another, but does not prohibit such acts if they are entered into by consenting adults. The statute does prohibit sexual assault and contributing to the sexual delinquency of a child.[143]

Thus Illinois typifies both the old criminal law reaction to homosexuality as well as the modern enlightened view as long as the homosexual practices are between consenting adults and are in private. Since 1961 a number of other states have joined Illinois in the decriminalization of homosexual practices between consenting adults in private (i.e., California, Colorado, Connecticut, Idaho, Oregon , Hawaii, Delaware, Texas, North Dakota, Georgia, Arkansas, Nevada, and Wisconsin).[144]

The Uniform Code of Military Justice still calls for a less than honorable discharge from the armed forces if a person admits to or is found to be a practicing homosexual. Further the military will not consider a homosexual suitable for military service. We have the cases of Air Force Sergeant Leonard Matlovich, PFC Barbara Randolph, and PVT Deborah Watson who were all given general discharges for revealing that they were practicing homosexuals according to article 125 of the USMJ.[145]

In 1969 the National Institute of Mental Health of the United States Department of Health, Education, and Welfare created a Task Force on Homosexuality. The task force concluded that the federal and state criminal codes should follow the recommendations of the Wolfenden Report of Great Britain and decriminalize homosexual behavior between consenting adults.[146] The District of Columbia in the Human Rights Act of 1973 bars discrimination on the basis of sexual orientation (i.e., homosexuality).[147]

The United States Supreme Court in a number of recent rulings has upheld the constitutionality of existing state laws (i.e., Virginia, Washington, and Missouri) that criminally penalize or civilly discriminate against practicing homosexuals, both male and female. The Virginia case dealt with banning the homosexual behavior of consenting adults. The Washington State case dealt with firing a teacher who admitted to being a homosexual, and the Missouri case dealt with the right of gay liberation groups to meet and organize on college campuses. This latter case was settled by the Court in favor of homosexual organizations being allowed to form campus organizations.[148]

Legal Definitions

According to Black, pederasty is the crime against nature which involves the carnal copulation of male with male, usually a man with a boy.[149] Black states that pederasty is a form of sodomy (i.e., sexual intercourse as performed by a man upon another male by penetration of the anus).[150]

Buggery is sexual intercourse of a man with another man and is equivalent to sodomy.[151] Fellatio or fellation is the offense of placing the male organ in the mouth of another male human being.[152] Cunnilingus is an act committed with the mouth of one female in contact with the female organ of another woman.[153]

All the crimes against nature defined by Black are terms used to describe some aspect of homosexuality. Homosexuality is defined as a compulsive sexual interest in another person of the same sex (i.e., male) while the same deviant behavior manifested by two females in each other is termed lesbianism.[154] Goode describes the bisexual as a male or female who is sexually interested in both members of one's own sex as well as members of the opposite gender.[155] Transvestites are males who dress like women and have feelings of eroticism when wearing feminine attire. Although the concept should not be confused with homosexuality or bisexuality, some transvestites are homosexuals and engage in acts of sodomy and fellatio with unsuspecting males who mistake these "female impersonators" as women.[156]

Homosexuality Statutes and Enforcement Policies

Homosexuality per se is not a crime in the United States. With the exception of the states previously mentioned that have decriminalized homosexual acts between consenting adults, a number of deviant sexual behaviors are considered criminal as applied to homosexuals (i.e., sodomy, fellation, cunnilingus, and mutual masturbation), whether in public or in private. All homosexual deviance between adults and juveniles is considered criminal. Most statutes governing homosexual behavior are usually enforced against males as female homosexuals (i.e., lesbians) are rarely mentioned in statutes or arrested by the police.[157]

Homosexual practices come under the sexual psychopaths chapter (i.e., 35) of the D.C. Code. A person shall be guilty of sodomy if one takes into his or her mouth or anus the sexual organ of any other person, or who shall place his or her sexual organ in the mouth or anus of any other person, or who shall have carnal copulation in an opening of the body except sexual parts with another person. Said person shall be fined not more than one thousand dollars or be imprisoned for a period not exceeding ten years. Any person committing such act with a person under the age of sixteen years shall be fined not more than one thousand dollars or be imprisoned for a period not exceeding twenty years. In any indictment for the commission of any of the acts declared to be offenses, it shall not be necessary to set forth the particular unnatural or perverted sexual practice with the commission of which the defendant may be charged, nor to set forth the particular manner in which said unnatural or perverted sexual practice was committed, but it shall be sufficient if the indictment set forth that the defendant committed a certain unnatural and perverted sexual practice with a person. Any penetration however slight is sufficient to complete the crime specified and proof of emission is not necessary.[158]

Any person who shall take or attempt to take any immoral, improper, or indecent liberties with any child of either sex, under the age of sixteen years with the intent of arousing, appealing to, or gratifying the lust or passions or sexual desires, either of said person or of such child, or of both such person and such child, or who shall commit or attempt to commit, any lewd or lascivious act upon or with the body, or any part or member thereof, of such child, with the intent of arousing, appealing to, gratifying the lust or passions or sexual desires, either of such person or of such child, or of both such person and such child shall be imprisoned not more than ten years. Any person who takes any such child or shall entice, allure, or persuade any such child, to any place whatever for the purpose either of taking any such immoral, improper, or indecent liberties with such child, with said intent or of committing any such lewd, or lascivious act upon or with the body, or any part or member thereof, of such child with said intent, shall be imprisoned not more than five years.[159]

The police generally do not arrest homosexuals unless the sexual deviance is flagrant or involves juveniles. On occasions when there is ample police manpower available and not needed elsewhere to deal with serious crimes, the police will entrap homosexuals in such places as public toilets, public meeting places such as parks, and bars and restaurants catering to homosexual trade. The entrapment issue has placed the police in a negative situation since the detectives have to involve themselves with homosexuals and the experience is demoralizing at the least and has led to bribery and violence on the part of certain officers. Thus most police policy today is moving away from entrapment.[160]

The discretionary power of the police in terms of who gets arrested in homosexual activities is biased in favor of the individual who is engaging in the act of sodomy fellatio. According to the criminal law both parties engaging in homosexual activities should be arrested. Thus many officers reason that the active participant is the "true" homosexual while the receiver of this deviant sex activity is not truly as perverted and need not be arrested.[161] The police tend to arrest three types of individuals for their involvement in homosexual acts. The active homosexual is one who actively seeks out homosexual encounters at gay bars, public toilets, and parks. The second type of homosexual arrested is one who frequents known homosexual hangouts and accepts invitations from the active type or "cruiser". The third type of person arrested is one who seeks out active or passive homosexuals as a way of getting kicks, is drunk, curious, and is intent on robbing or beating the homosexual. This situational offender under normal conditions would not have anything to do with homosexuals.[162]

The Los Angeles County study of the effects of the criminal justice system on homosexuals shows that most arrests were made in public or semi-public places rather than in a private residence. Most arrests were made in public toilets, in automobiles, in jails, in parks, in public baths, and on public beaches, in felony cases. Most misdemeanor arrests occurred in public toilets, autos, parks, theatres, bars, on the street, and in public baths. Most of the charges against those arrested were for fellation. Most offenders asked for a trial before a judge to avoid public exposure with most convictions being fines, suspended sentences, or charges reduced in most felony cases.[163]

The police rarely arrest the lesbian since she is typically not public in her expression of criminal deviance (i.e., most lesbian activity is in private, not public toilets, parked cars, parks, and beaches). Female homosexuals generally are not as aggressive as males in the solicitation process nor as in need of new partners so most law enforcement agencies do not have a special policy involving entrapment or harassment. Most lesbian bars are left alone and undercover police-women are rarely used in any entrapment process.[164]

Description of Homosexual Deviance

It would appear that males and females who take part in homosexual activities come from a cross section of American society (i.e., all social classes, races, ethnic groups, religions, regions, and marital statuses). There appears to be a concentration of homosexuals in the largest metropolitan areas which also contain the most open and militant of individuals.[165]

The gay or homosexual subculture allows these social deviants to create a community in which to establish their sexually deviant relations. The homosexual community consists of a variety of social networks according to Clinard (i.e., pairs of homosexually marrieds or singles; larger secondary groups; and individuals who are members of both primary and secondary groups). Members of these cliques, groups, and networks have all types of parties together and celebrate special events (i.e., anniversaries, birthdays, other special events).[166]

The homosexual or gay bar is another special institution which serves as a place for sexual exchange for short term sexual affairs, where friends can gather free of the prying eyes of "straights", where one can be socialized into homosexual value-attitudes, and where one can learn how to improve his life-style.[167] There are also voluntary organizations that cater to homosexuals such as Gay Activists Alliance, Mattachine Society, One Institute, Society for Individual Rights, and Metropolitan Community Church and which enter into settlement of disputes concerning civil rights, employment, discrimination, police harassment, and criminal law reform.[168]

The lesbian subculture differs in some important ways from that of homosexual subculture. Lesbians are more interested in personalized relationships rather than the promiscuous encounters of the typical gay. Most homosexuals consider that sex is the most important aspect of their interpersonal relationships while lesbians consider their companions personality and commitment to them more important than the sexual aspect of their relationship. Lesbians are more private in their relationships while gays are quite public in comparison in their quest for homosexual companionship. Lesbian bars serve the purpose of meeting friends and as a place for socialization compared to the overt search for sexual encounters in gay bars. Gays begin their sexual encounters at an earlier age than lesbians. The latter have much more heterosexual contacts, including marriages with offspring, than the former who may have had little sexual contact with women and do not want children.[169]

The bisexual is both heterosexual and homosexual depending on the type of sexual relationship they prefer at the moment. Thus a bisexual can be a single or married male or female and have supposedly satisfactory relationships with members of both sexes on the level of sexual encounters. Relatively few people are bisexuals and many homosexuals are convinced that a professed bisexual is really a latent homosexual but will not really admit their true sexual preferences.[170]

The homosexual prostitute is a young man who offers his services for a fee to older homosexuals who cannot attract younger men; offers services to homosexuals from another community who do not have the time to establish contacts since they are on a business trip; is a juvenile who is a runaway and needs the money; and a male who wants to be supported by a wealthy individual on a regular basis (i.e., akin to a mistress). These male prostitutes are either hustlers who consider their deviance as a temporary source of money and those who consider themselves as professionals (i.e., career-oriented).[171]

Prostitutes and strippers supposedly are oriented toward homosexuality because they are faced with contacts with men that are negative and exploitative. Thus these women spend much of their leisure time in the company of other exploited females and conclude that lesbianism is a warm and non-threatening relationship. Supposedly some strippers and prostitutes do not like men so their occupations are natural for the formation of affectional relationships with other women.[172]

Venereal Diseases

Legal History

The London Act of 1161 is the first recorded statute in England which forbade brothel keepers to employ prostitutes who had contracted gonorrhea (i.e., women suffering from the perilous infirmity of burning).[173] A London order of 1430 ordered brothel keepers to keep men suffering from gonorrhea (i.e., the so-called hidden disease) from visiting their prostitutes.[174] An ordinance of 1447 of Aberdeen, Scotland ordered all prostitutes to desist from their behavior or be branded since they were assumed to be the source of venereal disease.[175] The same city in 1507 passed a second regulation informing those persons infected with venereal disease to keep to themselves and stay at home until they are cured of the "Naples disease".[176]

Up until the nineteenth century a double standard prevailed concerning the punishment of those contracting venereal diseases. Males were at most looked upon as deviant while females were considered criminals. Prostitutes who contracted venereal diseases were placed in the public workhouses and made to wear yellow dresses to show how disgraceful they were to the community.[177] The Contagious Diseases Act of 1864 dealt with military personnel who contracted venereal diseases and the prostitutes who gave it to them. The women were given manditory examinations by the court and detained in specified hospitals.[178] A Ladies' National Association was formed in 1869 to try to help these lower class women accused of spreading the diseases and a Royal Commission was appointed in 1870 to investigate the alleged breach of constitutional guarantees of these unfortunate females. Finally a select committee of the House of Commons studied the issue and Parliament repealed the Act in 1886.[179]

Another Royal Commission was appointed in 1913 to study the problem of venereal diseases. It studied the issue until 1916 and based on its findings, Parliament passed the Venereal Disease Regulations the same year which set up public treatment centers that kept the identity of the patient confidential. Patients were advised to seek treatment on a voluntary basis but during and shortly after World War II public health authorities could force individuals through the use of the courts into manditory treatment.[180] The Matrimonial Causes Act of 1937 states that a marriage is null and void if a spouse knows that he or she has venereal disease at the time of marriage. The other spouse must be unaware that the other marriage partner was infected, stop sexual intercourse at the time of discovery, and institute divorce proceedings within a year of the wedding date.[181]

Venereal disease clinics were set up in 1948 under National Health Service in Great Britain.[182] In 1951 the British Federation against the Venereal Diseases was established as a private organization to educate the public concerning the prevention of the diseases. It worked closely with the Venereal Diseases and Treponematosis Division of the World Health Organization of the United Nations.[183] The Pharmaceutical Substances Act of 1956 made it manditory for all blood donors to have a blood test for syphilis.[184] Finally the Street Offenses Act of 1959 was in part an attempt to control the spread of venereal diseases from prostitution.[185]

The United States accepted the British practices concerning the prevention and control of venereal diseases without question from colonial times. The first indirect legislation dealing with the problem was the legislation of Congress known as the Comstock Law in 1873 which banned the mailing of contraceptives and information about them. Such information was deemed obscene by this federal statute.[186] The condom was such a birth control device and also effective in the prevention of venereal diseases. A congressional act of Congress banned prostitutes from entering this country as immigrants in 1875, thus indirectly stating that they were carriers of venereal diseases.[187] It was not until the Immigration Act of 1917 that Congress stated that persons who were infected with "loathsome or contagious diseases" should be denied entrance to the United States.[188]

The United States Court of Appeals in 1936 stated that contraceptives imported for a lawful purpose (i.e., prevention of venereal diseases) did not come under the Comstock Law. Connecticut passed the first statute requiring both prospective marriage partners to have blood tests for venereal disease in 1935. Rhode Island in 1938 required that all pregnant women be required to take prenatal blood tests to determine if they had contracted venereal disease.[189] Since 1968 several states have enacted laws allowing juveniles to be diagnosed and treated for venereal disease without the consent of their parents.[190] Finally in *Carey v. Population Services International,* the Supreme Court ruled that the New York statute forbidding the sale of contraceptives to those under age sixteen, and forbidding advertisement and display of same is unconstitutional. This 1977 ruling indirectly allows juveniles access to condoms which can be used as a preventative for venereal disease.[191]

Legal Definitions

Black defines venereal disease as one of several diseases identified with sexual intercourse.[192] Only the three most common diseases capable of being spread by the sex act are defined in law as venereal (i.e., gonorrhea, syphilis, and chancroid). Other venereal diseases or medical conditions associated with sexual intercourse are lymphogranuloma venereum, granuloma inguinale, non-specific urethritis, trichomonas vaginalis, scabies, genital warts, and lice.[193]

Venereal Disease Statutes and Enforcement Policies

The District of Columbia Code does not define specific venereal diseases but only states that communicable diseases shall be defined by the D.C. Council regulation.[194] The Director of Public Health is empowered to remove persons believed to be carriers of communicable diseases (i.e., venereal) if he has probable cause to believe that the person is affected with the disease or is a carrier and that the continuance of such person in the place where he may be is likely to be dangerous to the lives or health of other persons, or that by reason of the uncooperation or carelessness of such person the public health is likely to be endangered. Further the Director may by written order have the police detain such person in any place or institution so designated by the Director of Public Health.[195]

Detention of a person suspected of being affected or a carrier of venereal disease shall not exceed forty-eight hours unless a judge orders a continuance. A judge will set a hearing to determine whether the person detained is affected with venereal disease or is a carrier of communicable disease. If so ruled that the individual's release would be likely to endanger the lives or health of any other person, said person will be held in an institution designated by the Director of Public Health. If the detained person is not affected or a carrier, or is affected or a carrier but not likely to endanger the lives or health of others, that person shall be released by court order.[196]

It is unlawful for a person detained to leave a designated institution unless properly discharged by the authority of the Director of Public Health.[197] The Director of Public Health is empowered to seek a warrant from a judge for the arrest of any person who is affected by or a carrier of a communicable disease. The police under such warrant may break into the abode of the person in order to execute the warrant if the person refuses to admit the police.[198] It shall be unlawful for any person knowingly to obstruct, resist, oppose, or interfere with any person performing any duty or function under the authority of this statute.[199]

Any person who violates any of the provisions of the statute shall be fined not more than three hundred dollars or sentenced to imprisonment for not longer than ninety days, or both. The Court may also impose conditions upon any person found guilty. Such conditions may include submission to medical and mental examination, diagnosis, and treatment by proper health authorities or any licensed physician approved by the court.[200]

Any juvenile who appears in any clinic, hospital, or other facility of the Department of Public Health who is affected with a venereal disease or is a carrier of a venereal disease shall be detained by authority of the Director of Public Health. The juvenile will be allowed to consent to treatment and so treated if he agrees. Otherwise no treatment will be provided if said juvenile refuses such treatment. In such instance the Director of Public Health will search out said juvenile's parents or person standing in loco parentis to such minor in order to notify them that the juvenile is affected with a venereal disease or is a carrier of a venereal disease and whether said youth has received or refused to receive treatment.[201]

The Virginia Criminal Code states that persons of "ill fame", if found guilty of fornication, adultery, lewd and lascivious conduct, illicit cohabitation, sodomy are to be considered and declared to be reasonably suspected of having a venereal disease. No individual convicted of any such charges shall be released from custody until examined for venereal diseases. The state of Virginia also makes it a crime (i.e., one hundred dollar fine and/or six months in jail) for an individual who knows he or she has a venereal disease to spread it to other persons.[202]

The United States government under the National Venereal Disease Prevention and Control Act assists states to prevent and control venereal diseases. The United States Public Health Service aids the states in this matter and PHS personnel are empowered, with the aid of federal law enforcement agents, to deal with problems of venereal disease which are interstate in nature.[203]

Description of Specific Deviance

Several types of deviant individuals tend to have higher rates of venereal disease than the general population: (1) prostitutes (both heterosexual and homosexual); (2) homosexuals; (3) promiscuous persons (i.e., adulterers and fornicators); (4) juveniles (i.e., those who run away and engage in prostitution, both homo- and heterosexual, and those who engage in sexual intercourse); and (5) those who sexually assault or abuse children and/or adults and their victims (i.e., rapists, child molesters, and sexual abusers of children).[204]

The few studies dealing with the social background of individuals coming in for treatment of venereal disease indicates that there are essentially no differences in rates of infection between religious and ethnic groups, but differences between racial groups and social classes, although the diseases are not rare in any subculture within society.[205] The studies show a higher rate of venereal disease for the lower classes and Blacks than for middle/upper classes and whites. This may reflect the reporting techniques to a certain degree since most well to do persons go to a private doctor for treatment who may not report the case or all the social background data to the authorities while lower class and nonwhites generally seek out treatment at public facilities that report all the data to the proper authorities.[206] Venereal disease rates vary by age but appear to be highest among adolescents and young adults.[207] Morton states that venereal disease rates have increased faster for young women since the early 1960's than for young men. This finding also appears to be true in the United States.[208] The fact that the birth control pill gives no protection against venereal disease (while the condom does), plus the fact that young women are more sexually mature than previously and allowed more freedom of movement due to the effect of the woman's liberation ideology explains the raise of the venereal disease rate.[209]

It is estimated that the prevalence of venereal disease in the United States is about six million cases which is probably a conservative estimate. The rate of cases of gonorrhea is approximately four times greater than the rate of cases of syphilis. The U.S. Public Health Service estimates it cost six million dollars per year to maintain the syphilitic blind institutionally and another fifty million dollars to maintain the syphilitic insane. Thousands of babies and adults die each year due to the disease.[210]

Prostitution has long been considered the source of venereal diseases, since the women have contact with a number of clients on a daily basis, most of whom they never see again. It appears that streetwalkers have higher rates of venereal disease than massage parlor and house girls, while call girls have the lowest rate. The disease rates appear to be fairly low for prostitutes compared to females of the general population who are promiscuous.[211]

Homosexuals appear to have much higher rates of venereal diseases than heterosexuals. This is especially more true of gays than lesbians who tend not to be as promiscuous. Gays tend to have twice as many sexual contacts as heterosexual males. Further it appears that anal intercourse hinders the early detection of the diseases and this is the preference of most homosexuals.[212]

Individuals who engage in indiscriminate premarital or extramarital sexual intercourse usually have a higher rate of venereal disease than those who tend to seek out a long lasting relationship with one person. Thus those who are involved in the swinging singles scene as well as group sex (i.e., wife-swapping) appear to be maximizing their chances to contract venereal disease. The increased interest in experimentation with sexuality (i.e., oral sex, cunnilingus, and anal sex) coupled with the use of oral contraceptives increases the chances of contracting and spreading venereal disease. This new sexual freedom is accompanied with a lack of knowledge concerning the nature of venereal diseases since it is thought by many supposedly educated people that only immoral, dirty, or lower class individuals have venereal diseases.[213]

It appears that the greatest incidence of problems with venereal disease is among juveniles. Studies in Great Britain and the United States show that both males and females have greater freedom to do as they please. Despite the increased amount of sex education courses offered in the public schools, the establishment of free clinics that offer advice concerning birth control, and the creation of V.D. hotlines in the larger metropolitan areas, more and more adolescents contract a spectrum of venereal diseases each year. Many are afraid to inform their parents or seek out medical help so the disease gets worse. Often the infected youth is labeled as a delinquent and sent to training school where the problem of disease control is even more difficult for the authorities to deal with.[214]

Finally there are those who are the victims of sexual assaults by strangers, friends, or relatives. In the case of children who contract venereal disease, most do not know how they contracted the disease and are quite confused concerning the deviance surrounding the incident. Most adolescents are ashamed, afraid, and angry about the forced sexual relationship and resulting contraction of disease. Victims of incest are usually quite reluctant to admit what happened to them since they are afraid that the parent or relative will convince the police and/or juvenile authorities that they are promiscuous and should be sent to a training school. Rape victims who contract venereal disease are already suffering from the trauma of the sexual assault and often do not report this problem to the public health authorities or police since they do not want further involvement with the criminal justice system.[215]

Notes

[1] Robert Pursley, *Introduction to Criminal Justice*, Encino, California: Glenco Press, 1977, pp. 110-112; Marshall Clinard, *Sociology of Deviant Behavior*, New York: Holt, Rinehart and Winston, 1974, pp. 532-533; The President's Commission on Pornography and Obscenity, *Report of the Commission on Pornography and Obscenity*, New York: New York Times Book by Bantam Books, 1970.

[2] *United States v. One Book Called "Ulysses"*, 5 F. Supp. 182 (1933).

[3] United States Reports, *Miller v. California*, Washington, D.C.: Supreme Court of the United States, 1973; 354 U.S. 476 (1956).

[4] 370 U.S. 478 (1962).

[5] 378 U.S. 184 (1964).

[6] 383 U.S. 412 (1966); 383 U.S. 463 (1966); 383 U.S. 413 (1966).

[7] *Miller v. California, op. cit.;* 394 U.S. 557, 567 (1969).

[8] 413 U.S. 15 (1973).

[9] *Webster's New International Dictionary*, 3rd edition, unabridged, 1969; *The Oxford English Dictionary*, 1933.

[10] Henry Black, *Black's Law Dictionary*, St. Paul, Minnesota: West Publishing Company, 1968, p. 1227.

[11] Webster, *op. cit.;* Black, *op. cit.*, p. 1322.

[12] District of Columbia Code, 1973, supplement iv, 1977, 1437-1438.

[13] *Ibid.,* 1438.

[14] *Ibid.,* 1438.

[15] Interviews with Sergeant Abbott and Detective Benigas of the Metropolitan Police Department (D.C.) Obscenity Squad, 1977.

[16] *Ibid.*

[17] Bronislaw Malinowski, *The Sexual Life of Savages,* New York: Harcourt, Brace and World, 1929.

[18] The President's Commission, *op. cit.*

[19] *Ibid.,* pp. 25-30.

[20] *Ibid.*

[21] *Ibid.,* pp. 30-32.

[22] *Ibid.,* pp. 25-27.

[23] *Ibid.,* p. 27; Berl Kutchinsky, "The Effect of Easy Availability of Pornography on the Incidence of Sex Crimes: The Danish Experience," *Journal of Social Issues,* 1974.

[24] Michael Goldstein and Harold Kant, *Pornography and Sexual Deviance,* Los Angeles: University of California Press, 1973.

[25] Harold Greenwald, *The Elegant Prostitute: A Social and Psychoanalytic Study,* New York: Walker, 1970; Susan Hall, *Ladies of the Night,* New York: Simon and Schuster, 1973; Bruce Jackson, *In the Life: Versions of the Criminal Experience,* New York: New American Library, 1974; Larry Kleinman, *Sex Parlor,* New York: New American Library, 1973; Gail Sheehy, *Hustling,* New York: Delacorte Press, 1973; John Wells, *Tricks of the Trade,* New York: New American Library, 1970; Wayland Young, *Eros Denied: Sex in Western Society,* New York: Grove Press, 1966; Fernando Henriques, *Prostitution and Society,* New York: Grove Press, 1962; Harry Benjamin and R.E.L. Masters, *Prostitution and Morality,* New York: The Julian Press, 1964; Norman St. John-Stevas, *Law and Morals,* London: Burns and Oastes, 1964.

[26] William McDonald, "Stop and Frisk: An Historical and Empirical Assessment," in Robert Rich (ed.), *Essays on the Theory and Practice of Criminal Justice,* Washington, DC: University Press of America, 1977, pp. 51-52, 81-83.

[27] *Ibid.,* pp. 81-82.

[28] Kay Ann Holmes, "Reflections by Gaslight: Prostitution in Another Age," *Issues in Criminology,* 7 (Winter, 1972).

[29] *Ibid.*

[30] *Ibid.*

[31]Charles Winick and Paul Kinsie, *The Lively Commerce,* Chicago: Quadrangle Books, 1971, p. 212; Marshall Clinard, *Sociology of Deviant Behavior,* New York: Holt, Rinehart and Winston, 1974, pp. 513-514.

[32]Clinard, *op. cit.,* p. 514; Freda Adler, *Sisters in Crime: the Rise of the New Female Criminal,* New York: McGraw-Hill, 1975, pp. 223, 55-83.

[33]*Report of the Committee on Homosexual Offenses and Prostitution,* London: Her Majesty's Stationery Office, Cmnd. 247, 1957; Gilbert Geis, *Not the Law's Business,* Washington, DC: US Government Printing Office, 1972, pp. 187-189.

[34]Robert Bell, *Social Deviance,* Homewood, Illinois: The Dorsey Press, 1971, p. 229; T.C. Esselstyn, "Prostitution in the United States," *The Annals,* (March, 1968), pp. 123-135.

[35]Edwin Schur and Hugo Bedau, *Victimless Crimes,* New Jersey: Prentice-Hall, 1974.

[36]Bell, *op. cit.,* p. 229.

[37]Adler, *op. cit.,* pp. 220-221.

[38]Charles Rosenbleet and Barbara Pariente, "The Prostitution of the Criminal Law," *The American Criminal Law Review,* 11 (1973), pp. 373-427.

[39]Henry Black, *Black's Law Dictionary,* St. Paul, Minnesota: West Publishing Company, 1968, p. 1386.

[40]*Ibid.,* pp. 1306, 1373.

[41]District of Columbia Code, *District of Columbia Code Annotated,* Washington, DC: US Government Printing Office, 1973, 22-2701, 1177.

[42]Virginia State Criminal Code, *Virginia State Criminal Code,* 1975, 18.2-346.

[43]District Code, *op. cit.,* 1178.

[44]*Ibid.,* 1179.

[45]*Ibid.,* 1180.

[46]*Ibid.,* 1180-1181.

[47]*Ibid.,* 1181.

[48]*Ibid.,* 1182.

[49]*Ibid.,* 1178.

[50]*Ibid.,* 1179.

[51]*Ibid.,* 1180.

[52]*Ibid.*, 1180.

[53]*The Consolidated Laws of New York Annotated,* 1968, sections 230.08, 230.05, 230.10.

[54]*Code of Georgia Annotated,* X, 522-523; *Hawaii Revised Statutes,* VII, 886; *West's Wisconsin Statutes Annotated,* XLI, 356-357.

[55]*United States Code,* 18, 2421-2423.

[56]Interviews with Judge Norman of D.C. Superior Court, Assistant United States Attorney (D.C.) Rhea, Detective Grace, and Sergeant Ware of Vice Squad (Metropolitan Police Department, D.C.), Lt. Casey of Prostitution Detail (MPD, D.C.), Detective Robertson, Youth Division Prostitution and Perversion Squad (MPD, D.C.), 1977.

[57]International Association of Chiefs of Police, Research Division, *Prostitution II-Enforcement of Prostitution Laws,* Gaithersburg, Maryland: IACP, 1976: Denny Pace, *Handbook of Vice Control,* New Jersey: Prentice-Hall, 1971, pp. 65-72; Wayne LaFave, *Arrest: The Decision to Take a Suspect into Custody,* Boston: Little, Brown and Company, 1956, pp. 457-463; Paul Chevigny, Police Power: *Police Abuses in New York City,* New York: Random House, 1969; Jerome Skolnick, *Justice Without Trial: Law Enforcement in Democratic Society,* New York: John Wiley, 1966, pp. 103-112; The President's Commission on Law Enforcement and Administration of Justice, *Task Force Report: The Police,* Washington, DC: US Government Printing Office, 1967, p. 187.

[58]Hazel Kerper, *Introduction to the Criminal Justice System,* St. Paul, Minnesota: West Publishing Company, 1972, p. 82; Clinard, *op. cit.,* p. 522.

[59]Interviews with officers Ware, Casey, Robertson, and White of Metropolitan Police Department (D.C.), 1977.

[60]*Ibid.*

[61]*Ibid.*

[62]*Ibid.*

[63]Winick and Kinsie, *op. cit.*

[64]Uniform Crime Reports of FBI, *Crime in the United States-1976* Washington, DC: US Government Printing Office, 1977, p. 184.

[65]Interviews, *op. cit.*

[66]Clinard, *op. cit.,* p. 512; Bell, *op. cit.,* pp. 232-233, Erich Goode, *Deviant Behavior: An Interactionist Approach,* New Jersey: Prentice-Hall, 1978, pp. 333-340.

[67]Clinard, *op. cit.,* pp. 512-513; Bell, *op. cit.,* pp. 233-234; Goode, *op. cit.,* pp. 333-340.

[68]Interviews with anonymous members of the Alexandria, Virginia Police Department Vice Squad, 1977-1978; Goode, *op. cit.,* pp. 340-342.

[69]*Ibid.;* Albert Velarde and Mark Warlick, "Massage Parlors: the Sensuality Business," *Society,* 11 (1973), pp. 63-74.

[70]Goode, *op. cit.,* pp. 324-325.

[71]Interview with Captain George Henry, Watch Commander, Youth Division, MPD (D.C.), 1977; Clinard, *op. cit.,* p. 513; Diana Gray, "Turning Out: A Study of Teenage Prostitution," *Urban Life and Culture,* 1 (1973), pp. 401-425.

[72]Bell, *op. cit.,* p. 321; Goode, *op. cit.,* pp. 331-333.

[73]Goode, *op. cit.,* pp. 350-354; Bell, *op. cit.,* pp. 242-243; Robert Adelman and Susan Hall, *Gentlemen of Leisure,* New York: New American Library, 1972; Christina Milner and Richard Milner, *Black Players: The Secret World of Black Pimps,* Boston: Little, Brown, 1973.

[74]Morton Hunt, *The Natural History of Love,* New York: Alfred A. Knopf, 1959; G.R. Taylor, *Sex in History,* New York: The Vanguard Press, 1954; Isabel Drummand, *The Sex Paradox,* New York: G.P. Putnam's Sons, 1953; Morris Ploscowe, *Sex and the Law,* New Jersey: Prentice-Hall, 1951; John Gagnon and William Simon, *Sexual Deviance,* New York: Harper and Row, 1967.

[75]Norval Morris and Gordon Hawkins, *The Honest Politician's Guide to Crime Control,* Chicago: University of Chicago Press, 1969, p. 15.

[76]*Connecticut General Statutes, Annotated,* 1958, 28, 266-267.

[77]Sue Reid, *Crime and Criminology,* Hinsdale, Illinois: The Dryden Press, 1976, p. 35.

[78]1 James I, c. 11.

[79]4 and 5 William and Mary, c. 8.

[80]Reid, *op. cit.,* pp. 35-37.

[81]Robert Bell, *Social Deviance,* Homewood, Illinois: The Dorsey Press, 1971, p. 45.

[82]Henry Black, *Black's Law Dictionary,* St. Paul, Minnesota: West Publishing Company, 1968, p. 1427.

[83]*Ibid.,* p. 1563.

[84]*Ibid.,* p. 1563.

[85]*Ibid.,* p. 1563.

[86]*Ibid.,* pp. 743, 1563.

[87]*Ibid.,* p. 456.

[88]*Ibid.,* p. 1523.

[89] *Ibid.*, p. 326.

[90] *Ibid.*, p. 781.

[91] *Ibid.*, pp. 71-72.

[92] *Ibid.*, p. 206.

[93] Marshall Clinard, *Sociology of Deviant Behavior*, New York: Holt, Rinehart, and Winston, 1974, p. 523.

[94] *District of Columbia Code*, Annotated, Washington, DC: US Government Printing Office, 1973, 2, 22-3503, 1571.

[95] Black, *op. cit.*, p. 1052.

[96] *Ibid.*, p. 909; Clinard, *op. cit.*, p. 499.

[97] Clinard, *op. cit.*, p. 499.

[98] *Dorland's Illustrated Medical Dictionary*, Philadelphia: W.B. Saunders Company, 1957, p. 1502.

[99] Black, *op. cit.*, p. 1501; Dorland, *op. cit.*, p. 1202.

[100] Black, *op. cit.*, p. 1126; Dorland, *op. cit.*, p. 798.

[101] Dorland, *op. cit.*, p. 500.

[102] *Ibid.*, p. 1455.

[103] District of Columbia Code, *op. cit.*, 22-2801, 1499.

[104] *Ibid.*, 22-3502, 1570.

[105] *Ibid.*, 22-3001, 1524.

[106] *Ibid.*, 22-1002, 1376.

[107] *Ibid.*, 22-1112, 1381.

[108] *Ibid.*, 22-3501, 1567.

[109] *Ibid.*, 22-301, 1345.

[110] *Ibid.*, 22-601, 1368.

[111] Ploscowe, *op. cit.*; Ploscowe, "Sex Offenses: The American Legal Context," *Law and Contemporary Problems*, 25 (1960), pp. 217-225.

[112] Herbert Bloch and Gilbert Geis, *Man, Crime, and Society*, New York: Random House, 1970, pp. 255-269.

[113] Uniform Crime Reports of the FBI, *Crime in the United States—1976*, Washington, DC: US Government Printing Office, 1977, p. 184.

[114]*Ibid.*, p. 217.

[115]Herbert Packer, *The Limits of the Criminal Sanction,* Stanford, California: Stanford University Press, 1968, p. 304.

[116]P. Gebhard, J. Gagnon, W. Pomeroy, and C. Christenson, *Sex Offenders: An Analysis of Types,* New York: Harper and Row, 1965; "Sex Offenses," in *Law and Contemporary Problems,* 25 (1960), pp. 215-375; Bell, *op. cit.,* pp. 39-62; Clinard, *op. cit.,* p. 503; Ploscowe, *op. cit.;* Clellan Ford and Frank Beach, *Patterns of Sexual Behavior,* New York: Harper Colophon, 1972; Gagnon and Simon, *Sexual Deviance, op. cit.;* Gagnon and Simon (eds.), *The Sexual Scene,* Chicago: Aldine Publishing Company, 1970; Edward Sagarin and Donal MacNamera (eds.), *Problems of Sex Behavior,* New York: Thomas Y. Crowell Company, 1968.

[117]John Gagnon and William Simon, *Sexual Conduct: The Social Sources of Human Sexuality,* Chicago: Aldine-Atherton, 1973; Morton Hunt, *Sexual Behavior in the 1970's,* New York: Dell, 1975; Robert Sorensen, *Adolescent Sexuality in Contemporary America,* New York: World Publishing Company, 1973; Leslie Westoff, *The Second Time Around: Remarriage in America,* New York: Viking Press, 1977.

[118]Ira Reiss, "Premarital Sex as Deviant Behavior: An Application of Current Approaches to Deviance," *American Sociological Review,* 35 (1970), pp. 78-88.

[119]Hunt, *op. cit.*

[120]John Kanter and Melvin Zelnick, "Sexual Experiences of Young Unmarried Women in the United States," *Family Planning Perspectives,* 4 (1972), pp. 9-18; Charles Westoff and Norman Ryder, *The Contraceptive Revolution,* Princeton, New Jersey: Princeton University Press, 1976; Erich Goode, *Deviant Behavior: An Interactionist Approach,* New Jersey: Prentice-Hall, 1978, pp. 317-321; Robert Bell, *Premarital Sex in a Changing Society,* New Jersey: Prentice-Hall, 1966.

[121]Bell, *Premarital Sex in a Changing Society, op. cit.;* Bell, *Social Deviance, op. cit.,* pp. 50-62; Ira Reiss, *Premarital Sexual Standards in America,* New York: Free Press, 1960; Reiss, *The Social Context of Premarital Sexual Permissiveness,* New York: Holt, Rinehart, and Winston, 1967; Clinard, *op. cit.,* p. 537.

[122]Block and Geis, *op. cit.;* Gebhard et al., *op. cit.; Law and Contemporary Problems, op. cit.;* Gagnon and Simon, *Sexual Deviance, op. cit.;* Ploscowe, *op. cit.*

[123]John Macdonald, *Rape: Offenders and Their Victims,* Springfield, Illinois: Charles C. Thomas, 1971; Gebhard et al., *op. cit.;* Clinard, *op. cit.,* pp. 302-304.

[124]R. W. Bowling, "The Sex Offender and the Law," *Federal Probation,* 14 (1950), pp. 11-16; H.W. Dunham, *Crucial Issues in the Treatment and Control of Sexual Deviation in the Community,* East Lansing, Michigan: Michigan Department of Mental Health, 1951; Albert Ellis and Ralph Brancale, *The Psychology of Sex Offenders,* Springfield, Illinois: Charles C. Thomas, 1956;

Graham Hughes, "Consent in Sexual Offenses," *Modern Law Review*, 25 (1962), pp. 672-686; Benjamin Karpman, *The Sexual Offender and his Offenses*, New York: Julian, 1954; Larry Myers, "Reasonable Mistake of Age: A Needed Defense to Statutory Rape," *Michigan Law Review*, 64 (1965), pp. 105-135; Robert Sherwin, *Sex and Statutory Law*, New York: Oceana, 1949; Sherwin, "The Law and Sexual Relationships," *Journal of Social Issues*, 22 (1966), pp. 109-122.

[125]Edwin Sutherland and Donald Cressey, *Criminology*, Philadelphia: J.B. Lippincott, 1970, p. 161; Kark Schuessler (ed.), *Edwin H. Sutherland: On Analyzing Crime*, Chicago: University of Chicago Press, 1973, pp. 185-199.

[126]Bloch and Geis, *op. cit.*, pp. 261-262; Alfred Kinsey, C.W. Pomeroy, and Clyde Martin, *Sexual Behavior in the Human Male*, Philadelphia: W.B. Saunders, 1948, p. 370.

[127]Bloch and Geis, *op. cit.*, pp. 257-259.

[128]*Ibid.*

[129]*Lewd: The Inquisition of Seth and Carolyn*, Boston: Beacon Press, 1972; Fred Ilfeld and Roger Lauer, *Social Nudism in America*, New Haven, Connecticut: College and University Press, 1966.

[130]Libby Jones, *Striptease*, New York: Simon and Schuster, 1967; James Skipper and Charles McCaghy, "Stripteasers: the Anatomy and Career Contingencies of a Deviant Occupation," *Social Problems*, 17 (1970), pp. 391-405.

[131]Ford and Beach, *op. cit.*; Ploscowe, *op. cit.*; Bloch and Geis, *op. cit.*, pp. 259-261; Nathan Rickles, *Exhibitionism*, Philadelphia, J.B. Lippincott, 1950; Robert Smith et al., "Exhibitionism," *North Carolina Medical Journal*, 22 (1961), pp. 261-267.

[132]Bell, *op. cit.*, pp. 64-74; Ford and Beach, *op. cit.*, pp. 114-115; Reid, *op. cit.*, pp. 36-37; Gagnon and Simon, *op. cit.*; Sagarin and MacNamera, *op. cit.*

[133]Bell, *op. cit.*

[134]*Ibid.*, pp. 74-83; Clinard, *op. cit.*, pp. 523-529; Mary Walshok, "The Emergence of Middle-Class Deviant Subcultures: the Case of Swingers," *Social Problems*, 18 (1971), pp. 488-495; Charles and Rebecca Palson, "Swinging in Wedlock," *Society*, 9 (1972), pp. 28-37; Gilbert Bartell, *Group Sex*, New York: Peter H. Wyden Inc., 1971; Bartell, "Group Sex among the Mid-Americans," *Journal of Sex Research*, 6 (1970), pp. 113-130; James and Lynn Smith, "Co-Marital Sex and the Sexual Freedom Movement," *Journal of Sex Research*, 6 (1970), pp. 131-142; Duane Denfield and Michael Gordon, "The Sociology of Mate Swapping: On the Family that Swings Together Clings Together," *Journal of Sex Research*, 6 (1970), pp. 85-100.

[135]David Bailey, *Homosexuality and the Western Christian Tradition*, New York: David McKay Company, 1955; Roger Mitchell, *The Homosexual and the Law*, New York: Arco Publishing, 1969; A.L. Rowse, *Homosexuals in History*, New York: Macmillan Company, 1977; Robert Katz, "Notes on Religious History, Attitudes, and Laws Pertaining to Homosexuality," *National Institute of Mental Task Force on Homosexuality*, Rockville, Maryland: NIMH, 1972, p. 58.

[136]H.M. Hyde, *The Love that Dare not Speak its Name: A Candid History of Homosexuality in Britain*, Boston: Little, Brown, 1970.

[137]Robert Bell, *Social Deviance*, Homewood, Illinois: The Dorsey Press, 1971, pp. 288-289; Donald Cory, *The Lesbian in America*, New York: The Citadel Press, 1964; Marshall Clinard, *Sociology of Deviant Behavior*, New York: Holt, Rinehart and Winston, 1974, pp. 563-565; William Simon and John Gagnon, "The Lesbians: A Preliminary Overview," in Gagnon and Simon (eds.), *Sexual Deviance*, New York: Harper and Row, 1967, pp. 251-276; *Report of the Committee on Homosexual Offenses and Prostitution* (Wolfenden Report), London: Her Majesty's Stationery Office, Cmnd. 247, 1957.

[138]Alfred Kinsey et al., *Sexual Behavior in the Human Female*, Philadelphia: W.B. Saunders, 1953, p. 484.

[139]"The Constitutionality of Laws Forbidding Private Homosexual Conduct," *Michigan Law Review*, 72 (1974), p. 1613; Morris Ploscowe, *Sex and the Law*, New York: Ace Books, 1962; Mitchell, *op. cit.;* John Livingood (ed.), *National Institute of Mental Health Task Force on Homosexuality: Final Report and Background Papers*, Rockville, Maryland: National Institute of Mental Health, 1972; John Gallo et al., "The Consenting Adult Homosexual and the Law," *UCLA Law Review*, 13 (1966), pp. 643-832; Gilbert Cantor, "The Need for Homosexual Law Reform," in Ralph Weltge (ed.), *The Same Sex: An Appraisal of Homosexuality*, Philadelphia: Pilgram Books, 1969, pp. 83-88.

[140]Clinard, *op. cit.*, p. 546: Katz, *op. cit.*

[141]Wolfenden Report, *op. cit.*, pp. 25-26; Michael Buckley, *Morality and the Homosexual*, Westminister, Maryland: Newman Press, 1960; Bailey, *op. cit.;* Bailey (ed.), *Sexual Offenders and Social Punishment*, London; Church of England Moral Welfare Council, 1956, pp. 1-28; A.J. Ayer, "Homosexuals and the Law," *New Statesman*, 1960, p. 941; J.F. Wolfenden, "Ahead of Public Opinion," *New Statesman*, 1960, p. 941; J.E.H. Williams, "Sex Offenses: The British Experience," *Law and Contemporary Problems*, 25 (1960), pp. 334-360; Edwin Shur, "The Wolfenden Report," *American Sociological Review*, 28 (1963), p. 1055; Shur, *Crimes Without Victims: Deviant Behavior and Public Policy*, New Jersey: Prentice-Hall, 1965, pp. 107-114; Gilbert Geis, *Not the Law's Business*, Washington, DC: NIMH, US Government Printing Office, 1972; Bloch and Geis, *op. cit.*, p. 269; Robert Pursley, *Introduction to Criminal Justice*, Encino, California: Glencoe Press, 1977, pp. 115-116.

[142]*Honselman v. Illinois*, 48 N.E. 304, 305 (1897).

[143]American Law Institute, *Modal Penal Code*, proposed official draft, Philadelphia: American Law Institute, 1962; *Illinois Criminal Code*, 1961, 38, section 11-2.

[144]Pursley, *op. cit.*, 115; *Michigan Law Review*, *op. cit.;* Gallo, *op. cit.*

[145]Colin Williams and Martin Weinberg, *Homosexuals and the Military*, New York: Harper and Row, 1971; D.J. West, *Homosexuality*, Chicago: Aldine Publishing Company, 1967; Schur, *Crimes Without Victims, op. cit.*, pp. 83-84; Erich Goode, *Deviant Behavior: An Interactionist Approach*, New Jersey: Prentice-Hall, 1978, p. 360; *Washington Post*, March, 1975.

146Livingwood, *op. cit.;* Pursley, *op. cit.,* p. 116.

147*District of Columbia Human Rights Act,* title 34, 10, 1973.

148Goode, *op. cit.,* p. 360.

149Henry Black, *Black's Law Dictionary,* St. Paul, Minnesota: West Publishing Company, 1968, p. 1288.

150*Ibid.,* p. 1563.

151*Ibid.,* p. 243.

152*Ibid.,* p. 743.

153*Ibid.,* p. 456.

154Thomas Hoult, *Dictionary of Modern Sociology,* Totowa, New Jersey: Littlefield, Adams and Company, 1969, pp. 152, 185; The Dushkin Publishing Group, *Encyclopedia of Sociology,* Guilford, Connecticut: Dushkin Publishing Group, 1974, p. 128; Schur, *Crimes Without Victims, op. cit.,* pp. 69-70; Bell, *op. cit.,* p. 262.

155Goode, *op. cit.,* pp. 382-387.

156The Dushkin Publishing Group, *op. cit.,* p. 297.

157Clinard, *op. cit.,* pp. 546-547; Schur, *Crimes Without Victims, op. cit.,* pp. 77-79; Bell, *op. cit.,* pp. 250-251, 288-290; Ploscowe, *op. cit.,* p. 188.

158*District of Columbia Code,* Annotated, Washington, DC: US Government Printing Office, 1973, 2, 22-3502, 1570.

159*Ibid.,* 22-3501, 1567.

160Schur, *Crimes Without Victims, op. cit.,* pp. 74-82; Laud Humphreys, *Tearoom Trade: Impersonal Sex in Public Places,* Chicago: Aldine Publishing Company, 1975, pp. 84-88; Bloch and Geis, *op. cit.,* pp. 267-268; Benjamin Karpman, *The Sexual Offender and His Offenses,* New York: Julian, 1954; Bell, *op. cit.,* pp. 252-253.

161Paul Gebhard et al., *Sex Offenders,* New York: Harper and Row, 1965, pp. 324-325; Humphreys, *op. cit.*

162Gallo et al., *op. cit.,* p. 690.

163*Ibid.,* 707-708.

164*Ibid.,* pp. 693, 740.

165Clinard, *op. cit.,* p. 541; Bell, *op. cit.,* pp. 260, 299-305; Schur, *Crimes Without Victims, op. cit.,* pp. 91-94; William Helmer, "New York's Middle-Class Homosexuals," *Harpers,* (1963), p. 87; Marcel Saghir and Eli Robins, *Male and Female Homosexuality,* Baltimore: Williams and Wilkins,

1973; Michael Schofield, *Sociological Aspects of Homosexuality: A Comparative Study of Three Types of Homosexuals,* Boston: Little, Brown and Company, 1965; D.J. West, *Homosexuality,* Chicago: Aldine Publishing Company, 1967; Bryan Magee, *One in Twenty: A Study of Homosexuality in Men and Women,* New York: Stein and Day, 1966; Karla Jay and Alan Young (eds.), *After You're Out: Personal Experience of Gay Men and Lesbian Women,* New York: Links Books, 1975.

[166]Clinard, *op. cit.,* p. 559; Bell, *op. cit.,* pp. 260-278; Schofield, *op. cit.;* Martin Hoffman, *The Gay World: Male Homosexuality and the Social Creation of Evil,* New York: Basic Books, 1968; Donald Cory and John LeRoy, *The Homosexual and His Society: A View From Within,* New York: The Citadel Press, 1963; Barry Dank, "The Homosexuals," in Don and Patricia Spiegel (eds.), *The Outsiders,* New York: Rinehart Press, 1973; Donald Cory, *The Homosexual in America,* New York: Greenberg Publisher, 1951; Gordon Westwood, *Society and the Homosexual,* New York: E.P. Dutton, 1953; Wainwright Churchill, *Homosexual Behavior Among Males,* New Jersey: Prentice-Hall, 1971; Martin Hoffman, *The Gay World,* New York: Basic Books, 1968; Arno Karlen, *Sexuality and Homosexuality,* New York: Norton, 1971; C.A. Tripp, *The Homosexual Matrix,* New York: New American Library, 1976; Martin Weinberg and Colin Williams, *Male Homosexuals,* New York: Oxford University Press, 1974; Evelyn Hooker, "The Homosexual Community," in John Gagnon and William Simon (eds.), *Sexual Deviance,* New York: Harper and Row, 1967; Edwin Schur, *Crimes Without Victims, op. cit.,* pp. 85-86, 88-89; Maurice Leznoff and William Westley, "The Homosexual Community," *Social Problems,* 3 (1956), pp. 257-263; James McCaffrey (ed.), *The Homosexual Dialectic,* New Jersey: Prentice-Hall, 1972.

[167]Nancy Achilles, "The Development of the Homosexual Bar as an Institution," in Gagnon and Simon, *op. cit.;* Schur, *Crimes Without Victims, op. cit.,* pp. 86-88.

[168]Edward Sagarin, *Odd Man In: Societies of Deviants in America,* Chicago: Quadrangle Books, 1969.

[169]Clinard, *op. cit.,* pp. 567-568; Bell, *op. cit.,* pp. 294-300; Goode, *op. cit.,* pp. 387-392; Jack Hedblom, "The Female Homosexual: Social and Attitudinal Dimensions," in McCaffrey, *op. cit.;* Magee, *op. cit.;* William Simon and John Gagnon, "The Lesbians: A Preliminary Overview," in Gagnon and Simon, *op. cit.;* Frank Caprio, *Female Homosexuality,* New York: Grove Press, 1962; Philip Blumstein and Pepper Schwartz, "Lesbianism and Bisexuality," in Erich Goode and Richard Troiden (eds.), *Sexual Deviance and Sexual Deviants,* New York: William Morrow, 1974; Saghir and Robins, *op. cit.;* Siegrid Schafer, "Sexual and Problems of Lesbians," *The Journal of Sex Research,* 12 (1976), pp. 50-69; Charlotte Wolff, *Love Between Women,* New York: Harper Colophon, 1973; Donald Cory, *The Lesbian in America,* New York: The Citadel Press, 1964.

[170]Blumstein and Schwartz, *op. cit.;* Martin Duberman, "The Bisexual Debate," *New Times,* (June, 1974), pp. 34-41; Louise Knox, "The Bisexual Phenomenon," *Viva* (July, 1974), pp. 42-45, 88, 94; Robert Stoller, "The Bedrock of Masculinity and Feminity: Bisexuality," *Annals of General Psychiatry,* 26 (1972), pp. 207-212.

[171]Schur, *Crimes Without Victims, op. cit.,* pp. 89-91; Cory and LeRoy,

op. cit., p. 96; Albert Reiss, "The Social Integration of Queers and Peers," *Social Problems,* 9 (1961), pp. 102-120; H.L. Ross, "The Hustler in Chicago," *Journal of Student Research,* 1 (1959), pp. 13-14; Simon Raven, "Boys Will Be Boys: The Male Prostitute in London," in Hendrik Ruitenbeek (ed.), *The Problem of Homosexuality in Modern Society,* New York: E.P. Dutton, 1963.

[172]Charles McCaghy and James Skipper, "Lesbian Behavior as an Adaptation to the Occupation of Stripping," *Social Problems* (1969), pp. 262-270; Gebhard ct al., *op. cit.,* p. 30; Bell, *op. cit.,* p. 244.

[173]R.S. Morton, *Venereal Diseases,* Baltimore: Penguin Books, 1966, p. 20; A. Fessler, "Advertiscments in the Treatment of Venereal Disease and the Social History of Venereal Disease," *British Journal of Venereal Diseases,* 25 (1949), p. 84; S.M. Laird, *Venereal Disease in Britain,* Baltimore: Penguin Books, 1943; Theodore Rosbury, *Microbes and Morals: The Strange Story of Venereal Disease,* New York: Viking Press, 1971.

[174]Morton, *op. cit.,* p. 20.

[175]*Ibid.,* p. 24.

[176]*Ibid.*

[177]Fessler, *op. cit.,* p. 84; Morton, *op. cit.,* p. 30.

[178]Morton, *op. cit.,* p. 30.

[179]*Ibid.*

[180]*Ibid.,* p. 31.

[181]*Ibid.,* p. 140.

[182]*Ibid.,* p. 32.

[183]*Ibid.,* p. 136.

[184]*Ibid.,* p. 141.

[185]*Ibid.,* p. 163.

[186]Robert Bell, *Social Deviance,* Homewood, Illinois: Dorsey Press, 1976, p. 93.

[187]Ralph Thomlinson, *Population Dynamics,* New York: Random House, 1976, p. 298.

[188]*Ibid.,* pp. 298-299.

[189]Bell, *op. cit.,* pp. 94, 115; Norman St. John-Stevas, "History and Legal Status of Birth Control," in Edwin Schur (ed.), *The Family and the Sexual Revolution,* Bloomington, Indiana: Indiana University Press, 1964, pp. 337-338.

[190]Bell, *op. cit.,* p. 261.

[191]*Carey v. Population Services International,* 1977.

[192]Henry Black, *Black's Law Dictionary,* St. Paul, Minnesota: West Publishing Company, 1968, p. 1726.

[193]Morton, *op. cit.,* pp. 15-18.

[194]*District of Columbia Code,* Annotated, Washington, D.C.: U.S. Government Printing Office, 1973, 1, 6-119, 610.

[195]*Ibid.,* 6-119a, 610.

[196]*Ibid.,* 6-119b, 610-611.

[197]*Ibid.,* 6-119d, 612.

[198]*Ibid.,* 6-119e, 612.

[199]*Ibid.,* 6-119g, 612.

[200]*Ibid.,* 6-119h, 613.

[201]*Ibid.,* 6-119j, 613-614.

[202]*Code of Virginia,* 5A, title 32-94, Charlottesville, Virginia: The Michie Company, 1950.

[203]*United States Code,* title 42, Washington, DC: US Government Printing Office, 1971, 247.

[204]Morton, *op. cit.,* pp. 112-123; Bell, *op. cit.,* pp. 260-263; William Brown et al., *Syphilis and Other Venereal Diseases,* Cambridge, Massachusetts: Harvard University Press, 1970; Steward Brooks, *The V.D. Story,* New York: A.S. Barnes Company, 1971; Margaret Hyde, *V.D.: The Silent Epidemic,* New York: McGraw-Hill, 1973; Robert Helmer, *The Venus Dilemma,* Los Angeles: Nash Publishing Company, 1974; Robert Richards, *Venereal Diseases and Their Avoidance,* New York: Holt, Rinehart and Winston, 1974; Celia Deschin, "Teenagers and Venereal Disease: A Sociological Study of 600 Teenagers in New York City's Social Hygiene Clinics," *American Journal of Nursing,* 1963; Richard Stiller, *The Love Bugs,* New York: Thomas Nelson, 1974; Eric Johnson, *V.D.,* Philadelphia: J.B. Lippincott, 1973; Louis Lasagna, *The V.D. Epidemic,* Philadelphia: Temple University Press, 1975; A.J. King and C.S. Nichol, *Venereal Diseases,* London: Cassell, 1964; M. Schofield, *The Sexual Behavior of Young People,* London: Longmans, 1965.

[205]Morton, *op. cit.,* p. 114.

[206]Deschin, *op. cit.*

[207]Brown, *op. cit.,* p. 78; Morton, *op. cit.,* p. 115.

[208]Deschin, *op. cit.;* Morton, *op. cit.,* p. 116; Schofield, *op. cit.*

[209]Bell, *op. cit.,* p. 263.

[210]*Ibid.*, pp. 259-260; Lawrence Galton, "VD: Out of Control?," *Medical Aspects of Human Sexuality,* (January, 1972), pp. 18-22.

[211]Stiller, *op. cit.,* p. 56; Morton, *op. cit.,* pp. 119-123.

[212]Lasagna, *op. cit.,* pp. 8-9; Morton, *op. cit.,* pp. 128-130; E.R. Trice, "Venereal Disease and Homosexuality," *Medical Aspects of Human Sexuality,* (January, 1969), pp. 70-71.

[213]Johnson, *op. cit.,* p. 79; Stiller, *op. cit.;* Brown, *op. cit.;* Brooks, *op. cit.;* Hyde, *op. cit.;* Helmer, *op. cit.;* Richards, *op. cit.*

[214]Deschin, *op. cit.;* Morton, *op. cit.,* pp. 115-119; Schofield, *op. cit.*

[215]Interviews with Captain Clayton Clark and officer Selma Partner, Sex Offender Branch, Metropolitan Police Department of Washington, D.C., 1977, 1978.

Chapter 6

Domestic Deviance

Family Conflicts

Legal History

The legal status of members of the family stems from Roman Law as interpreted by ecclesiastical law after the time of the Code of Justinian.[1] The Code of Aethelberht (600 A.D.) in England states that problems of a domestic nature were to be treated as torts and handled as both family and church matters.[2] Thus the English Common Law that deals with family conflicts (i.e., domestic relations) is based primarily on church law and later on equity or chancery law.[3]

According to the Common Law, all acts of deviance in connection with the institution of the family were torts (i.e., husband/wife, parent/child, affinal and consanguinal relations) with the exceptions of adultery and incest. These crimes were handled by ecclesiastical law in England.[4] Bigamy was not a crime until the time of King James I when it was made a felony.[5] Such family problems as child and wife abuse were dealt with by family members, a fact that has legal status going back to Roman Law. The Common Law allowed the husband to deal with wife and children as he wished which included deprivation of liberty and corporal punishment short of death.[6]

Adultery, incest, and bigamy were punished in the ecclesiastical courts in the early period of the Common Law in England. Adultery and incest were considered criminal acts and both parties were considered liable except in cases of incest where the child was under age seven. The reasons for the severity of punishment for adultery and incest were the probable creation of illegitimate offspring that threatened family stability, violated the sanctity of the marriage contract, and created challenges to the legitimate heirs to the family estate. Further at Common Law illegitimate children could not inherit from either the mother or father although there were challenges made on behalf of bastards of the upper classes. Finally illegitimate children could not obtain support from their fathers at Common Law.[7]

In Colonial New England of the seventeenth century, statutes were passed making adultery punishable by death and fornication punishable by public whipping. Usually the offender was fined, sometimes whipped, rarely branded, and never hanged.[8] The Puritans tried to resolve their problems concerning illegitimacy by passing statutes making the father of the child responsible for its upbringing.[9]

At Common Law, domestic relations problems were under the jurisdiction of the ecclesiastical courts who had jurisdiction over all problems of marriage and also dealt with divorce. It was not until the nineteenth century that the traditional authoritarian relationship of the husband legally dominating wife and children was challenged in England by the chancery or equity court. This institution was absent or incorporated into the civil court structure in the early United States.[10] Until 1857 England had no satisfactory solution for individuals who wished to divorce and this was a continual source of problems from adultery to desertion.[11] The divorce laws were not any better in colonial America. In 1682 the colony of Pennsylvania allowed divorce if one spouse was convicted of adultery. This statute was later expanded to allow divorce on the grounds of incest, bigamy, and homosexuality. Divorces were granted by the colonial governor and later the colonial legislatures of Pennsylvania, New Jersey, and New Hampshire.[12]

After independence from Great Britain, the United States government allowed each state to decide the divorce issue for itself. Legislative divorce was only allowed in the South and very rarely granted so the problems of adultery, bigamy, seduction, fornication and prostitution continued. All the states in the North (i.e., Pennsylvania, Massachusetts, New York, New Jersey, all the other New England states and Tennessee) had general divorce laws by 1800.[13] For example New York only allowed divorce for adultery; this law remained basically unchanged from 1787 until the early 1970's. Vermont in 1798 allowed divorce for adultery, desertion, and other grounds while Rhode Island allowed divorce for any type of sexual deviance (i.e., homosexual as well as heterosexual).[14]

Desertion of the family by a husband was dealt with indirectly by the Common Law as the wife and children were to be cared for by other members of the immediate family. According to the Common Law, a wife did not have legal standing outside of the marital context (i.e., her legal existence disappeared in favor of her husband).[15] The states had to makc allowances for wives who were deserted so that they could sell the family land and other possessions in order to pay bills and live without going on welfare. This first happened in Massachusetts in 1787 and by 1850 several states allowed married women some legal rights.[16] Thus the gradual move toward legal equality for married women was not motivated by ideological principles but by the pragmatic concern about keeping deserted women and children off of welfare.

The poor house was essentially the same in eighteenth and nineteenth century America as it had been in England since 1601. Parents who neglected or deserted their children could not be held liable for taking care of them so the states allowed dependent youths to be apprenticed or be trained as servants (i.e., the former for boys and the latter for girls). Abuses by masters of their wards were notorious but little in the way of legislation took place until well into the nineteenth century. It was not until 1899 that the Illinois legislature passed the first Juvenile Court Act in America that brought together under one jurisdiction all cases of child neglect, dependency, and delinquency.[17]

It was not until 1920 that the Nineteenth Amendment to the U. S. Constitution allowed women the right to vote. This did not alter to a great degree their legal status in the family since husbands still dominated the marital context in terms of divorce settlements.[18] It was not until the Civil Rights Act of 1964 that sex discrimination was outlawed by Congress. This aided in pushing the states to modernize their divorce and dependency statutes but the pending Equal Rights Amendment to the Constitution has speeded up the concern by many states in the problems of spouse and child abuse.[19]

Legal Definitions

Black defines adultery as the voluntary sexual intercourse of a married individual with someone other than the offender's spouse. A distinction is sometimes made between one or both parties being married (i.e., single and double adultery respectively). Open and notorious adultery constitutes the flagrant and public living together as husband and wife of individuals one of whom is married.[20] Bigamy is the crime of deliberately marrying a second person while knowingly still married to another spouse. By statute the second marriage is not legal and any children of the void marriage are considered by law to be illegitimate.[21]

Black defines abuse of a child as ill treatment which may be injurious, improper, hurtful, or sexually offensive.[22] Another name for the maltreatment of juveniles by parents or guardians is the battered-child syndrome.[23] An abandoned child is one who is deserted by his or her parents or guardian and who is without proper care or the ability to pay for his or her proper care. A neglected child is one who is not receiving proper care, education, and upbringing from his or her parents or guardian according to the statutes for such care established by law in a given jurisdiction.[24]

Desertion is the actual abandonment or cessation of matrimonial cohabitation by either spouse and a refusal to fulfill the duties and obligations of the marital relationship, with an intent to abandon or give up entirely and not to return to or resume the marital relationship, occuring without legal justification either in the consent or the wrongful conduct of the other party. Constructive desertion arises when an existing cohabitation is ended by the misconduct of one spouse providing that the misconduct is itself a legal ground for divorce.[25]

Divorce is the legal separation of husband and wife effected for cause by the judgment of a court, either totally dissolving the marriage (i.e., *a vinculo matrimonii*) or suspending its effects so far as concerns the cohabitation of both spouses (i.e., *a mensa et thoro* or from bed and board).[26]

One who is illegitimate is usually a term applied to a child whose parents were not married legally.[27] Black defines a bastard as an illegitimate child or one born of an unlawful intercourse and before the legal marriage of his or her parents. The term also describes a child born after marriage but under circumstances which make it impossible that the husband of his mother can be his father.[28] There are two types of the latter situation (1) adulterine or adulterous bastards (i.e., children produced by an illegal sexual liaison between two people who, at the time when the child was born, were either of them or both married to some other individual) and (2) incestuous bastards (i.e., children produced by an illegal sexual liaison between two people who are relations within the guidelines prohibited by law).[29]

Incest is the crime of sexual intercourse or cohabitation between a man and a woman who are related to each other within the guidelines set up by the jurisdiction that prohibit marriage between the two by law.[30]

Statutes and Enforcement Policy

Whoever commits adultery shall on conviction be punished by a fine not exceeding five hundred dollars, or by imprisonment not exceeding one year, or both; and when the act is committed between a married woman and an unmarried man, both parties to such act shall be found guilty of adultery; and when such act is committed between a married man and an unmarried woman, the man shall only be guilty of adultery.[31] A person who has a living husband or wife and who marries another shall be guilty of bigamy, and on conviction shall be imprisoned for not less than two nor more than seven years. This statute shall not apply to any person whose spouse has been continually absent for five successive years next before such marriage without being known to such person to be living within that time, or whose marriage to said living spouse shall have been dissolved by a valid decree of a competent court, or shall have been pronounced void by a valid decree of a competent court on the ground of the nullity of the marriage contract.[32]

Cruelty to children is defined as any act of torture, beating, abuse, or otherwise willfully maltreating any child under the age of eighteen years; or any individual having the custody or possession of a child under the age of fourteen years who shall expose, or aid and abet in exposing such child in any highway, street, field, house, or other place, with the intent to abandon said child; or any person having in his custody or control a child under the age of fourteen years who shall in any way dispose of said child with a view to its being employed as an acrobat, or a gymnast, or a contortionist, or a circus rider, or a rope-walker, or in any exhibition of like dangerous character, or as a beggar, or merchant, or pauper, or street singer, or street musician; or any person who shall take, receive, hire, employ, use, exhibit, or have in custody any child of the age last named for any of the purposes enumerated shall be deemed guilty of a misdemeanor and upon conviction shall be fined not more than two hundred and fifty dollars or imprisoned for a term not exceeding two years, or both.[33]

Any person of sufficient financial ability who shall refuse or neglect to provide for any child under the age of fourteen years of which he or she shall be the parent or guardian, such food, clothing, and shelter as will prevent the suffering and secure the safety of such child shall be guilty of a misdemeanor and upon conviction shall be fined not more than one hundred dollars or imprisoned not more than three months, or both.[34]

The District of Columbia has no specific statute dealing with spouse abuse since a wife or husband can file charges of assault, battery, and/or false imprisonment. Divorce and desertion are not crimes but behavior that is causal in creating the grounds for divorce may be (i.e., adultery, bigamy, seduction, etc.) It is not a crime to be illegitimate but the behavior that produces the illegitimate issue may be criminal (i.e., adultery or incest). In most states it is a crime for a husband to fail to support his wife and/or children.[35]

If any individual related to another person within and not including the fourth degree of consanguinity computed according to the rules of the Roman or civil law shall marry or cohabit with or have sexual intercourse with such other so-related individual, knowing him or her to be within said degree of relationship, the individual so offending shall be found guilty of incest and upon conviction shall be punished by imprisonment for not more than twelve years.[36]

Most of the offenses against the family and children are quite difficult for the agencies of law enforcement to enforce. This is due to the fact that most members of the community do not care about these offenses since they are so common. Thus the public prosecutor does not press the police for more stringent enforcement of the statutes since he is usually reluctant to prosecute most types of cases (i.e., adultery, spouse abuse, child abuse, and even bigamy and incest). Desertion cases are rarely prosecuted since the husband who has failed to provide for wife and children would serve no useful purpose to the state if he goes to jail.[37]

Most of the cases of child abuse and sexual assaults on children in the District of Columbia originate through reports of Children's Hospital and other private and public hospitals that investigate suspicious cases. Cases of spouse abuse are usually reported by either the spouse who has been injured or a neighbor who calls the police. In some cases the Department of Social Services will refer a case to the police but more likely the social worker will refer an abused wife to the House of Ruth which provides counselling and treatment for battered wives.[38]

The Corporation Counsel's Office, Juvenile Section of the District of Columbia government reports that there were 548 cases of child abuse and sexual assault on children in 1976. According to the Metropolitan Police Department Sex Offense Branch and Youth Division, this figure is approximately five times lower than the actual incidence of offenses but they are not reported to the police. The police receive 24 percent of the reported cases while Children's and D. C. General report the majority of cases of abuse and neglect. Other reporting agencies are the schools, social workers, neighbors, relatives, the child himself, parent or guardian, and private social agencies.[39]

The Prevention of Child Abuse and Neglect Act of 1977 (D.C.) requires that every physician, psychologist, medical examiner, dentist, chiropractor, registered nurse, licensed practical nurse, person involved in care and treatment of patients, police officer, school administrator, classroom teacher, social worker, day care worker, and mental health professional, who knows or has reasonable cause to suspect that a child known to him or her in his or her professional or official capacity has been or is in immediate danger of being a mentally or physically abused or neglected child shall immediately report or have a report made to the Metropolitan Police Department or the Child Protective Service Division of the D.C. Department of Human Resources. Also any person, hospital, or institution participating in good faith in the making of a report shall have immunity from liability, civil or criminal. Neither the husband/wife privilege nor the physician/patient privilege shall be grounds for excluding evidence. Any person who willfully fails to make such a report shall be fined not more than one hundred dollars or imprisoned not more than thirty days, or both.[40]

One percent of those arrested in 1976 were for alleged offenses against family and children. Ninety percent of these offenses were perpetrated by males and ten percent by females.[41] Of all those held for prosecution for offenses against family and children (i.e., 5,766) fifty percent plead guilty to the original offense, two percent plead guilty to a lessor charge, twenty-four percent were acquitted or had the case dismissed, and twenty-four percent of the cases were referred to juvenile court.[42]

Description of Specific Deviance

There are no specific profiles on the typical individuals who commit adultery, bigamy, or get divorced. Adultery is quite common today and individuals from all social classes, races, ethnic groups, and religions are guilty of this victimless crime. Co-marital sex or swinging is popular with many middle and upper class couples.[43] Bigamy is quite rare in today's society since divorce laws allow a person who has been deserted to remarry after the requisite number of years of desertion have elapsed. Divorce is quite common in American society and cuts across all subcultural lines and age groups, although marriages are also broken by annulment, voluntary separation, as well as desertion. Divorce rates are increasing for those under thirty-five and those over fifty-five for a variety of reasons, both criminal and noncriminal. Post-marital sex is seen as more normal than deviant for the formerly married individual of either sex.[44]

Spouse abuse (i.e., usually wife abuse) is a serious and growing problem in the United States. Battered wives have usually kept the incidents of violence directed towards them by husbands to themselves for a variety of reasons (i.e., fear of further violence, shame and guilt, need for financial support for themselves and their children, and feelings that the police will be ineffective in resolving the problem). The Office of Abused Persons of the Montgomery County, Maryland Department of Social Services states that 263 women were served in 1977. Counselling services and shelter capabilities are offered to these women. The House of Ruth, Battered Women Program in the District of Columbia also offers similar services.[45]

Child abuse is becoming an increasingly serious problem in the United States. It is estimated that more than one million children are victims of physical and/or sexual abuse and neglect by parents, relatives, or guardians in the United States. Of these abused children approximately two thousand die yearly from the effects of abuse and/or neglect. These figures are quite conservative as most cases go unreported or are reported as accidents.[46]

Persons who are child abusers are parents, guardians, close relatives (i.e., uncles, aunts, siblings, cousins), and friends of the family. These people are typically mentally unstable, drug addicts, alcoholics, and/or sexual deviants.[47]

The types of injuries to children are physical, sexual, and psychological in nature. Burns, beatings, whippings, starving, sexual assaults, and various degrees of psychological torment are perpetrated upon children every day leading to permanent injury and death. A number of selected case studies will show the diversity of the problem of child abuse. A nine year old girl was subjected for a period of two weeks to hot baths with liquid clorox poured into the water which were administered to her by her stepmother. Between these baths the child was whipped on a regular basis. Two days before the child died the stepmother beat the child so severely that she was covered with open wounds. The stepmother proceeded to pour clorox and peroxide into these wounds and then scrubbed the wounds with an SOS pad. The child died from shock the next day.[48]

An eleven year old girl was subjected to sexual abuse by the boyfriend of the mother who allowed him to live with her and her children. The mother did not discover the fact that her daughter and boyfriend were having sexual relations until approximately a year's time elapsed. The boyfriend had taken the daughter on shopping trips where he bought her presents and then to motels where he had sexual intercourse with her. She was told not to tell her mother or the boyfriend would take all the gifts away from her. At the time the mother discovered the relationship, her daughter already had experienced her menstrual cycle and could have gotten pregnant. The mother was upset that her boyfriend was sleeping with her daughter, not that the child was regularly exposed to sex and could have gotten pregnant.[49]

A five year old girl living with her drug addict aunt and her alcoholic grandfather was brought to the hospital by a neighbor. The little girl complained of severe pains eminating from her urinogenital tract. Upon examination the girl was found to have a severe case of gonorrhea. Investigation of the case by the police revealed that the girl had been abandoned by her addict mother and given to her sister who said she would take care of her niece. The aunt in turn began to drink and take drugs and left the child in the care of the alcoholic grandfather. He and his drinking buddies would then drunk take liberties with the little girl who subsequently contracted venereal disease. The aunt and grandmother paid no attention to the medical problem of the child until the neighbor brought her to the hospital.[50]

A mother brought her eighteen month old son to the hospital where the child upon examination was shown to be suffering from what appeared to be a rare skin disease. Closer medical examination showed that the child had been severely burned upon his face with a hot iron and that his body was encrusted with layers of dirt (i.e., the mother had never bathed the child). The mother complained that her son was "mean" just like his father and that she punished him by neglecting him and then burning him when he cried too much. The mother was committed to the public mental hospital and her son placed in a foster home. The mother upon release began to drink heavily and subsequently wanted her child back. She was very upset when the case worker would not allow her to ever see her child again.[51]

Incest is another crime that is rarely discussed in public but occurs with a frequency that would surprise the average member of the community. Most often these crimes occur between father and daughter, brother and sister, and sometimes between mother and son. A parent or sibling will endulge in sexual activities with another member of the immediate family because of psychological problems, problems with one's spouse who denies one access to acceptable sexual relations, adolescent experimentation where there is no proper parental authority present to prevent such activity, and perverted interest in sexual intercourse with members of the nuclear family.[52] The Guyon Society of Alhambra, California is a group dedicated to the practice of incest among members of the nuclear family. This society believes that the parent is the logical person from whom the child should learn about sexuality. Members of this society take contraceptive precautions so that daughters, sisters, and mothers will not become pregnant.[53]

Abortion

Legal History

The English Common Law says nothing about abortions until after the time of fetal "quickening" (i.e., fetal movement which usually occurs between the sixteenth and twentieth week of pregnancy). The ecclesiastical court also ignored the abortion issue. Thus both legal and illegal abortions were fairly commonplace in Great Britain for centuries.[54] In eighteenth century America, the colonial assemblies followed the English example and allowed the pregnant woman to terminate her pregnancy before quickening.[55]

Parliament in 1803 passed Lord Ellenborough's Act which declared all abortions criminal except those performed to save the life of the prospective mother. The act specifically dealt with abortions performed by poisoning either before or after quickening. In practice very few persons were convicted of this crime which called for life imprisonment.[56] The United States followed the English example several years later when Connecticut passed an abortion statute in 1821 which was based on the English act of 1803. Most states still allowed abortions before quickening until the time of the Civil War although some states like New York passed abortion statutes that allowed abortion only when necessary to save the mother's life (1828).[57]

It was not until 1938 that the 1803 English Act was challenged in the famous case of *Rex v. Bourne*. This case set the tone for future abortions performed by a physician for the sake of saving the life of the prospective mother.[58] The Abortion Law Reform Association starting in 1952 lobbied

Parliament to introduce several abortion bills which all failed to be enacted. In the United States, The Planned Parenthood Federation in 1955 drafted a model abortion statute.[59] The American Law Institute drafted a model abortion statute in 1962.[60]

The Abortion Act of 1967 passed by Parliament was quite liberal. The Act provided for legal termination of pregnancy if two licensed physicians agreed that continuation of pregnancy would involve risk to the life of the prospective mother, or injury to her physical or mental health, or to any children in the family. Abortion was also permitted if there was great risk that the child would be physically or mentally abnormal if born. The Act had no provision dealing with rape.[61]

Colorado and California both reformed their abortion statutes in 1967 which made them quite similar to the British Act of 1967. Colorado allowed abortions in the cases of rape and incest while California did not. The protection of the mental health of the woman was accepted as grounds for abortion in California. New York in 1970 allowed abortions for any reasons at all (i.e., abortion on demand).[62] Hawaii, Alaska, and Washington followed the New York example and approved liberal abortion statutes in 1970. Eleven other states also liberalized their abortion statutes to coincide with either the Colorado or California examples.[63]

In 1973 the United States Supreme Court ruled that abortion is legal in this country and that any woman has the right to have an abortion. In *Roe v. Wade* the Court held that the right to privacy is broad enough to encompass a woman's decision whether or not to terminate her pregnancy. The right of privacy is not absolute and a state can decide at some point to regulate a pregnancy. The Court ruled that prior to the end of the first trimester of pregnancy the state may not interfere with or regulate an attending physician's decision reached in conjunction with his patient that a pregnancy should be terminated. After the first trimester and until the point when the fetus becomes viable the state may only regulate an abortion procedure to the extent that such regulation relates to the preservation and protection of maternal health. After the fetus is viable the state may prohibit abortions altogether except when necessary to preserve the life or health of the mother. Last the fetus is not included within the definition of person as used in the Fourteenth Amendment of the Constitution.[64]

In *Doe v. Bolton* (1973), the Court struck down requirements that abortion must be approved by a hospital committee and that two licensed doctors must confirm the attending physician's recommendations to abort.[65] Thus both 1973 decisions allowed abortion on demand and states did not need to keep an abortion statute.

In 1976, the Supreme Court ruled in *Planned Parenthood of Missouri v. Danforth* that Missouri's requirement of spousal consent was unconstitutional because it granted the husband the right to prevent unilaterally and for whatever reason, the effectuation of his wife's and her doctor's decision to terminate her pregnancy.[66] The Court also ruled the same year that a minor under the age of eighteen does not need her parents' consent to have an abortion. States may require written informed consent from the woman prior to abortion, but they may not prohibit use of the saline method of abortion after the first trimester of pregnancy.[67]

The Supreme Court in 1977 ruled that the Equal Protection Clause of the Constitution does not require a state participating in the medicaid program to pay the expenses incident to nontherapeutic abortions for indigent women simply because it has made a policy choice to pay expenses incident to childbirth. The Connecticut regulation does not impinge upon the fundamental right of privacy recognized in the *Roe* decision. An indigent woman desiring an abortion is not disadvantaged by Connecticut's decision to fund childbirth; she continues as before to be dependent on private abortion services.[68]

A number of attempts to override the 1973 Supreme Court decisions have been made in the United States Congress. These pieces of legislation would be in the form of a constitutional amendment. As of this date all attempts have failed (i.e., right-to-life, states rights, fetus-as-persons, Burdick Amendment, Church Amendment, Helms Amendment, and Hogan-Froelich Amendment).[69]

Legal Definitions

Black defines abortion as the unlawful destruction or bringing forth of the fetus before the natural time of birth; causing or procuring an abortion is the actual crime.[70] A criminal abortion can take place only after the fetus is viable and the life of the mother is not endangered. It is the illegal destruction of a fetus by the use of drugs, instruments, or manipulation.[71]

Abortion Statutes and Enforcement Policy

Whoever by means of any instrument, medicine, drug, or other means whatever, procures or produces, or attempts to procure or produce an abortion or miscarriage on any woman, unless the same were done as necessary for the preservation of the mother's life or health and under the direction of a competent licensed physician, shall be imprisoned not less than one year or not more than ten years; or if the death of the mother results therefrom, the person procuring or producing, or attempting to procure or produce the abortion or miscarriage shall be guilty of second degree murder.[72]

Since the 1973 and 1976 Supreme Court decisions the number of arrests and prosecutions for illegally performed abortions has all but ended in the District of Columbia.[73] Since the Supreme Court decision allowing states not to elect to pay for nontherapeutic abortions in 1977, there might be a return to illegal abortions and associated deaths among the lower class poor in society once again. In New York alone there were estimated to have been 50,000 illegal abortions annually before 1974 which resulted in the deaths of twenty-five women annually.[74]

Thus the Supreme Court ruling of 1977 discriminates against the poor who can least afford a legal, let alone an illegal abortion. Since the poor cannot pay much they will have to seek out abortionists who are not skilled and utilize unsanitary instruments and facilities. Thus the poor woman who cannot get funding for a non-therapeutic abortion will either try to self-induce abortion or be at the mercy of those offering illicit services under dangerous conditions. This situation might bring back a more disreputable version of the abortion mill and/or ring as Schur described.[75]

A lengthy literature has been developed concerning the criminal abortion and the problems of law enforcement.[76] First of all the woman seeking an abortion must find an abortionist and poor women have a harder time finding one since they lack the money to seek out a legal nontherapeutic abortion at a licensed clinic or hospital. The indigent female must resort to seeking out paramedical and non-medical hospital staff such as practical nurses, orderlies, and maintenance staff who have access to medical supplies and have a little knowledge of medical practices but are not really able to do any more for a desperate pregnant woman that she can do for herself.[77]

The police today are not looking for the abortionist but come across the abortion problem when a woman is found dead or dying from a self-induced abortion or one performed by the "cheap" abortionist. Thus the problem is one for the police homicide squad rather than for a special detail assigned to discover and break up abortion mills and rings as in the past when abortions were illegal. There is apparently little police corruption concerning illegal abortion operations since a licensed doctor can earn more than enough money performing legitimate abortions. Therefore the problem of obtaining evidence through undercover work, presenting the case at trial, and trying to get a conviction are relatively rare today. The current problem today is the proper inspection of abortion clinics by public health authorities to see that instruments, staff, and operating rooms meet proper health standards and have proper licenses to perform abortions. This is a task that the police do not perform. The local medical society can suspend or revoke a doctor's license to practice medicine if he or she performs improper abortions but it is almost impossible to prove that a patient died due to deliberate criminal negligence of the physician (i.e., refer to the 1977 case of Dr. Sherman whose patient died after an incomplete abortion was performed).[78]

Description of Specific Deviance

The majority of women who seek abortions are unmarried women with teenagers accounting for an estimated forty percent of all abortions. It is estimated that medicaid financed approximately thirty percent of all abortions in the United States until 1978. It is estimated that without medicaid support, poor women would seek out abortionists who are not licensed or make the attempt themselves with the result that up to 250 deaths would result and possibly 25,000 complications would occur requiring hospitalization at public expense.[79]

The assumption can be safely made that most women who seek illegal nontherapeutic abortions today are from the lower classes and are probably urban nonwhites to a great extent (i.e., Blacks, Puerto Rican-Americans, and Mexican-Americans). Since most of these women are poor and not married, they are singled out by the state legislatures, United States Congress, and Supreme Court as socially deviant and penalized for their lack of information about birth control on the one hand and their high rate of illegitimate births with subsequent need for public welfare aid on the other hand. Even with public hospitals offering free non-therapeutic abortions, most poor women would be turned away due to lack of staff and space to perform all the abortions.

Women who have attempted self-induced abortions have used a variety of methods such as oral (i.e., chlorox, turpentine, quinine, tea, gin, and various pills), insertion (i.e., catheter into the uterus or knitting needles, coat-hangers, wire), and insertion of liquids into the uterus (i.e., chlorox, lye, turpentine, douche). Most of these attempts fail to produce an abortion and the chances for serious medical consequences are one thousand times greater than if an abortion were performed by a licensed doctor.[80]

Public opinion polls conducted from 1973 through 1976 consistently show that those polled (approximately 54 percent) are in favor of the continuation of legalized abortions in the United States. Three polls in particular broke down their samples by religion (i.e., National Data Program for the Social Sciences, Devries Poll, and National Opinion Research Survey). All three showed that Catholic-Americans were opposed to abortions for single women, poor women, and women not wanting more children. Protestant-Americans were more favorably inclined to grant abortions to these categories of women while Jewish-Americans were the most favorably inclined toward nontherapeutic abortions for all women.[81]

A number of organizations have been active in the abortion issue throughout the years. In 1931 a number of organizations came out in favor of birth control (i.e., Federal Council of the Churches of Christ,

American Neurological Association, the Eugenics Society, and the Central Conference of Rabbis).[82] The Roman Catholic Church has opposed abortion since 1930 when Pope Pius XI spoke on Christian Marriage. The 1968 Papal Encyclical of Human Life did not ease the controversy.[83] The American Medical Association approved of birth control in 1937.[84] At the present time almost all Protestant and Jewish leaders are in favor of therapeutic abortions and most also favor nontherapeutic abortions.[85]

At present there are a number of organizations organized for and against the continued legalization of abortions in America. The National Abortion Rights Action League, the Religious Coalition for Abortion Rights, Planned Parenthood Federation of America, and Zero Population Growth Inc. are in favor of legalized abortions while the National Conference of Catholic Bishops, Committee for Pro-Life Activities, leads the opposition to abortion. Since 1972 the Committee for Pro-Life Activities has sponsored a respect life program (i.e., Respect Life Sunday in October of every year). On January 22, 1976 approximately fifty thousand people marched in Washington, DC., to persuade Congress to pass a constitutional amendment forbidding abortion. In April and June of 1977 Pro-Life rallies were also held in Washington to protest Congress' inaction on the abortion issue. President Carter's opposition to federal funds being used for nontherapeutic abortions has caused problems for the abortion supporters for the poor since Congress appears to be somewhat unsure about federal funding for all types of abortions for the poor.[86]

Euthanasia

Legal History

The first mention of mercy killing or euthanasia is an article published in 1870 in England. The first appeal for legalizing the practice of euthanasia also occurred in England in 1901 when a bill was rejected by Parliament. Ohio in 1906 was the first state where an attempt was made to legalize euthanasia but the legislation never passed the state legislature. A second attempt to get Parliament to enact euthanasia legislation failed in England in 1931. In 1938 the Euthanasia Society of America was founded and began the difficult task of lobbying legislatures and educating the general public on this issue.[87]

The first court case involving a doctor took place in 1950 when he was tried for killing a terminally ill cancer patient. The judge declared that the euthanasia issue had no place in the trial but the jury acquitted the physician. Most cases of mercy killing that go to court end with the jury either acquitting the defendant or refusing to indict the offender.[88]

The New Jersey State Supreme Court in 1976 rendered a decision that recognized the legality of passive, involuntary euthanasia for a patient whose mental and physical health has irrevocably declined to a level of vegetative existence. The Court noted that the state has an interest to preserve life and allows the physician the decision on how best to accomplish this end but there is a point in time when the interest of the state must give way to the individual's right to privacy. The Court based its ruling on *Roe v. Wade* (410 U.S. 113 (1973)) which guarantees the right of privacy and in certain instances protects a person's decision to terminate medical care. The New Jersey Supreme Court refused to order the state to terminate medical care for the terminally ill in this decision.[89]

The Court had to decide the issue of whether passive euthanasia constitutes criminal homicide. The Court rejected this view and felt that death resulting from discontinuation of life support systems constitutes expiration from natural causes, not homicide. The Court set up guidelines by which a life support system of a terminally ill patient could be withdrawn in order to protect the rights of the patient and relieve the doctor of legal responsibilities. First the doctor must state that there is no possibility that the patient will recover. Second the doctor with concurrence of the family or guardian must determine that the life support system be stopped. Last a hospital board must agree that the attending physician's decision to terminate life support is correct.[90]

As of this date there is still no legal basis for distinguishing euthanasia from homicide since the *Quinlan* case dealt specifically with the technical aspects of death.

Legal Definitions

Black defines euthanasia as the act or practice of painlessly killing people suffering from incurable and distressing disease (i.e., an easy or agreeable death).[91] The concept of euthanasia can be divided into two categories: voluntary or non-voluntary (i.e., the former involving the consent of the person while the latter term applies where the person is not capable of making a rational decision) and active or passive (i.e., the former involves some positive act of commission while the latter term involves an act of omission).[92]

An issue closely related to euthanasia is the legal definition of death. Black defines death as the cessation of life or the total stoppage of the circulation of the blood (i.e., natural death).[93] Medical technology has advanced our definition of death beyond that expressed by a legal authority like Black (i.e., an absence of spontaneous respiration and cardiac function). There is currently disagreement among medical, psychological, and sociological experts as to what constitutes death (i.e., cellular, physiologic, intellectual, spiritual, and social).[94] This disagreement concerns certain categories of people such as the terminally ill, the deformed, and those suffering from permanent brain damage.

A new definition of death has ben proposed by Harvard Medical School and a number of states including Virginia and Maryland have adopted this definition (i.e., six additional states have adopted the Harvard definition and fifteen other states have legislation pending). Brain death is defined as unreceptivity and unresponsiveness to external stimuli; no movement or breathing for one hour, or three minutes on a respiratory machine; no reflexes; and a flat electroencephalogram for a time period varying from ten minutes to twenty-four hours.[95]

Statutes and Enforcement Policy

There are no criminal statutes dealing specifically with euthanasia. There are only statutes dealing with homicide and aiding or abetting a suicide.[96] A person who practices euthanasia will most likely be charged with homicide or manslaughter if the matter is brought to the attention of the police department.[97] This is because the beneficial intention of the person practicing euthanasia on another must be disregarded in a court of law since the offender knows that his act can cause death of another and malice aforethought is assumed since his intention is to cause the death of another.[98]

The practice of euthanasia rarely comes to the attention of the police as performed by physicians although relatives or close friends may be exposed as practitioners if an autopsy is requested by the coroner's office as to cause of death. Only a small percentage of doctors are ever charged for practicing euthanasia by the public prosecutor although most friends or relatives are charged with murder or manslaughter. Very few juries will convict a physician or relative for a mercy killing. Those who are convicted are usually given suspended sentences by presiding judges.[99]

Description of Specific Deviance

Three groups of people have been identified with the euthanasia issue. People who are terminally ill with only a short time to live would obviously benefit from euthanasia. This category is the easiest to deal with since there is no hope that they will survive. Most are in great physical pain and a great number would like to end their suffering rather than be kept alive in such a horrible state. The second group of people who could benefit from euthanasia are persons considered defective or degenerate. This group includes those who are in a permanent unconscious vegetative state (i.e., through disease or accident), those who are severely retarded and unable to care for themselves, those who are hopelessly mentally ill, the senile, and those suffering from gross physical defects. There are difficulties in dealing with some members of this category on ethical and religious grounds. The third category of people who could benefit from euthanasia are infants and young children with gross physical or mental defects.[100]

Recent polls show that a sizeable minority of people are in favor of some form of legalized euthanasia.[101] This is in part due to the activities of numerous organizations, both secular and religious. The Roman Catholic Church issued a statement in 1957 concerning euthanasia. Both Protestant and Jewish groups have also taken a stand on the euthanasia issue, some positive and others opposed.[102] The Euthanasia Education Council was established in 1972 as part of the Euthanasia Society of America to educate citizens and lobby for legislation. As to date, eight states have enacted right-to-die laws (i.e., California, New Mexico, Idaho, Nevada, Oregon, Texas, Arkansas, and North Carolina). The statutes are basically the same with the person determining his or her future and no doctor or nurse having to take any action contrary to their personal beliefs. These statutes deal only with passive euthanasia. Currently Idaho, Montana, and Oregon are considering legislation making active euthanasia legal.[103]

The American Hospital Association in 1973 prepared a patient's bill of rights which allows the patient to receive that information necessary to give informed consent and to refuse treatment to the extent permitted by law. The concept of utilizing the hospice was also brought over from England. Hospice care involves making a dying patient comfortable, both physically and mentally, with family and friends, away from hospital life support systems and the impersonality of hospital rules and regulations.[104]

Suicide

Legal History

Suicide was a crime at Common Law in England. The deceased's body was treated with disrespect as it was allowed to be mutilated by the public, dragged through the streets, and exhibited in public as a warning to others not to commit suicide. The offender's corpse was denied Christian burial by the church and what remained of the mutilated corpse was denied burial in hallowed ground. The property of the suicide was confiscated by the King. This was apparently the situation by the time of King William in the eleventh century since by the time of Henry II in the twelfth century suicide was a felony and attempted suicide was a misdemeanor punishable by fine and possible imprisonment.[105]

Over the centuries in England, the suicide was given an ignominious burial in the crossroads of the public highway with a stake driven through the body and lost all his personal and real property to the Crown.[106] The colony of Massachusetts followed the Common Law and in 1660 passed a statute requiring suicides be buried by a highway under a load of stones so that all could see the infamous grave. The colony of North Carolina in 1715 accepted the same practice.[107]

Upon independence from England and the passage of the United States Constitution after 1789, the states stopped dealing with suicides in terms of ignominious burial and forfeiture of estats as punishment for the crime.[108] Massachustts repealed its statute of 1660 in 1823 but most states still carried criminal laws against suicide attempts.[109] In 1824 Parliament passed an Act stopping the centuries old practice of burying suicides by the highway with a stake through the body and provided for burial in churchyards but without religious ceremony and only at night between nine p.m. and midnight.[110] Attempted suicide was a crime in England from 1854 until 1961 (i.e., a misdemeanor punishable initially by a short jail sentence and up to six months for a second attempt).[111] In 1870 Parliament repealed the statute confiscating the property of suicides.[112] In 1882 Parliament passed an act allowing suicides normal burial with religious rites.[113]

In the United States during the late nineteenth and early twentieth centuries, a number of states began examining their statutes concerning suicide and attempted suicide. As early as 1877 Massachusetts stated that suicide was a crime (i.e., *malum in se*) though not punishable if self-murder is accomplished. Similar conclusions were reached by the state courts in Alabama, New Jersey, and South Carolina.[114] New York and Illinois recognized suicide as a grave public wrong but did not consider it a crime.[115] Several states like Iowa, Indiana, and Texas have no common law crimes so suicide could not be considered a criminal act.[116] Massachusetts in 1816 ruled that one who aids and abets another in, or is accessory before the fact to, self-murder is also a criminal.[117] Alabama and Tennessee cases concluded that if two parties agree to kill themselves together and only one succeeds in dying, the other can be charged with the crime of murder.[118] South Carolina ruled that an individual who attempts to commit suicide but accidently kills another is guilty of a crime.[119] Until recently in New Jersey, and South Dakota, attempted suicide was a crime.[120]

The Suicide Act of 1961 passed by Parliament rescinded the law in England that made suicide a crime and thus attempted suicide could no longer be considered criminal either. But the Act did make it a crime to aid, abet, counsel, or procure the suicide of another individual.[121]

Legal Definitions

Black defines suicide as the deliberate termination of one's life while in possession and enjoyment of one's mental faculties (i.e., self-destruction).[122] Other definitions state that suicide is the intentional act of voluntarily taking your own life.[123] Durkheim defined suicide as "all cases of death resulting directly or indirectly from a positive or negative act of the victim himself, which he knows will produce the result".[124] Cavan defines suicide as either "the intentional taking of one's life or the failure when possible to save oneself when death threatens" (i.e., self-murder).[125]

Statutes and Enforcement Policy

At present there are no statutes making suicide or attempted suicide a crime in the United States.[126] In the state of South Dakota, it is a crime to willfully, in any manner, advise or wilfully furnish another individual with any deadly weapon or poisonous drug knowing that such person intends to use the same in taking his own life, and in the case such person thereafter uses the same in taking his own life, one is guilty of aiding suicide which is punishable by imprisonment for not less than seven years.[127] Anyone who willfully aids another in the attempt to take his own life in any manner but does not succeed in actually taking his own life is guilty of a felony punishable by imprisonment not to exceed two years or by fine not to exceed one thousand dollars, or both.[128] It is no defense to a person who aides a suicide or attempts to aid a suicide who is unsuccessful in the attempt that the individual committing suicide or attempting to commit suicide was not capable of committing the crime himself.[129] These statutes are similar to the English Suicide Act of 1961.

According to Captain Clark and Lieutenant Morris of the Metropolitan Police Department (District of Columbia), there are a number of problems that the police have to deal with where suicides or attempted suicides are concerned. The police have to consider whether the individual acted alone while in complete control of his faculties, whether the individual was under the influence of alcohol, narcotics, and other dangerous drugs, or whether the situation involved other individuals (i.e., homicide-suicide).[130]

The police officer has to take into consideration the nature of the suicide attempt in order to best deal with the individual. Thus the officer is faced with a dilemma of whether to approach the potential suicide with compassion and in an attempt to help or to interpret the situation as potentially prone to violence and take appropriate protective measures. If the potential suicide is not in possession of his mental faculties, the officer can take him into protective custody as mentally ill and dangerous and deliver the person to a public hospital for diagnosis and observation.[131] If the potential suicide is under the influence of alcohol, drugs, or both, the officer is in potential danger for his life and the life of others around the vicinity of the suicidal person. Thus the person could have a hand gun or rifle and be shooting aimlessly so as to draw attention to himself, or be trying to jump off a bridge or building, or driving a vehicle in a reckless manner. The officer has a real problem in dealing with this type of potential suicide since many innocent bystanders as well as the officer could be injured or possibly killed in the attempt to stop the potential suicide from completing his act of self-destruction.

The individual who has committed a homicide and then kills himself before the police can respond to the scene poses no additional threat to third parties or the police. Unfortunately all too often there are individuals who kill another and then wait for the police to respond to the incident. These anomic murderers want the police to shoot them and in reality are using the police as the mechanism for completing the suicide act since this type of individual must kill someone else in order to force himself into a confrontation with the police where they will hopefully kill him in a shoot-out.[132]

A considerable number of murder-suicide offenders usually have a close relationship with those whom they murder (i.e., parent killing a child, mercy killings, death pacts, and accidental deaths initiated from family quarrels). Individuals who become this type of criminal tend to have violent personalities and are also self-destructive. Murder-suicide offenders tend to have very close ties with nuclear family members and are usually forced by circumstance to commit suicide rather than planning to end their lives without harming others.[133]

Police officers have a suicide rate approximately six times greater than that of the general population. Many officers find that dealing with criminals and other social deviants on a daily basis causes problems for them and members of their families when they are off-duty. Officers find that they must protect themselves psychically from the realities of their work and they become too cynical, serious, emotionally withdrawn from immediate family members, cold, and authoritarian. The fact that officers must carry their guns while off-duty and are technically on-call if the need arises makes it hard to relax away from work. This job-related problem coupled with the fact that the enforcement bureaucracy is some-what authoritarian (i.e., officers must accept orders and shift changes without question) creates a need in the officer to find a way to escape the tensions of his job. Some officers become alcoholics, others become drug abusers, and some take out their frustrations on wives and children. All these deviant solutions which are caused by the demands of police work leave the officer a prime candidate for suicide if the pressures reach the breaking point. Thus a police officer becomes susceptable to suicide before retirement, when his marriage is breaking up, if his children are a major source of anxiety, or if he becomes sick (i.e., physically or emotionally).[134]

Description of Specific Deviance

The current estimated suicide rate for the United States is eleven per one hundred thousand population.[135] It is estimated that this figure is probably under-reported by as much as forty percent. Of those who commit suicide approximately one-third had attempted suicide. Thus there are approximately twenty-five thousand suicides each year and probably a ratio of 8 to 1 in terms of attempted suicide to completed suicide during the same twelve month period.[136]

Males tend to have a high rate of suicide while females have a low rate of suicide but make more attempts at suicide than men.[137] More older people (i.e., age cohorts 55-64 and 75 and older) tend to commit suicide than younger.[138] More whites and American Indians commit suicide than Blacks and other minorities.[139] Divorced individuals have a higher rate of suicide than married people.[140] Protestants have a higher suicide rate than either Catholics or Jews.[141] Individuals of both high and low social status tend to commit suicide more often than people of average social status. Also individuals who are downwardly mobile socially are more apt to commit suicide than either those who are socially stable or upwardly mobile.[142] Supposedly there is some correlation between mental health and suicide but the data appears to be inconculsive. The most one can conclude is that individuals who are depressed over long periods of time tend to be more suicidal than those who are not. There also appears to be a link between alcoholism and drug abuse and suicide.[143] Both the West and Central parts of America have more suicides than the North and South. Central city residents tend to be more suicidal than surburban residents.[144]

The first organization to become concerned about suicides was the Royal Humane Society in 1774 in England.[145] The National Save-a-Life League was founded in the United States in 1906. The first of the Suicide Prevention Centers to appear in recent years in this country was founded in 1958 in Los Angeles. Today there are a variety of formal organizations and voluntary associations that deal with suicide prevention (i.e., Suicide Prevention Service, Call-for-Help Clinics, Crisis Call Centers, Rescue, Inc., Dial-a-Friend, and Suicides Anonymous).[146] The District of Columbia operated a suicide hotline until 1977 but transferred the service to the emergency mental health admitting office at D. C. General Hospital.[147]

The Center For Studies of Suicide Prevention was established by the National Institute of Mental Health in 1967 and also began publication of the *Bulletin of Suicidology*. The Institute conducts and supports research on the various aspects of suicide prevention and provides support to public and private organizations that deal with this topic.[148]

Mental Disorders

Legal History

The Common Law of England indicates from earliest times (i.e., after 1226) that a person under age seven is not liable for criminal responsibility or intent (i.e., *mens rea*) since he does not know right from wrong; between seven and fourteen the individual is also not criminally liable if he does not know right from wrong. If an individual above age fourteen does not appear to be able to function at least to that mental age, he is deemed mentally incompetent and termed a lunatic under the Common Law. This doctine applied to violent crimes such as murder with malice aforethought where the offender could plead lunacy as a defense and be pardoned by the Crown.[149]

By 1536 under Henry VIII the first law was passed placing the poor insane under the care of the local governments. This practice was expanded under the law of Elizabeth I in 1601 whereby the crown took responsibility for the destitute insane. Thus a policy evolved in England by the seventeenth century allowing violent criminals to plead lunacy in order to avoid criminal prosecution while non-criminal lunatics who happened to be poor were placed in the workhouses and jails along with alcoholics, vagrants, and the unemployed poor. Thus during the American colonial period and well into the nineteenth century in the United States the insane were treated in the same manner as other social deviants who were jailed.[150]

It was not until 1843 that a legal test was accepted for dealing with the criminally insane. This was the *M'Naghten* case and the rule derived from this case states that a defendant who knows the difference between right and wrong is legally sane.[151] In an 1868 Iowa case, the irresistible impulse or wild beast test was stated. An offender who knows that his criminal act was wrong but was driven to it by an uncontrollable and irresistible impulse arising from his insanity could not be held responsible for his actions.[152] A third rule was developed in two New Hampshire cases in 1869 and 1871. The test stated that insanity was a valid defense to a crime if the defendant suffered from a mental disease (i.e., was mentally ill). Thus all tests of mental disease were questions of legal fact to be decided by juries. This test allowed for the introduction of testimony by psychiatrists.[153] In 1890 the New York state legislature passed a statute making provision for hospitals and the care for the legally insane.[154] The first psychopathy law enacted in the United States was the Briggs Act of Massachusetts in 1911, and dealt with so-called defective delinquents.[155]

The first statute authorizing the sterilization of criminals, the insane, feeble-minded, and epileptics was passed in Indiana in 1907. The law was declared unconstitutional in 1921 since it denied due process of law to the offender.[156] Another similar statute was passed in Indiana in 1927.[157] The same year the U. S. Supreme Court ruled that a feeble-minded Virginia girl could be sterilized on order of the superintendent of a state mental hospital in her best interest and that of society.[158] The first sexual psychopath statute was passed by Michigan in 1937.[159]

The Supreme Court in 1942 rejected an Oklahoma statute that required sterilization of habitual criminals.[160] The National Mental Health Act of 1946 passed by Congress established the National Institute of Mental Health which was to assist states and community mental health facilities in developing their programs, and to encourage and fund research into the prevention, causes, and treatment of mental illness.[161] In 1954, the *Durham* rule was the result of a federal court case and stated that an offender is not criminally responsible if his crime was the product of mental disease or defect.[162] In 1959 Parliament passed the Mental Health Act which provides for the detention of the mentally ill under certain circumstances.[163]

The Joint Commission on Mental Illness and Health reported its findings on American mental hospitals and made its recommendations in 1961.[164] The Model Penal Code of 1962 proposed a test of insanity that dealt with mental disease or defect, incompetency, or unsoundness of mind. In particular the test states that an individual is not responsible for criminal conduct if at the time he commits a crime such conduct is due to mental disease or defect and that the offender does not have the capacity to either appreciate the criminality of his conduct or conform to the requirements of the criminal law.[165]

The Community Mental Health Centers Act was passed by Congress in 1963 which funded the construction and staffing of community centers that offered in-patient, out-patient, and emergency care in addition to counseling and education programs.[166] In 1970 the Supreme Court upheld a Nebraska statute permitting sterilization as a condition for release from a mental hospital but this was a situation involving voluntary sterilization of a mental patient.[167] In 1972 the federal courts rejected the *Durham* rule and accepted the Model Penal Code test in its place.[168] Also the same year the Supreme Court ruled that both the due process and equal protection clauses of the Constitution require that a defendant who is found incompetent to stand trial must receive procedural civil requirements; involuntary civil commitment standards must be met before one can be subjected to prolonged commitment; and the defendant must be released when he no longer meets civil commitment standards.[169] Finally in 1973 the federal courts ruled that the sexual psychopath laws are unconstitutional since they do not protect the procedural safeguards of the defendant.[170]

Legal Definitions

As Clinard points out, there are many problems in attempting to define mental illness or disorder.[171] Since this discussion deals with crimes without victims, we will examine the legal definition of insanity rather than the medical (i.e., psychiatric) definition. This is an extremely difficult task since medical jurisprudence plays a key role in the legal determination of criminality.

Black defines insanity as unsoundness of mind, madness, mental alienation or derangement, or a morbid psychic condition. Insanity also involves the intellect, the emotions, the will, and the moral sense.[172] In criminal law, the term means such a perverted and deranged condition of the mental and moral faculties as to render the individual incapable of distinguishing right from wrong, or to render one at the time unconscious to the nature of the act one is committing, or, if conscious of the act in terms of right and wrong, unable to control oneself to prevent the commission of the crime. Thus an insane individual is so mentally deranged or incompetent that he cannot be charged with criminal intent since he cannot control his will in order to avoid perpetrating a crime.[173]

Other terms synonymous with insanity are derangement, lunacy, and *non compos mentis*. Derangement is all the forms of mental unsoundness except idiocy.[174] Lunacy is the common law term for one who has completely lost his memory and understanding. The term is a general description of all forms of derangement or mental unsoundness.[175] *Non compos mentis* is a term applicable to all insane individuals of whatever type of insanity.[176]

Legal insanity refers to a disorder of the intellect (i.e., a disease of the brain rendering one incapable of distinguishing right from wrong with respect to the crime committed).[177] Moral insanity is a morbid perversion of the feelings, affections, or propensities but without any illusions or derangement of the intellectual faculties. It is the irresistable impulse or incapacity to differentiate between what is moral and immoral. Moral insanity is not usually an acceptable defense to a crime.[178] A psychopath or sociopath (i.e., sociopathic personality) is one having mental disorders not amounting to insanity but characterized by a defect of basic personality character (i.e., social-self), eccentricity, emotional instability, inadequacy or perversity of conduct, suspiciousness, lack of social feeling, lack of self-control, or lack of truthfulness.[179]

Delirium tremens or settled insanity is a legal form of insanity and may be of such nature or intensity as to render the individual incapable of committing a crime. It is produced by alcoholism over a long period of time so that the habitual drunk cannot abstain from drinking or else suffer a nervous disorder that cannot be easily treated. The term is distinguished from temporary insanity or drunkenness which directly results from too much liquor at a particular time.[180]

Paranoia is the delusionary insanity of an individual who is rational mentally except in certain circumstances (i.e., a particular delusion causes the person to react in an insane manner).[181] Mania is a form of insanity where the individual is subject to hallucinations and illusions that are accompanied by a high state of excitement that may amount to complete loss of control.[182] Homicidal mania is the irresistable impulse to murder another person brought about by an insane delusion (i.e., self-defense, revenge, or the instrument of justice).[183] Kleptomania is the inability to stop from stealing.[184] Dipsomania or toxicomania is the irresistible impulse to excessive use of alcohol, opiates, cocaine, or other drugs.[185] Pyromania is the irresistible urge to set fires to property.[186]

Statutes and Enforcement Policy

The D.C. Code defines mental illness as a psychosis or other disease which substantially impairs the mental health of a person. A mentally ill person is defined as one who has mental illness but does not include a person committed to a private or public hospital by order of a court in a criminal proceeding.[187]

Any person may apply to a public or private hospital for admission as a voluntary patient for the purposes of observation, diagnosis, and treatment of a mental illness. Upon the request of any person over eighteen years of age or in the case of a person under eighteen with consent of his spouse, parent, or legal guardian, he or she shall be examined by the admitting psychiatrist to determine whether the individual should be admitted or not.[188] A voluntary patient admitted to a hospital shall be released within forty-eight hours after making a written request to leave if he is over eighteen years of age. A voluntary patient under eighteen may be released if his spouse, parent, or guardian makes the written request. A voluntary patient may be released by the chief of service if he determines that the patient has recovered and continued hospitalization would no longer be useful.[189]

A friend or relative of one believed to be suffering from a mental illness may apply on behalf of that person to the admitting psychiatrist of a hospital by presenting the person together with a reference from a practicing doctor. The admitting psychiatrist shall admit the alleged mentally ill patient if he feels the need for examination and treatment is indicated. The patient must state in writing that he does not object to hospitalization.[190] A police officer or a physician of the person in question who has reason to believe that the person is mentally ill and because of the illness is likely to injure himself or others if he is not immediately detained may without a warrant take the person into custody, transport him to a private or public hospital, and make application for his admission thereto for purposes of emergency observation and diagnosis. The application shall reveal the circumstances under which the person was taken into custody and the reasons therefor.[191]

A police officer may apprehend and detain a person whom he believes to be a mentally ill person and found under suspicious circumstances. Said apprehended person shall be brought before a United States commissioner for a hearing and if said commissioner is not available to be taken to St. Elizabeth's Hospital where the superintendent may detain the person pending a hearing before a United States commissioner. The hearing shall be within seventy-two hours of detention. The hearing can be at St. Elizabeth's Hospital if it is medically determined that the person should not be moved as a health or safety factor.[192] The superintendent shall promptly examine a person committed and if not found to be mentally ill shall discharge him, or if found to be mentally ill shall return him to the state of his residence or to his relatives, if practicable.[193]

The term sexual psychopath means a person, not insane, who by a course of repeated misconduct in sexual matters has evidenced such lack of power to control his sexual impulses as to be dangerous to other persons because he is likely to attack or otherwise inflict injury, loss, pain, or other evil on the objects of his desire.[194] Other statutes dealing with sexual psychopaths deal with examination by psychiatrists, hearing-commitment to St. Elizabeth's Hospital, parole-discharge, and stay of criminal proceedings.[195]

In all states and the District of Columbia commitment of the mentally ill is a civil procedure. Thus the police are prohibited by statute from taking a suspected mentally ill person to jail. In many states the commitment laws specify that the mentally ill do not have to be dangerous, just in need of care and treatment for involuntary commitment. Some states even make the welfare and needs of persons other than the prospective patient (i.e., family members) a sufficient criterion for involuntary commitment. Only a minority of states continue to use the term "dangerous" or require the likelihood of injury to self or others in order for the police to bring the person to a hospital for involuntary commitment.[196]

The mentally ill are not the only individuals that the police deal with in terms of commitment to a public or private hospital for psychiatric observation and diagnosis. The police are also authorized in thirty-seven states to deal with mentally defective or deficient individuals (i.e., idiots and imbeciles). The same number of states also allow alcoholics to be committed; thirty-four states deal with drug addicts and abusers in the same manner; and a few states even subject epileptics to confinement in mental hospitals.[197]

Finally the criminal justice system also has to deal with those criminals who are adjudicated criminally insane. Thus individuals who are deemed incompetent to stand trial or enter a plea of guilty, defendants found guilty by reason of insanity, individuals found guilty of violation of certain statutes like sexual psychopath or defective delinquent laws, convicted and sentenced offenders who become mentally ill while in prison or jail, and the mentally ill who pose a danger to medical personnel in the course of their diagnosis and treatment are all sent to special institutions for the criminally insane. There are presently seventy-three such institutions in America today.[198]

Description of Specific Deviance

NIMH estimates for 1970 state that approximately three million Americans are treated for mental disorders of which approximately six hundred thousand are institutionalized.[199] There were more than four hundred thousand admissions to state and county mental hospitals in 1972 of which forty percent were involuntary. There are 501 mental hospitals in the United States of which 312 are state and county institutions, 39 are Veterans Administration neuropsychiatric hospitals, and 150 are private hospitals. There are also an estimated thirteen hundred general hospitals that contain psychiatric treatment facilities. There are also approximately 2100 outpatient clinics throughout the country that deal with mental health problems.[200] This is in addition to the 73 correctional institutions for the criminally insane, already noted elsewhere.

It is estimated that the medical treatment, incarceration, and loss of work costs due to mental illness exceed twenty billion dollars per year in the United States.[201] If one considers all the social stresses that most Americans are subjected to every year and the resulting deviant solutions to these stresses (i.e., drug addiction and abuse, alcoholism, over-eating, child and spouse abuse, suicide, and violent criminal acts), the costs of mental illness are truly astronomical.

Weinberg's review of several urban studies of mental disorders shows that the overall rates of psychoses and of schizophrenia are highest near the central business districts and transitional areas of inner cities and decline as one moves outward toward the suburbs where the rates of neurosis increases significantly.[202] Social mobility appears to be related to mental illness (i.e., both upward and downward).[203] There also appears to be a positive correlation between social class and mental illness (i.e., lower class persons tend to be psychotic and middle/upper class people tend to be neurotic).[204]

There appears to be little difference in the prevalence of mental illness among males and females in society. Rates of mental disorders tend to increase as the typical individual goes through the life cycle with neuroses occuring most frequently before middle age and psychoses occuring most often during middle age or early old age although schizophrenia occurs most often before middle age.[205] Jews tend to be more neurotic while Catholics tend to be more psychotic but these findings are quite tentative. The rate of mental illness is higher for whites than for nonwhites although Blacks, Mexican-Americans, and American Indians do suffer a disproportionate amount of mental problems. Finally rates of mental disorders are higher for the divorced and separated than for those who are married.[206]

The Hospital of St. Mary of Bethlehem in London was used after 1400 as an insane asylum.[207] In 1776 Virginia became the first state to open an asylum. It was not until 1890 that the New York legislature passed a statute establishing hospitals that offered specialized care for the legally insane.[208] Up to 1960 almost ninety percent of those in mental hospitals and institutions for the criminally insane were involuntarily committed.[209] Until the early 1970's, most individuals were kept in an institution whether public or private, punitive or rehabilitative for several years.[210] The practice is currently to use outpatient services except for the most difficult cases. These services include a whole range of activities from counseling, individual and group therapy, and medical treatment by both professionals (i.e., psychiatrists, psychologists, social workers) and volunteers of concerned nonprofessionals. There are also halfway houses for ex-mental patients and social organizations like Recovery Incorporated that help ex-mental patients meet others with similar backgrounds in order to discuss and overcome common problems in adjusting to the community. Sometimes nursing and foster homes are utilized as alternatives to hospitalization for the elderly mentally ill as well as the juvenile mental patient.[211]

Notes

[1]Henry Maine, *Ancient Law*, Boston: Beacon Press, 1963, pp. 153-154.

[2]*Ibid.*, p. 140.

[3]Arthur Diamond, *The Evolution of Law and Order*, Westport, Connecticut: Greenwood Press, 1951, p. 148.

[4]Morton Hunt, *The Natural History of Love*, New York: Alfred A. Knopf, 1959; G. R. Taylor, *Sex in History*, New York: Vanguard Press, 1954; Isabel Drummand, *The Sex Paradox*, New York: G. P. Putnam's Sons, 1953; Morris Ploscowe, *Sex and the Law*, New Jersey: Prentice-Hall, 1951.

[5]1 James I, c. 11.

[6]Maine, *op. cit.*

[7]*Ibid.*

[8]Edmund Morgan, "The Puritans and Sex," in Michael Gordon (ed.), *The American Family in Social-Historical Perspective*, New York: St. Martin's Press, 1973, pp. 284-290.

[9]*Ibid.*, pp. 289-291.

[10]Lawrence Friedman, *A History of American Law*, New York: Simon and Schuster, 1973, pp. 179-184.

[11]Gerhard Mueller, "Inquiry into the State of a Divorceless Society: Domestic Relations Law and Morals in England from 1660 to 1857," *University of Pittsburgh Law Review*, 18 (1957), p. 545.

[12]Nelson Blake, *The Road to Reno: A History of Divorce in the United States*, 1962, pp. 34-47.

[13]*Ibid.*, p. 50.

[14]*Ibid.*

[15]Friedman, *op. cit.*, pp. 184-185.

[16]*Ibid.*, pp. 185-186.

[17]Ibid., pp. 188-191; Robert Rich, *Juvenile Delinquency: A Paradigmatic Perspective*, Washington, DC: University Press of America, 1978, pp. 221-222.

[18]Robert Bell, *Social Deviance*, Homewood, Illinois: The Dorsey Press, 1971, p. 320.

[19]*Ibid.*, pp. 386-387.

[20]Henry Black, *Black's Law Dictionary*, St. Paul, Minnesota: West Publishing Company, 1968, pp. 71-72; The Dushkin Publishing Group, *Encyclopedia of Sociology*, Guilford, Connecticut: The Dushkin Publishing Group, 1974, p. 4.

[21]Black, *op. cit.*, p. 206; Dushkin, *op. cit.*, p. 21.

[22]Black, *op. cit.*, p. 25.

[23]Dushkin, *op. cit.*, p. 37.

[24]Henry Fairchild (ed.), *Dictionary of Sociology*, Paterson, New Jersey: Littlefield, Adams and Company, 1962, p. 39; Black, *op. cit.*, p. 533.

[25]Black, *op. cit.*, pp. 532-533; Dushkin, *op. cit.*, pp. 77-78.

[26]Black, *op. cit.*, p. 566; Dushkin, *op. cit.*, p. 83.

[27]Fairchild, *op. cit.*, p. 149.

[28]Black, *op. cit.*, pp. 192-193.

[29]*Ibid.*, pp. 71-904.

[30]Black, *op. cit.*, p. 904; Fairchild, *op. cit.*, p. 150; Dushkin, *op. cit.*, p. 135.

[31]*District of Columbia Code,* Annotated, Washington, DC: US Government Printing Office, 1973, 2, 22-301, 1345.

[32]*Ibid.*, 22-601, 1368.

[33]*Ibid.*, 22-901, 1374.

[34]*Ibid.*, 22-902, 1375.

[35]Martin Haskell and Lewis Yablonsky, *Criminology: Crime and Criminality*, Chicago: Rand McNally, 1978, p. 114.

[36]D. C. Code, *op. cit.*, 22-1901, 1437.

[37]Haskell and Yablonsky, *op. cit.*, pp. 114-115.

[38]Interview with Officer Selma Partner, Sex Offense Branch, Metropolitan Police Department of Washington, DC, 1978; Interview with Captain George Henry, Watch Commander, Youth Division, Metropolitan Police Department of Washington, DC, 1978; Interview with Dr. Veronica Maz, Battered Women Program, House of Ruth, Washington, DC, 1978.

[39]*Ibid.*

[40]*Prevention of Child Abuse and Neglect Act*, Washington, DC: Council of the District of Columbia, 1977, pp. 1-22.

[41]Uniform Crime Reports of the FBI, *Crime in the United States-1976*, Washington, DC: US Government Printing Office, 1977, p. 184.

[42]*Ibid.*

[43]Dushkin, *op. cit.*, p. 4.

[44]Bell, *op. cit.*, pp. 82-86; Dushkin, *op. cit.*, p. 83; Morton Hunt, *The World of the Formerly Married*, New York: McGraw-Hill, 1966.

[45]Haskell and Yablonsky, *op. cit.*, p. 115; Interview with Dr. Maz, *op. cit.*; Interview with Cynthia Anderson, Coordinator, Office of Abused Persons, Department of Social Services, Montgomery County, Maryland, 1978.

[46]Haskell and Yablonsky, *op. cit.*, p. 114.

[47]Henri Raffalli, "The Battered Child: An Overview of a Medical, Legal, and Social Problem," *Crime and Delinquency* (April, 1970), pp. 139-150: David Gill, *Violence Against Children*, Cambridge, Massachusetts: Harvard University Press, 1975; Joseph Goldstein et. al., *Beyond the Best Interests of the Child*, New York: MacMillan, 1973; C. H. Kempe, *Helping the Battered Child and His*

Family, Philadelphia: J. B. Lippincott, 1972; Leontine Young, *Wednesday's Children*, New York: McGraw-Hill, 1964; Vincent Fontana, *Somewhere a Child is Crying*, New York: MacMillan, 1973; E. R. Helfer, *Child Abuse and Neglect*, Washington, DC: Report to the Subcommittee of Children and Youth, Committee of Labor and Public Welfare, United States Senate, 1973; Claire Nissenbaum, "A Child is Dead," *Reaction* (1972), *Symposium on Child Abuse*, Denver: The American Humane Association-Children's Division, 1972; W. T. Downs, "The Meaning and Handling of Child Neglect — A Legal View," *Child Welfare* (March, 1963), pp. 131-134.

48Case studies based on officer reports of the Youth Division and Sex Offense Branch, Metropolitan Police Department (D.C.), 1978.

49*Ibid.*

50*Ibid.*

51*Ibid.*

52Paul Gebhard and John Gagnon, "Male Sex Offenders Against Very Young Children," *American Journal of Psychiatry*, 121 (1964), pp. 576-580; R.E.L. Masters, *Patterns of Incest*, New York: The Julian Press, 1963; S. K. Weinberg, *Incest Behavior*, New York: Citadel Press, 1955; Irving Kaufman et al., "The Family Constellation and Overt Incestuous Relations Between Father and Daughter," *American Journal of Orthopsychiatry*, 24 (1954), pp. 266-277; Hector Cavallin, "Incestuous Fathers: A Clinical Report," *American Journal of Psychiatry*, 122 (1966), pp. 1132-1138; C. Bagley, "Incest Behavior and Incest Taboo," *Social Problems*, 16 (1969), pp. 505-519.

53Haskell and Yablonsky, *op. cit.*, p. 349.

54Gilbert Geis, "Criminal Abortion," in Simon Dinitz et al., (eds.), *Deviance: Studies in Definition, Management, and Treatment*, New York: Oxford University Press, 1975, p. 320; David Granfield, *The Abortion Decision*, Garden City, New York: Doubleday, 1969, pp. 73-76.

55Robert Bell, *Social Deviance*, Homewood, Illinois: The Dorsey Press, 1971, p. 122; Granfield, *op. cit.*

56Geis, *op. cit.*, p. 320; Granfield, *op. cit.*

57Bell, *op. cit.*, p. 122; Geis, *op. cit.*; Granfield, *op. cit.*

58Mary Calderone (ed.), *Abortion in the United States*, New York: Paul B. Hoeber, 1958, pp. 193-194.

59Edwin Schur, *Crimes Without Victims: Deviant Behavior and Public Policy*, New Jersey: Prentice-Hall, 1965, p. 57.

60American Law Institute, *Model Penal Code*, Philadelphia: American Law Institute, 1962, pp. 189-190.

61Granfield, *op. cit.*, p. 107; Geis, *op. cit.*, p. 321.

62Geis, *op. cit.*, pp. 316-319; Granfield, *op. cit.*, pp. 76, 112.

[63]Geis, *op. cit.*, pp. 319-320.

[64]*Roe v. Wade*, 410 U.S. 113 (1973).

[65]*Doe v. Bolton*, 410 U.S. 179 (1973).

[66]*Planned Parenthood of Missouri v. Danforth*, 428 U.S. 52, 70-71 (1976).

[67]*Bellotti v. Baird*, 428 U.S. 132, 147 (1976).

[68]*Maher, Commissioner of Social Services of Connecticut v. Roe et al.*, 75-1440, June 20, 1977, Washington, DC: Supreme Court of the United States, I-II of Syllabus.

[69]Susan Lowe, "The Right to Choose: Facts On Abortion," *Family Planning Perspectives*, 7 (1975), p. 225.

[70]Henry Black, *Black's Law Dictionary*, St. Paul, Minnesota: West Publishing Company, 1968, p. 20.

[71]Henry Fairchild (ed.), *Dictionary of Sociology*, Paterson, New Jersey: Littlefield, Adams and Company, 1962, p. 1.

[72]*District of Columbia Code*, Annotated, Washington, DC: US Government Printing Office, 1973, 2, 22-201, 1085.

[73]Interview with Captain Joseph O'Brien, Homicide Squad, Metropolitan Police Department of Washington, DC, 1977.

[74]J. Pakter et al., "Impact of the Liberalized Abortion Law in New York City on Deaths Associated with Pregnancy: A Two-Year Experience," *Bulletin of the New York Academy of Medicine*, 49 (1973), p. 804.

[75]Schur, *op. cit.*, pp. 31-34; Jerome Bates, "The Abortion Mill: An Institutional Analysis," *Journal of Criminal Law and Criminology*, 45 (1954), pp. 157-163; Jerome Bates and E. S. Zawadzski, *Criminal Abortion: A Study in Medical Sociology*, Springfield, Illinois: Charles C. Thomas, 1964.

[76]Bell, *op. cit.*, pp. 139-143; Schur, *op. cit.*, pp. 31-38; Abraham Rongy, *Abortion: Legal or Illegal,* New York: Vanguard Press, 1933; Lucy Freeman, *The Abortionist*, New York: Doubleday and Company, 1962; National Committee on Mental Health, *The Abortion Problem*, Baltimore: Williams and Wilkins Company, 1944; Glanville Williams, *The Sanctity of Life and the Criminal Law*, New York: Alfred A. Knopf, 1957; Calderone, *op. cit.*; Zad Leavy and Jerome Kummer, "Criminal Abortion: Human Hardships and Unyielding Law," *Southern California Law Review*, 35 (1962), pp. 139-140; Russell Fisher, "Criminal Abortion," *Journal of Criminal Law and Criminology*, 42 (1951), pp. 246-150; Paul Gebhard et al., *Pregnancy, Birth, and Abortion*, New York: Paul B. Hoeber, 1958; Nancy Howell, *The Search for an Abortionist*, Chicago: University of Chicago Press, 1969; Roy Lucas, "Federal Constitutional Limitations on the Enforcement and Administration of State Abortion Statutes," *The North Carolina Law Review*, (July, 1969), pp. 730-778; Alice Rossi, "Abortion Laws and Their Victims," *Trans-Action*, (September, 1966), pp. 7-12.

[77]Freeman, *op. cit.*; Howell, *op. cit.*

[78]Ex-Abortionist is Probed by U.S. Attorney, *Washington Post*, October 26, 1977.

[79]Lowe, *op. cit.*; Zero Population Growth, *15 Facts You Should Know About Abortion*, Washington, DC: Zero Population Growth, Inc., 1976; Bell, *op. cit.*, pp. 132-139; Schur, *op. cit.*, pp. 45-51.

[80]Polgar and Fried, *op. cit.*, pp. 126-127.

[81]National Abortion Rights Action League, *Public Opinion Polls Since the Supreme Court Decisions of 1973*, Washington, DC: NARAL, 1976.

[82]Norman St. John-Stevas, "History and Legal Status of Birth Control," in Edwin Schur (ed.), *The Family and the Sexual Revolution*, Bloomington, Indiana: Indiana University Press, 1964, pp. 377-378.

[83]Bell, *op. cit.*, p. 131.

[84]St. John-Stevas, *op. cit.*

[85]Bell, *op. cit.*, p. 131.

[86]*Washington Post*, September 29, 1977; *Washington Star*, October 18, 1977; *Washington Post*, September 28, 1977.

[87]Glanville Williams, *The Sanctity of Life and the Criminal Law*, New York: Alfred A. Knopf, 1957; O. R. Russell, *Freedom to Die: Moral and Legal Aspects of Euthanasia*, New York: Human Sciences Press, 1975; Charles and Diane Triche, *The Euthanasia Controversy: 1812-1974*, Troy, New York: Whetson Publishing Company, 1975; Jerry Wilson, *Death By Decision: The Medical, Moral and Legal Dilemmas of Euthanasia*, Philadelphia: Westminister Press, 1975.

[88]Russell, *op. cit.*, pp. 258-260.

[89]Marvin Kohl, "On Death, Dying, and the Karen Ann Quinlan Case," *The Humanist*, 16 (1976), pp. 18-19; "In Re Quinlan: Defining the Basis for Terminating Life Support under the Right of Privacy," *Tulsa Law Journal*, 12 (1976), pp. 150-167; Congressional Research Service, Library of Congress, *The Right to Die*, HU-6251-c3 (June 2, 1976), pp. 16-20.

[90]*Ibid.*

[91]Henry Black, *Black's Law Dictionary*, St. Paul, Minnesota: West Publishing Company, 1968, p. 654; Henry Fairchild (ed.), *Dictionary of Sociology*, Paterson, New Jersey: Littlefield, Adams and Company, 1962, p. 109.

[92]Russell, *op. cit.*, pp. 20-22.

[93]Black, *op. cit.*, p. 488.

[94]Henry Beecher, "Ethical Problems Created by the Hopelessly Unconscious Patient," *The New England Journal of Medicine*, 284 (1971), p. 260; Orville Brim et al., (eds.), *The Dying Patient*, New York: Russell Sage Foundation, 1970.

[95]Harvard Medical School Ad Hoc Committee to Examine the Definition of Death, "A Definition of Irreversible Coma," *Journal of the American Medical Association*, 205 (1968), pp. 85-88; Wilson, *op. cit.*; Donald Culter (ed.), *Updating Life and Death: Essays on Ethics and Medicine,* Boston: Beacon Press, 1969; John Behnke and Sissela Bok, *The Dilemma of Euthanasia,* New York: Doubleday, 1975.

[96]*District of Columbia Code*, Annotated, Washington, DC: US Government Printing Office, 1973, 2, 22-2401, 2402, 2403, 2404, 2405, 1463-1488.

[97]Interview with Captain Joseph O'Brien, Homicide Squad, Metropolitan Police Department of Washington, DC, 1977.

[98]Eike-Henner Kluge, *The Practice of Death*, New Haven: Yale University Press, 1975; Marvin Kohl, *The Morality of Killing*, New York: Humanities Press, 1974.

[99]Williams, *op. cit.*; "Legal Aspects of Euthanasia," *Albany Law Review,* 36 (1972), pp. 679-686; "Right to Die," *Houston Law Review*, 7 (1970), pp. 667-670; E. J. Gurney, "Is There a Right to Die?—a Study of the Law of Euthanasia," *Cumber-Sam Law Review*, 3 (1972), pp. 245-248; "Right to Die," *California Western Law Review*, 10 (1974), pp. 613-627; Morris Forkosch, "Privacy, Human Dignity, Euthanasia—Are These Independent Constitutional Rights?," *University of San Fernando Valley Law Review*, 3 (1974), pp. 1-20; Richard Delgado, "Euthanasia Reconsidered—The Choice of Death as an Aspect of the Right of Privacy," *Arizona Law Review*, 17 (1975), pp. 474-494; Daniel Maguire, "Death: Legal and Illegal," *Atlantic*, 833 (1974), pp. 72-77; David Meyers, "The Legal Aspects of Medical Euthanasia," *Bioscience*, 23 (1973), pp. 467-470; Joseph Sanders, "Euthanasia: None Dare Call It Murder," *The Journal of Criminal Law and Criminology*, 60 (1969), pp. 351-359.

[100]Group for the Advancement of Psychiatry, *The Right to Die: Decision and Decision Makers*, Philadelphia: Group for the Advancement of Psychiatry, 1973; A. B. Downing (ed.), *Euthanasia and the Right to Death*, Los Angeles: Nash Publishing Company, 1969; Richard Trubo, *An Act of Mercy: Euthanasia Today*, Los Angeles: Nash Publishing Company, 1973; Robert Williams (ed.), *To Live and to Die: When, Why and How*, New York: Springer-Verlag, 1973; Melvin Grant, *Dying and Dignity: The Meaning and Control of a Personal Death*, Springfield, Illinois: Charles C. Thomas, 1974; Mary Mannes, *Last Rights*, New York: William Morrow and Company, 1974; Milton Heifetz, *The Right to Die: A Neurosurgeon Speaks of Death with Candor*, New York: G. P. Putnam's Sons, 1975; Marvin Kohl (ed.), *Beneficient Euthanasia*, Buffalo, New York: Promethus, 1975; Eric Cassell, "Permission to Die," *Bioscience*, 23 (1973), pp. 475-478; R. S. Duff and A. G. Campbell, "Moral and Ethical Dilemmas in the Special Care Nursery," *New England Journal of Medicine*, 289 (1973), pp. 890-894.

[101]U. S. Senate Special Committee on Aging, *Death With Dignity: an Inquiry into Related Public Issues*, Hearings, 92nd Congress, 2nd Session, Washington, DC: US Government Printing Office, 1972.

[102]Russell, pp. 200-214; Immanuel Jacobovits, *Jewish Medical Ethics*, New York: Bloch Publishing Company, 1959; Charles McFadden, *Medical Ethics*, Philadelphia: F. A. Davis, 1967; American Friends Service Committee,

Who Shall Live? Man's Control Over Birth and Death, New York: Hill and Wang, 1970; Paul Ramsey, *The Patient as Person: Explorations in Medical Ethics*, New Haven: Yale University Press, 1970; Daniel Maguire, *Death By Choice*, New York: Doubleday, 1974.

[103]*Euthanasia News*, 3 (1977), New York: Euthanasia Education Council, pp. 1-5.

[104]L. K. Altman, "Doctor and Patient: Bill of Rights, a Break with old Paternalism," *New York Times*, January 1, 1973, p. 1; Sheila Kast, "Hospice: A New Way to Combat Loneliness of a Loved One's Final Days of Life," *Washington Star*, November 28, 1977, pp. B1-2.

[105]C. Ray Jeffery, "The Development of Crime in Early English Society," in Chambliss (ed.), *Crime and the Legal Process*, New York: McGraw-Hill, 1969, pp. 23-28; Leon Radzinowicz, *A History of English Criminal Law*, London: Macmillan, 1948-53.

[106]Normal St. John-Stevas, *Life, Death and the Law,* Bloomington, Indiana: Indiana University Press, 1961; Louis Dublin, *Suicide: A Sociological and Statistical Study,* New York: Ronald Press, 1963; Jack Gibbs (ed.), *Suicide,* New York: Harper and Row, 1968; Erwin Stengel, *Suicide and Attempted Suicide,* Middlesex, England: Pelican Books, 1969; G. L. Williams, *The Sanctity of Life and the Criminal Law*, New York: Alfred A. Knopf, 1957; William Lecky, *A History of European Morals,* New York: Appleton-Century-Crofts, 1906; Edmund Cahn, *The Moral Decision,* Bloomington, Indiana: Indiana University Press, 1959; "Crime of Suicide," *The Economist*, 196 (1960), pp. 871-872; Kenneth Robinson, "Suicide and the Law," *The Spectator*, March 4, 1958, p. 317.

[107]*Ibid.*

[108]*American and English Encyclopedia of Law and Practice*, volume 24, section II, pp. 490-491; *Corpus Juris Secundum*, 1953, 871-875; *American Jurisprudence*, 1968, section 583.

[109]Marshall Clinard, *Sociology of Deviant Behavior*, New York: Holt, Rinehart and Winston, 1974, p. 630; Robert Bell, *Social Deviance*, Homewood, Illinois: Dorsey Press, 1976, p. 211; Gibbs, *op. cit.*, p. 53.

[110]4 George IV, c. 52, s. 1.

[111]Williams, *op. cit.*, p. 280.

[112]Herbert Bloch and Gilbert Geis, *Man, Crime and Society*, New York: Random House, 1970, p. 64.

[113]*Ibid.*

[114]*Commonwealth v. Mink*, 123 Mass. 422; *State v. Carney*, 69 N.J. Law 478, 55A. 44; *Southern Life and Health Ins. Co. v. Wynn*, 29 Ala. App. 207, 194 So. 421; *State v. Levelle*, 13 S.E. 314, 34 S.C. 120.

[115]*Hundert v. Commercial Travelers' Mut. Acc. Ass'n. of America*, 244 App. Div. 459, 279 N.Y.S. 555, 556; *Burnett v. People of State of Illinois*, 204 Ill. 208, 68 N.E. 505, 510.

[116]*State v. Campbell*, 217 Iowa 848, 251 N.W. 717, 92 A.L.R. 1176; *Prudential Ins. Co. of America v. Rice*, 52 N.E. 2nd 624, 222 Ind. 231; *Grace v. State*, 69 S. W. 529 Texas.

[117]*Commonwealth v. Bowen*, 13 Mass. 356.

[118]*McMahan v. State*, 968 Ala. 70, 53 So. 89; *Turner v. State*, 119 Tenn. 663, 108 S.W. 1139, 15 L.R.A., N.S.

[119]*State v. Levelle, op. cit.*

[120]Williams, *op. cit.*, p. 283.

[121]Clinard, *op. cit.*, p. 632; Bloch and Geis, *op. cit.*, pp. 65-66; "Crime of Suicide," *op. cit.*

[122]Henry Black, *Black's Law Dictionary*, St. Paul, Minnesota: West Publishing Company, 1968, p. 1602.

[123]Henry Fairchild (ed.), *Dictionary of Sociology*, Paterson, New Jersey: Littlefield, Adams and Company, 1962, p. 312; The Dushkin Publishing Group, *Encyclopedia of Sociology*, Guilford, Connecticut: Dushkin Publishing Inc., 1974, p. 289.

[124]Emile Durkheim, *Suicide*, New York: Free Press, 1951, p. 44.

[125]Ruth Cavan, *Suicide*, Chicago: University of Chicago Press, 1928, p. 3.

[126]Williams, *op. cit.*, p. 283.

[127]*American Jurisprudence*, *op. cit.*, 22-16-37.

[128]*Ibid.*, 22-16-38.

[129]*Ibid.*, 22-16-39.

[130]Interviews with Captain Clayton Clark and Lieutenant Anthony Morris, Metropolitan Police Department, Washington, D.C., 1977.

[131]General Order number 308.4, Metropolitan Police Department, Washington, D.C.

[132]Marvin Wolfgang, *Patterns in Criminal Homicide*, Philadelphia: University of Pennsylvania Press, 1958, p. 274; Donald West, *Murder Followed by Suicide*, Cambridge, Massachusetts: Harvard University Press, 1966; Stengel, *op. cit.*; Andrew Henry and James Short, *Suicide and Homicide*, New York: Free Press, 1965; Manfred Guttmacher, *The Mind of the Murderer*, New York: Farrar, Straus, 1960; T. Dorpat, "Suicide in Murderers," *Psychiatry Digest* (1966), pp. 51-55.

[133]West, *op. cit.*, pp. 145-146.

[134]Edward Shev, *Good Cop/Bad Cops: Memoirs of a Police Psychiatrist*, Los Angeles: S.F. Book Company, 1977; Interviews with Captain Clark and Ltd. Morris, *op. cit.*

135Department of Health, Education, and Welfare, *Statistical Abstracts of the United States*, Washington DC: US Government Printing Office, 1972, p. 59.

136Bell, *op. cit.*, p. 213; Gibbs, *op. cit.*, pp. 53, 61-63; James Wilkins, "Suicidal Behavior," *American Sociological Review*, 32 (1967), pp. 286-298.

137Gibbs, *op. cit.*, pp. 57-73; Dublin, *op. cit.*, pp. 22-29; Ronald Maris, *Social Forces in Urban Suicide*, Homewood, Illinois: Dorsey Press, 1969, pp. 91-98, 107-108; Calvin Schmid and Maurice Van Arsdol, "Completed and Attempted Suicides: a Comparative Analysis," *American Sociological Review*, 20 (1955), pp. 273-283.

138*Ibid.*; "Suicide Among Youth," Special Supplement, *Bulletin of Suicidology*, 1971, pp. 2, 19, 37.

139Warren Breed, "The Negro and Fatalistic Suicide," *Pacific Sociological Review*, 13 (1970), pp. 156-162; Maris, *op. cit.*, pp. 100-107; Gibbs, *op. cit.*, pp. 64-67; Dublin, *op. cit.*, pp. 30-35.

140Maris, *op. cit.*, pp. 91-98; Dublin, *op. cit.*, pp. 22-29; Gibbs, *op. cit.*, pp. 63-66, 227-245.

141Maris, *op. cit.*, pp. 101-102; Gibbs, *op. cit.*, pp. 64-67; Dublin, *op. cit.*, pp. 74-79.

142Maris, *op. cit.*, pp. 122-123; Warren Breed, "Occupational Mobility and Suicide Among White Males," *American Sociological Review*, 28 (1963), pp. 179-188; Gibbs, *op. cit.*, pp. 68-69; Dublin, *op. cit.*, pp. 61-66.

143Bell, *op. cit.*, p. 218; Stengel, *op. cit.*; Jack Douglas, *The Social Meaning of Suicide*, Princeton, New Jersey: Princeton University Press, 1967; Douglas, *Deviance and Respectability*, New York: Basic Books, 1970, pp. 192-228; Edwin Schneidman and Norman Farberow (eds.), *Clues to Suicide*, New York: McGraw-Hill, 1957.

144Dublin, *op. cit.*, pp. 49-55, 223-225; Gibbs, *op. cit.*, p. 66; Maris, *op. cit.*, pp. 136, 156; Schmid and Van Arsdol, *op. cit.*, p. 276.

145James Coleman, *Abnormal Psychology and Modern Life*, Glenview, Illinois: Scott, Foresman and Company, 1972, pp. 347-348.

146Clinard, *op. cit.*, p. 654.

147Interview with Doris Loughlin, Chief of Mental Health Services, D. C. General Hospital, Washington, D. C., 1977.

148Clinard, *op. cit.*, p. 654.

149Michel Foucault, *Madness and Civilization: A History of Insanity in the Age of Reason*, New York: Random House, 1973; Albert Deustch, *The Mentally Ill in America*, New York: Columbia University Press, 1949; Samuel Brakel and Ronald Rock, (eds.), *The Mentally Disabled and the Law*, Chicago: University of Chicago Press, 1971; Nicholas Kittrie, *The Right to be Different*, Baltimore: The Johns Hopkins University Press, 1971; C. Ray Jeffery, "The Development of Crime in Early English Society," in Chambliss (ed.), *Crime and the Legal Process*, New York: McGraw-Hill, 1969, p. 28; Hazel Kerper, *Introduction to the Criminal Justice System*, St. Paul: West Publishing Company, 1972, pp. 70-73.

[150]*Ibid.*; Robert Dreher, "Origin, Development, and Present Status of Insanity as a Defense to Criminal Responsibility in the Common Law," *Journal of History of Behavioral Sciences*, 3 (1967), pp. 47-57.

[151]*M'Naghten's Case,* 8 Eng. Rep. 718 (1843); Sue Reid, *Crime and Criminology*, Hinsdale, Illinois: The Dryden Press, 1976, pp. 169-170; Lawrence Friedman, *A History of American Law*, New York: Simon and Schuster, 1973, pp. 514-515; Martin Haskell and Lewis Yablonsky, *Criminology: Crime and Criminality*, Chicago: Rand McNally, 1978, p. 42; Kerper, *op. cit.*, pp. 73-74.

[152]*State v. Felter*, 25 Iowa 67, 82 (1868); Friedman, *op. cit.*, p. 515; Kerper, *op. cit.*, pp. 73-74.

[153]*State v. Pike*, 49 N.H. 399, 442 (1869); Friedman, *op. cit.*, p. 515; *State v. Jones*, 50 N.H. 369, 398 (1871); Reid, *op. cit.*, p. 170.

[154]Paul Horton and Gerald Leslie, *The Sociology of Social Problems*, New Jersey: Prentice-Hall, 1974, p. 526.

[155]Kittrie, *op. cit.*, p. 65; Harry Allen and Clifford Simonsen, *Corrections in America: An Introduction*, Beverly Hills, California: Glencoe Press, 1975, p. 347.

[156]Reid, *op. cit.*, p. 166; *Williams v. Smith*, 131 N.E. 2 (1921).

[157]*Burns Indiana Statutes*, Annotated, 16-13-13-1 (22-1601).

[158]*Buck v. Bell*, 274 U.S. 200, 207 (1927); Reid, *op. cit.*, pp. 166-167.

[159]Edwin Sutherland, "The Diffusion of Sexual Psychopath Laws," in Chambliss (ed.), *op. cit.*, p. 74; Allen and Simonsen, *op. cit.*, pp. 347-349.

[160]*Skinner v. Oklahoma*, 316 U.S. 535, 539, 541 (1942); Reid, *op. cit.*, p. 167.

[161]Horton and Leslie, *op. cit.*, p. 526.

[162]*Durham v. United States*, 214 F.2d 862, 871 (1954); Reid, *op. cit.*, p. 170; Haskell and Yablonsky, *op. cit.*, p. 42; Kerper, *op. cit.*, p. 74.

[163]P. J. Fitzgerald, *Criminal Law and Punishment*, London: Oxford University Press, 1962, p. 131.

[164]Joint Commission on Mental Illness and Health, Action For Mental Health, *Final Report*, New York: Basic Books, 1961.

[165]*Model Penal Code*, sections 4.01, 4.02, 1962; Kerper, *op. cit.*, pp. 75-77; Haskell and Yablonsky, *op. cit.,* p. 43; Reid, *op. cit.*, p. 170.

[166]Horton and Leslie, *op. cit.*, pp. 526-527; Clinard, *op. cit.*, p. 619; President's Commission on Law Enforcement and the Administration of Justice,

Challenge of Crime in a Free Society, Washington, D.C.: US Government Printing Office, pp. 228-229.

[167]*State v. Cavitt*, 157 N.W. 2d 171 (1968); 396 U.S. 996 (1970); Reid, *op. cit.*, pp. 167-168.

[168]*United States v. Browner*, 471 F.2d 969 (1972); Reid, *op. cit.*, p. 170.

[169]*Jackson v. Indiana*, June 7, 1972 (number 70-5009).

[170]*Davy v. Sullivan*, 354 F. Supp. 1320.

[171]Clinard, *op. cit.*, pp. 587-597.

[172]Henry Black, *Black's Law Dictionary*, St. Paul, Minnesota: West Publishing Company, 1968, p. 929.

[173]*Ibid.*, p. 935.

[174]*Ibid.*, p. 930.

[175]*Ibid.*

[176]*Ibid.*, p. 931.

[177]*Ibid.*, p. 932.

[178]*Ibid.*

[179]*Ibid.*, p. 1392.

[180]*Ibid.*, pp. 931, 933.

[181]*Ibid.*, p. 931.

[182]*Ibid.*, p. 934.

[183]*Ibid.*

[184]*Ibid.*, p. 1011.

[185]*Ibid.*, pp. 933, 935.

[186]*Ibid.*, p. 935.

[187]*District of Columbia Code*, Annotated, Washington, DC: US Government Printing Office, 2, 1973, 21-501, 1287.

[188]*Ibid.*, 21-511, 1289.

[189]*Ibid.*, 21-512, 1289-1290.

[190]*Ibid.*, 21-513, 1290.

[191]*Ibid.*, 21-521, 1290.

[192]*Ibid.*, 21-903, 1315.

[193]*Ibid.*, 21-905, 1315.

[194]*Ibid.*, 22-3503, 1571.

[195]*Ibid.*, 22-3506 to 22-3510.

[196]Brackel and Rock, *op. cit.*, p. 36; Egon Bittner, "Police Discretion in Apprehending the Mentally Ill," *Social Problems*, 14 (1967), pp. 278-292.

[197]Brackel and Rock, *op. cit.*, p. 37.

[198]Allen and Simonsen, *op. cit.*, p. 345.

[199]National Institute of Mental Health, *Mental Illness and Its Treatment*, U.S. Public Health Service, Washington, DC: US Government Printing Office, 1970.

[200]Alan Stone, *Mental Health and the Law*, NIMH Crime and Delinquency Issues, U. S. Public Health Service, Washington, DC: US Government Printing Office, 1976, p. 43.

[201]*Mental Illness and Its Treatment, op. cit.*

[202]Kirson Weinberg (ed.), *The Sociology of Mental Disorders*, Chicago: Aldine Publishing Company, 1967; Thomas Scheff (ed.), *Mental Illness and Social Process*, New York: Harper and Row, 1967; E. G. Jaco, *The Social Epidemiology of Mental Disorders*, New York: Russell Sage Foundation, 1960; H. W. Dunham, *Community and Schizophrenia: An Epidemiological Analysis*, Detroit: Wayne State University Press, 1965.

[203]Robert Faris and Warren Dunham, *Mental Disorders in Urban Areas*, Chicago: University of Chicago Press, 1939; August Hollingshead and Frederick Redlich, *Social Class and Mental Illness*, New York: John Wiley, 1958; Hollingshead et al., "Social Mobility and Mental Illness," in Weinberg, *op. cit.*, pp. 48-53; Leo Srole and Thomas Langner, "Socioeconomic Status Groups: Their Mental Health Composition," in Weinberg, *op. cit.*, pp. 33-47; Langner and Stanley Michael, *Life Stress and Mental Health*, New York: Free Press, 1963; James Rinehart," *Social Problems*, 15 (1968), pp. 478-488.

[204]Faris and Dunham, *op. cit.*, pp. 23-81, 143-150; Hollingshead and Redlich, *op. cit.*, pp. 220-302, 186-213; Dunham, *op. cit.*, pp. 86-198; Leo Srole et al., "Mental Health in the Metropolis," in Silverstein (ed.), *The Social Control of Mental Illness*, New York: Thomas Y. Crowell, 1968; Frank Riessman et al., *Mental Health of the Poor*, New York: Free Press, 1964; Jaco, *op. cit.*, pp. 125-173.

[205]Faris and Dunham, *op. cit.*, pp. 38-81; Jaco, *op. cit.*, pp. 32-39; Langner and Michael, *op. cit.*, p. 77; Reissman, *op. cit.*, pp. 33-34; Stephen Spitzer and Norman Denzin (eds.), *The Mental Patients: Studies in the Sociology of Deviance*, New York: McGraw-Hill, 1968.

[206]Langer and Michael, *op. cit.*, pp. 77-79; Jaco, *op. cit.*, pp. 40-59, 109-124; Spitzer and Denzin, *op. cit.*, pp. 121-147.

[207]Black, *op. cit.*, p. 196; Horton and Leslie, *op. cit.*, p. 526.

[208]Horton and Leslie, *op. cit.*, p. 526.

[209]Deutsch, *op. cit.*, p. 425; Kittrie, *op. cit.*, p. 55; U. S. Congress, Senate Committee on the Judiciary, Subcommittee on Constitutional Rights, *Hearings on Constitutional Rights of the Mentally Ill*, 87th Congress, 1st Session, Washington, DC: US Government Printing Office, 1961, p. 43.

[210]David Mechanic, *Mental Health and Social Policy*, N.J.: Prentice-Hall, 1969; Brackel Rock, *op. cit.*, pp. 36-45; Kittrie, *op. cit.*, p. 79; *Challenge of Crime in a Free Society*, *op. cit.*, pp. 228-229.

[211]Clinard, *op. cit.*, pp. 618-624; M. Greenblatt and B. Simon (eds.), *Rehabilitating of the Mentally Ill*, Washington, DC: American Association for the Advancement of Science, 1969; Shirley Angrist et al., *Women After Treatment: A Study of Former Mental Patients and Their Normal Neighbors*, New York: Appleton-Century-Crofts, 1968; David Landy and Sara Singer, "The Social Organization and Culture of a Club for Former Mental Patients," in Spitzer and Denzin, *op. cit.*, pp. 449-476; Francine Sobey, *The Nonprofessional Revolution in Mental Health*, New York: Columbia University Press, 1970; William Henry et al., *The Fifth Profession*, San Francisco: Jossy-Bass, 1971; Harry Gottesfeld (ed.), *The Critical Issues in Community Mental Health*, New York: Behavioral Publications, 1972; Arthur Bindman and Allen Spiegel (eds.), *Perspectives in Community Mental Health*, Chicago: Aldine, 1969.

Chapter 7

Gambling

Legal History

The first recorded lottery in England was in 1569 during the time of Elizabeth I. A good part of the monies raised by the lottery was to go toward the construction and maintenance of public works. In 1612 James I gave his permission for the establishment of a lottery in the colony of Virginia. Lotteries were held in London in 1627, 1631, and 1689 in order to raise money for public works projects. Under William and Mary, the crown took charge of all lotteries.[1]

In colonial America in addition to the lottery established in Virginia, there were lotteries in Boston but some Quakers in Philadelphia were opposed to a lottery for Pennsylvania in 1699. In the eighteenth century, lotteries were used as a way to finance public works projects (i.e., road building, construction of bridges and canals, and the establishment of schools and colleges). Philadelphia in 1748 held a lottery in order to purchase cannons for the defense of the city. Connecticut held a lottery to make additions at Yale in 1750. Several other colleges like Harvard, Dartmouth, Brown, William and Mary, and Union benefited from public lotteries during the eighteenth century in several colonies. The construction of Washington, DC. was partially financed by lottery.[2]

By 1832 approximately 420 lotteries were drawn in eight states. The popularity of these lotteries lead to the organization of a lottery business run by the forerunners of organized crime. Some deviant operators of lotteries sold large blocks of tickets with no intention of holding a raffle and thus obscounded with the proceeds. Others would arrange for confederates to be the winners or would award more inferior prizes than those advertised. Thus in response to the growing criminal influence in the lottery business, Pennsylvania and Massachusetts passed statutes prohibiting the sale of lottery tickets and the operation of lotteries in 1833. New York state followed with its prohibition against lotteries in 1834 and by 1840 most states had prohibitions against lotteries.[3]

While the majority of states enacted legislation banning lotteries by the time of the Civil War, Louisiana built its lottery into a large interstate project that brought in millions of dollars annually. The United States Congress in 1890 passed legislation that forbade the distribution of lottery machines and tickets through the mail. Finally in 1895 congressional statutes forbade interstate transportation of lottery tickets. This put an end to the Louisiana lottery.[4]

By the beginning of World War I, gambling had become a crime in the United States although more people than ever had an active interest in this form of social deviance. Gambling became the greatest source of revenue for organized crime. It controlled and expanded its interests from lotteries (i.e., numbers and bolita), off-track betting, bets on sports events and large dice games, to illegal casinos.[5]

The federal government began dealing with illegal gambling on a national basis in 1948 when Congress passed a statute prohibiting the operation of gambling ships off the coasts of the United States.[6] The Special Senate Committee to Investigate Organized Crime in Interstate Commerce headed by Senator Kefauver began hearings in 1950. It produced a number of statutes aimed at organized crime and in particular prohibited the interstate transportation of gambling devices. The series of statutes enacted were known as the Johnson Act.[7] During the 1950s the federal government tried to control the spread of gambling by creating statutes that allowed the Internal Revenue Service to monitor and tax betting through the use of excise and occupational stamp taxes.[8]

The United States Department of Justice in the early 1960s began seriously looking into the organized crime aspect of gambling. The federal government believed that illegal gambling provided much of the revenue for most organized crime operations. Congress passed three statutes which attacked interstate gambling facilities and prohibited the use of public communications facilities to transmit wagering information on an interstate basis.[9] In 1960 Parliament enacted the first of a series of laws legalizing gambling in Great Britain. The Omnibus Crime Control and Safe Streets Act passed by Congress in 1968 allowed the F.B.I. to use wiretapping in order to catch bookmakers.

The Organized Crime Control Act of 1970 expanded federal control over interstate gambling.[10] The Act defined a gambling business as one that involves five or more persons in the conducting, financing, directing, managing, or ownership of a business doing a gross volume of two thousand dollars per day or which operates continuously over a thirty day period and which is in violation of the law of the state where it occurs.

The Act also prohibits conspiracy to obstruct justice on the part of those involved in these operations.[11]

The federal lottery statutes were strengthened to restrict those operating lotteries from using postal, mass media, and interstate commerce facilities. The intent of these statutes was to protect the public from corrupt and fraudulent practices on an interstate level.[12] In 1975 these statutes of the United States Code were not applied to the various states that had legislated legal lotteries into operation (i.e., New Hampshire established its lottery in 1964, followed by Delaware, Illinois, Maine, Connecticut, Maryland, Massachusetts, Michigan, New Jersey, New York, Ohio, Pennsylvania, and Rhode Island).[13]

Legal Definitions

Black defines gambling as the playing or gaming for money or other stakes (i.e., to stake money or other valuables on an uncertain event). Gambling not only involves chance but the hope of gaining more money than one originally wagered. A gambler is a person who practices games of chance with the expectation of earning a living from this activity. A gambling device is an apparatus that is used and employed in gambling so that one may win or lose money or other valuables in the process of utilizing the device.[14] A gaming (i.e., gambling) house is any building, place, or room kept for the purpose of gambling. A gaming table is any table that could be used for playing any game of chance for money or valuables.[15] A lottery is a chance for a prize for a price (i.e., a scheme whereby one person pays another money and becomes entitled to receive more money or nothing in return as some formula of chance may determine; a game of chance in which small sums of money are bet for the chance of obtaining a larger sum of money.)[16] A numbers game is a game of chance in which one person selects any number and makes a bet on that number and gives amount of bet and number to the runner who enters it on a pad, the player receiving a copy, and whereby the winning number is determined each day by computation based upon prices paid on the horse races, stock market, etc. that are published in a newspaper, and the holder of the winning number receives approximately 500 times the amount of the bet.[17]

Statutes and Enforcement Policy

Any person keeping, setting up, or promoting, or being concerned as owner, agent, or clerk, or in any other manner, in managing, carrying on, promoting, or advertising, directly or indirectly, any policy lottery, policy shop, or any lottery, or shall sell or transfer any chance, right, or interest, tangible or intangible, in any policy lottery, or any lottery or shall sell or transfer any ticket, certificate, bill, token, or other device, purporting or intended to guarantee or assure to any person or entitle one to a chance of drawing or obtaining a prize to be drawn in any lottery, or in a game or device commonly known as policy lottery or policy or shall for himself or another person sell or transfer, or have in his possession for the purpose of sale or transfer, a chance or ticket in or share of a ticket in any lottery or any such bill, certificate, token, or other device, shall be fined for each said offense not more than one thousand dollars or be imprisoned not more than three years or both.[18]

Any person knowingly having in his possession or under his control, any record, notation, receipt, ticket, certificate, bill, slip, token, paper, or writing, current or not current used or to be used in violating the other provisions dealing with gambling will for each offense be fined not more than one thousand dollars or be imprisoned not more than one year, or both.[19]

Any individual knowingly permitting on any premises under his control, the sale of any chance or ticket in or share of a ticket in any lottery or policy lottery, or policy shop on such premises, shall be fined not less than fifty dollars nor more than five hundred dollars, or be imprisoned not more than one year, or both.[20]

Whoever shall set up or keep any gaming table, or any house, vessel, or place, on land or water, for the purpose of gaming, or gambling device (commonly called A, B, C, faro bank, E), roulette, equality, keno, thimbles, or little joker, or any kind of gaming table or gambling device adapted, devised, and designed for the purpose of playing any game of chance for money or property, or shall induce, entice, and permit any individual to bet or play at or upon any such gaming table or gambling device, or on the side of or against the keeper thereof, shall be imprisoned for a term of not more than five years.[21]

It shall be unlawful for any individual knowingly, as owner, lessee, agent, employee, operator, occupant, or otherwise, to maintain or aid or permit the maintaining of any gambling premises. All monies, vehicles, furnishings, fixtures, equipment, stock (including without limitation, furnishings and fixtures adaptable to non-gambling uses, and equipment and stock for printing, recording, computing, transporting, safekeeping, or communication) or other things of value used or to be used in carrying on or conducting any lottery, or the game or device commonly known as a policy lottery or policy, contrary to the provisions of the statute; in setting up or keeping any gaming table, bank, device contrary to the provisions of this statute; in maintaining any gambling premises, shall be subject to seizure by any member of the Metropolitan Police Department for the jurisdiction, and any property seized regardless of its value shall be proceeded against in the Courts by libel action brought in the name of the jurisdiction by the public attorney, and shall, unless good cause be shown to the contrary, be forfeited to the jurisdiction, and shall be made available for the use of any agency of the government or otherwise disposed of as may, by order or by regulation. Whoever violates this statute shall be imprisoned not more than one year or fined not more than one thousand dollars, or both, unless the violation occurs after one has already been convicted of a previous violation of this statute, in which case he may be imprisoned for not more than five years, or fined not more than two thousand dollars, or both.[22]

Whoever shall deal, play, or practice, or be in any manner accessory to the dealing or practicing of the confidence game or swindle known as three-card monte, or of any such game, play, or practice, or any other confidence game, play, or practice, shall be punished by a fine not exceeding one thousand dollars and by imprisonment for not more than five years.[23]

It shall be unlawful for any individual, or association of people, to purchase, possess, own, or acquire any chance, right, or interest, tangible or intangible, in any policy lottery, or any lottery, or to make or place a bet or wager, accept a bet or wager, gamble or make books or pools on the result of any athletic contest (i.e., football, baseball, softball, basketball, hockey, polo, tennis, golf, wrestling, boxing, trotting, running of horses, running of dogs, or any other sporting or athletic event or contest). Any person or association found guilty shall be fined not more than one thousand dollars or imprisoned not more than one year, or both.[24]

Bucketing or bucket-shopping is the making of or offering to make any contact respecting the purchase or sale, either upon credit or upon margin, of any securities or commodities wherein both parties thereto intend, or such keeper intends, that such contract shall be, or may be, terminated, closed, or settled according to or upon the basis of the public market quotations of prices made on any board of trade or exchange upon which said securities or commodities are dealt in and without a bona fide purchase or sale of the same. Bucketing is also the making of or offering to make any contract respecting the purchase or sale, either upon credit or upon margin, of any securities or commodities, wherein both parties intend, or such keeper intends, that such contract shall be, or may be, deemed terminated, closed, or settled when such public market quotations of prices for the securities or commodities named in such contract shall reach a certain figure without a bona fide purchase or sale of the same. Finally bucketing is the making of or offering to make any contract respecting the purchase or sale, either upon credit or upon margin, of any securities or commodities wherein both parties do not intend, or such keeper does not intend, the actual or bona fide receipt or delivery of such securities or commodities, but do intend, or such keeper does intend, a settlement of such contract based upon the differences of such public market quotations of prices at which said securities or commodities are or are asserted to be bought and sold.[25]

The individual who makes or offers to make any contract or who is the keeper of any bucket-shop shall upon conviction be fined a sum not exceeding one thousand dollars or by imprisonment for not more than one year. Any person convicted of a second offense shall be imprisoned for not more than five years. The continuing of the keeping of a bucket-shop by any person after the first conviction shall be deemed a second offense. If a domestic corporation shall be convicted of a second offense, it shall be dissolved. If a foreign corporation shall be convicted of a second offense, it shall be restrained from doing business in the jurisdiction.[26]

Any individual who shall communicate, receive, exhibit, or display in any manner any statement of quotations of prices of any securities or commodities with the intent to make, or offer to make, or to aid in making, or offering to make any contract prohibited shall be fined not more than one thousand dollars or imprisoned for not more than one year for the first offense.[27]

It is unlawful for one to pay or give, or agree to pay or give, or to promise or offer, any valuable thing to any individual with intent to influence such individual to lose or cause to be lost, or to attempt to lose or cause to be lost, or to limit or attempt to limit his or his team's margin of victory or score in any professional or amateur athletic contest in which said individual is or may be a contestant or participant; or with intent to influence such individual, in the case of any professional or amateur athletic contest in connection with which such individual (i.e., manager, coach, owner, second, jockey, trainer, handler, groom, etc.) has or will have any duty or responsibility with respect to a contestant, participant, or team who or which is engaging or may engage therein, to cause or attempt to cause the loss of such athletic contest by such contestant, participant, or team; or the margin of victory or score of such contestant, participant, or team to be limited; or with intent to influence such individual, in the case of any professional or amateur athletic contest in connection with which such individual is to be or may be a referee, judge, umpire, linesman, starter, timekeeper, or other similar official, to cause or attempt to cause the loss of such athletic contest by any contestant, participant, or team who or which is engaging or may engage therein; or the margin of victory or score of any such contest, participant, or team to be limited. Whoever violates this statute shall be punished by imprisonment for not less than one year nor more than five years and fined not more than ten thousand dollars.[28]

It shall be unlawful for any person to solicit or accept, or agree to accept, any valuable thing or a promise or offer of any valuable thing to influence such individual to lose or cause to be lost, or to attempt to lose or cause to be lost, or to limit or attempt to limit his or his team's margin of victory or score in, any professional or amateur athletic contest in which such individual is or may be a contestant or participant; or to influence such individual, in the case of any professional or amateur athletic contest in connection with which such individual (i.e., manager, coach, owner, second, jockey, trainer, handler, groom, etc.) has or will have any duty or responsibility with respect to a contestant, participant, or team who or which is engaging or may engage therein, to cause or attempt to cause the loss of such athletic contest by such contestant, participant, or team; or the margin of victory or score of such contestant, participant, or team to be limited; or to influence such individual, in the case of any professional or amateur athletic contest in connection with which such individual is to be or may be a referee, judge, umpire, linesman, starter, timekeeper, or other similar official, to cause or attempt to cause the loss of such athletic contest by any contestant, participant, or team who or which is engaging or may engage therein; or the margin of victory or score of any such contestant, participant, or team to be limited. Whoever violates any provision of this section of the statute will be imprisoned for not more than one year and by a fine of not more than five thousand dollars.[29]

Whoever is found in a gambling establishment or an establishment where intoxicating liquor is sold without a license or any narcotic drug is sold, administered, or dispensed without a license, if he knew that it was such an establishment and if he is unable to give a good account of his presence in said establishment shall be imprisoned for not more than one year or fined not more than five hundred dollars, or both.[30]

Most of the responsibility for enforcement of anti-gambling laws rests with the Metropolitan Police Department although the Federal Bureau of Investigation does enter the picture if a huge gambling operation is uncovered. Gambling enforcement has been a traditional source of serious problems to the police. Enforcement efforts have never had more than a minimal impact on illegal gambling because of public enthusiasm for the activity. Investigations of police corruption usually show that gambling is the prime source of this problem in police departments.[31]

The Gambling Branch of the Morals Division of the Metropolitan Police Department (District of Columbia) deals with all gambling law violations. Gambling squad officers serve a two year tour of duty. A large percentage of the investigations by the gambling squad is initiated as a result of unhappy bettors who have not been paid off when they have won the lottery. Many other gambling investigations are initiated based on information supplied by informants. There is a selective enforcement policy towards gambling activities by the gambling section as they would like to obtain evidence against those who organize gambling operations rather than arrest those who gamble so that gambling activities can be completely shut down.[32]

The broadness of the gambling statutes and the difficulty in obtaining evidence that stands up in court (i.e., paid informers and wire taps) have caused members of the criminal justice system to approach gambling in a predictable pattern. The members of the gambling section of the Metropolitan Police Department work with the Major Violators Branch of the United States Attorney's Office and the F.B.I. The common problem of gambling in an urban area with the generality of the statutes allows both the prosecutor and the defendant much latitude in resolving the case. Most prosecutors allow the offender to plead guilty to lesser offenses in order to get a quick conviction. The gambler knows this and readily accepts the plea to a lesser charge since many of those arrested are repeat offenders (i.e., compulsive gamblers) and sometimes cooperate with the police in gaining information on especially corrupt gambling operations. The fact that the gambling statutes carry more severe punishment for repeat offenders does not stop gamblers since they know they will only be fined the minimum or have the original charge reduced by the prosecutor.[33]

Thus the criminal justice system really prefers to arrest those in organized crime who set up and provide the money to initially conduct the various types of gambling operations in a metropolitan area. For the most part those constantly arrested are the average persons who gamble. Therefore the public prosecutor allows the typical defendant to plead guilty to a lesser charge, judges usually impose fines or dismiss the charges rather than heavily fine or imprison offenders, and gambling continues to be a common problem in the jurisdiction.[34]

The District of Columbia has a conviction rate of approximately fifty-two percent for gambling violations although less than three percent of those convicted received jail sentences. Forty-eight percent of the cases were dismissed by the prosecutor or the judge. Thus police administrators feel that their use of manpower and financial resources are best used in attempting to make strong cases against organized crime figures involved in gambling operations or use their resources for other work than that of enforcement of gambling laws.[35]

Only one percent of those arrested for all crimes in 1976 were for gambling according to the F.B.I.[36] A sample of jurisdictions in 1976 that showed the disposition of all cases indicates that out of 6,259 arrests for gambling, seventy-five percent of those arrested plead guilty to the offense charged, three percent plead guilty to a lesser offense, nineteen percent were acquitted of the charge or had their cases dismissed, and three percent were referred to juvenile court.[37]

Description of Specific Deviance

According to the National Gambling Commission, more than sixty percent of all adult Americans gamble, both legally and illegally. It is estimated that at least thirty billion dollars has been wagered in any given year during the 1970s with approximately one-third going to organized crime. At present thirty-three states have some form of legalized gambling (i.e., Nevada and New Jersey have legalized almost every form of gambling; paramutual betting is legal in thirty-three states; bingo is legal in eleven states; five states allow slot machines; poker is legal in Gardena, California; and gambling type pinball machines are legal in Illinois).[38]

It appears that most individuals gamble with friends. Approximately one in twenty individuals who gamble are of the compulsive type. This type of person ultimately has problems with his or her family or marriage, commits the crime of embezzlement, or gets involved with loan sharks who represent organized crime. Despite these forms of deviance attributed to gambling, most people surveyed are in favor of some form of legalized gambling in their state.[39]

Most gambling operations in metropolitan areas of the United States have been established and are controlled by organized crime. An elaborate hierarchy has been created where the customer places his bet with the small operator who in turn turns over the money collected and policy slips to runners who in turn deliver the money and slips to district offices. Those at the district level turn the money over to persons at the main office. The profits that eventually go into other organized crime operations such as loan sharking are passed from so many levels of the organization that it is virtually impossible to trace those at the top who make decisions as to where the illicit funds ultimately should be best put to use. The telephone has been used widely for lottery and sports betting. The gambling syndicate is structured in such a way so as to prevent heavy losses (i.e., more money may be bet on a number or sports event than an operator can pay off if the number should win). To counteract this problem operators bet some of their own money on that number or game. This "layoff" betting is performed through a network of local, regional, and national layoff personnel who take bets from the street level of gambling operations.[40]

Notes

[1] John Ashton, *A History of English Lotteries,* London: Leadenhall Press, 1893; John Ezell, *Fortune's Merry Wheel,* Cambridge, Massachusetts: Harvard University Press, 1960; Robert Herman (ed.), *Gambling,* New York: Harper and Row, 1967; Commission on the Review of the National Policy Toward Gambling, *Gambling in America,* Washington, D. C.: Government Printing Office, 1976.

[2] *Ibid.*

[3] *Ibid.*

[4] Ezell, *op. cit.,* pp. 13-14.

[5] Herbert Marx, "Gambling in America," *The Reference Shelf,* 23 (1952); Fred Cook, "Gambling, Inc.," *The Nation,* 191 (1960); Henry Chafitz, *Play the Devil,* New York: C. N. Potter Publishing Company, 1960; "Gambling," *The Annals,* 269 (1950); The President's Commission on Law Enforcement and Administration of Justice, *Task Force Report: Organized Crime,* Washington, DC: US Government Printing Office, 1967, p. 2.

[6] *United States Code,* title 18, section 1083.

[7] *United States Code*, title 15, sections 1171-1177.

[8] *United States Code*, title 26, sections 4401-4411.

[9] *United States Code*, title 18, sections 1084, 1952, 1953.

[10] Public Law 91-452, 84 Stat. 922, October 15, 1970.

[11] *United States Code*, title 18, sections 1955, 1511.

[12] *United States Code*, title 18, sections 1301-1304; 1307; 1953; title 39, section 3005.

[13] *Gambling in America, op. cit.*; Congressional Research Service, Library of Congress, *Legalized Gambling in the United States: A Survey*, August 11, 1971, pp. 1-3.

[14] Henry Black, *Black's Law Dictionary*, St. Paul, Minnesota: West Publishing Company, 1968, p. 808.

[15] *Ibid.*, p. 809.

[16] *Ibid.*, p. 1097.

[17] *Ibid.*, p. 1218.

[18] *District of Columbia Code*, Annotated, Washington, DC: US Government Printing Office, 1973, 2, 22-1501, 1407.

[19] *Ibid.*, 22-1502, 1411.

[20] *Ibid.*, 22-1503, 1415.

[21] *Ibid.*, 22-1504, 1415.

[22] *Ibid.*, 22-1505, 1416-1417.

[23] *Ibid.*, 22-1506, 1419.

[24] *Ibid.*, 22-1508, 1419-1420.

[25] *Ibid.*, 22-1509, 1420-1421.

[26] *Ibid.*, 22-1510, 1421.

[27] *Ibid.*, 22-1511, 1421.

[28] *Ibid.*, 22-1513, 1422.

[29] *Ibid.*

[30] *Ibid.*, 22-1515, 1423.

[31] Lawrence Sherman (ed.), *Police Corruption: A Sociological Perspective*,

Garden City, New York: Anchor Books, 1974; *Gambling In America, op. cit.*; Task Force Report, Organized Crime, *op. cit.*, p. 2.

[32]Interview with Inspector Charles Light, commander, morals division of Metropolitan Police Department of Washington, DC, 1977; interview with Lt. Richard Simmonds, commander, gambling section, M.P.D. (D.C.), 1977; interview with Sergeant William Martin, gambling squad, M.P.D. (D.C.), 1977.

[33]*Ibid.*

[34]Ibid.; Donald Cressey, *Theft of the Nation: The Structure and Operations of Organized Crime in America,* New York: Harper and Row, 1969, pp. 74-77, pp. 267-268.

[35]*Ibid.*; Cressey, *op. cit.*, pp. 283-287.

[36]Uniform Crime Reports of the F.B.I., *Crime in the United States—1976,* Washington, DC: US Government Printing Office, p. 184.

[37]*Ibid.*, p. 217.

[38]Gambling in America, *op. cit.*; Rufus King, *Gambling and Organized Crime,* Washington, D.C: Public Affairs Press, 1969; Herbert Bloch, "The Gambling Business: An American Paradox," *Crime and Delinquency,* 8 (1962), pp. 355-364; Robert Pursley, *Introduction to Criminal Justice,* Encino, California: Glencoe Press, 1977, p. 99.

[39]Bloch, *op. cit.*; *Gambling in America, op. cit.*; Ned Polsky, *Hustlers, Beats, and Others,* Garden City, New York: Anchor Books, 1969; Louis Lawrence, "Bookmaking," *The Annals,* 269, (1950), pp. 46-54; Herman, *op. cit.*; Cook, *op. cit.*; Irving Zola, "Observations on Gambling in a Lower Class Setting," in Howard Becker (ed.), *The Other Side,* New York: Free Press, 1964, pp. 247-260; George McCall, "Symbiosis: The Case of Hoodoo and the Numbers Racket," in Becker, *The Other Side,* pp. 51-66.

[40]King, *op. cit.*; Cressey, *op. cit.*; *Task Force Report: Organized Crime, op. cit.*; Pursley, *op. cit.*; Marshall Clinard and Richard Quinney, *Criminal Behavior Systems: A Typology,* New York: Holt, Rinehart and Winston, 1973, pp. 224-226, 239-241, 247; Herbert Bloch and Gilbert Geis, *Man, Crime and Society,* New York: Random House, 1970, pp. 190-216; "Combating Organized Crime," *The Annals,* 347 (1963); Estes Kefauver, *Crime in America,* Garden City, New York: Doubleday, 1951; "Organized Crime", *Crime and Delinquency,* 8 (1962), pp. 325-407; Gus Tylor (ed.), *Organized Crime in America: A Book of Readings,* Ann Arbor, Michigan: University of Michigan Press, 1962; Permanent Subcommittee on Investigations, Senate Committee on Government Operations, *Gambling and Organized Crime,* Senate Report number 1310, 87th Congress, 2nd Session, Washington, DC: US Government Printing Office, 1962.

Chapter 8

Drug Abuse and Addiction

Alcoholism

Legal History

The English Common Law did not define an alcoholic as a criminal and his drunken behavior was tolerated in public or private as long as he did not breach the peace or become disorderly. The church had jurisdiction over the chronic alcoholic since his behavior showed a lack of moral character. In 1606, Parliament passed the Intoxication Act (I James) which made public intoxication a crime. Colonial America accepted drunkenness as criminal although most alcoholics were not really treated the same as other criminals.[1]

The first Congress of the United States was lobbied to impose prohibitive tariffs on the importation of alcoholic beverages into the country by members of the temperance movement which based their beliefs on puritan doctrines. By the 1830s there was an ideological war between the prohibitionists who wanted to stop the manufacture and sale of alcohol and the manufacturers and consumers of spirits. By the 1850s approximately forty percent of the states prohibited the manufacture and sale of alcohol but most of these laws were rescinded or modified by the 1860s. The Habitual Drunkards Act was passed by Parliament in 1879. It authorizes confinement in a retreat, upon the person's own application and admission that one is an habitual drunkard who cannot manage one's own affairs and is a danger to oneself and others in the

191

community.[2] Another attempt at prohibiting the manufacture and sale of alcoholic beverages through legislation came during the 1880s when eight states enacted statutes that were prohibitionist in nature.[3]

After 1890, the prohibitionists (i.e., Women's Party, the Woman's Christian Temperance Union, The National Temperance League of America, Prohibition Party, Anti-Saloon League and the International Order of Good Templars) attempted to get the state legislatures to pass statutes that curtailed the manufacture and sale of alcohol. These state laws failed to stop the sale of alcoholic beverages between states so the prohibitionists lobbied for congressional action. In 1913 Congress passed the Webb-Kenyon law that prevented the shipping of alcohol from "wet" states to "dry" jurisdictions. The Jones-Randall law was enacted in 1917 which made it a crime to use the United States mail to send liquor advertisements to people who lived in states that prohibited the manufacture and sale of alcohol. In 1918 Congress passed the Eighteenth Amendment to the Constitution which prohibited the manufacture, sale, and public consumption of alcohol. The Volstead Act passed by Congress in 1919 enforced the Amendment by defining what an intoxicating beverage was and forbade the wholesale manufacture, transportation, and sale of liquor but not the buying, using, or making of it for private use.[4]

By 1929 the problem of dealing with the Volstead Act made the federal government appoint a commission to study the problems of enforcement of the Act and the growing disrespect for the Eighteenth Amendment by both respectful members of the community and organized crime which provided the illicit alcohol. The Wickersham Commission reported in 1931 that there was a breakdown of federal enforcement of the liquor laws and an increase of crime and corruption on the state level concerning control of alcohol. In 1933 Congress repealed the Eighteenth Amendment and passed the Twenty-First Amendment which was adopted by the states in the same year. Thus control of liquor reverted to the states which could remain dry or become wet as each legislature decided.[5]

The campaign to change the legal status of alcoholics began in a series of test cases in the District of Columbia in 1964. Four test cases were dropped by the public prosecutor before the *Easter* case was heard in court.[6] The District of Columbia Court of Appeals in 1966 stated that a chronic alcoholic cannot be convicted of the crime of public drunkenness which should be handled as a public health problem. The Court stated that chronic alcoholism is a sickness and a good defense to a drunkenness charge since the defendant lacks the necessary criminal intent to be guilty of a crime and cannot be punished under the criminal law.[7] The District Court of Appeals ruled in the *Driver* case that the Eighth Amendment (i.e., rules against cruel and unusual punishment) applies to chronic alcoholics as they cannot be convicted of public drunkenness.[8]

Congress passed the Hagan Act (i.e., District of Columbia Alcoholic

Rehabilitation Act) in 1967 which repealed the public intoxication statute and established a comprehensive detoxification system under the civil law. Hawaii became the first state in 1968 to abolish public drunkenness as a crime and replace it with civil statutes dealing with rehabilitation of the alcoholic.[9] The President's Commission on Law Enforcement and Administration of Justice Task Force Report on Drunkenness recommended alternatives to incarceration for alcoholics in 1967.[10]

The United States Supreme Court in 1968 upheld the Texas trial court conviction of Powell for the crime of public drunkenness but agreed with the decisions reached by the lower courts in the *Easter* and *Driver* cases. The Court concluded that they could not decide whether alcoholism is a disease or not and that the defendant was not found guilty because he was an alcoholic but because he was drunk in public; and that defendant's conviction did not violate his Eighth Amendment rights. The Court also stated that until rehabilitation centers are created, a jail sentence can be of some use in sobering the alcoholic, and indefinite civil commitment for treatment purposes would be worse than a criminal sentencing. The Court felt that it did not have the expertise to decide whether an alcoholic lacks the necessary criminal intent to be guilty of a crime.[11] The Supreme Court's decision in *Powell* is somewhat confusing when compared to the lower courts' findings in *Easter* and *Driver*.

In 1966 the National Center for Prevention and Control of Alcoholism was established in the National Institute of Mental Health of H.E.W. to develop and deal with programs concerning the use of alcohol in society. In 1968 Congress passed the Alcoholic and Narcotic Addict Rehabilitation Act. Congress passed the Comprehensive Alcohol Abuse and Alcoholism Prevention, Treatment, and Rehabilitation Act and established the National Institute on Alcohol Abuse and Alcoholism within NIMH in 1970.[12]

The Amercian Medical Association defined alcoholism as a form of drug dependence and an illness in 1970.[13] The American Bar Association and the American Medical Association Joint Committee on Alcoholism published a model act in 1971 that stated that the laws against public drunkenness should be rescinded except where the individual is disorderly. All alcoholics who were not disorderly should be handled at civil detoxification centers.[14] This was one of the recommendations of the Task Force on Drunkenness of the President's Commission of 1967. Also in 1971, the National Conference of Commissioners, representing the fifty state governments adopted the Uniform Alcoholism and Intoxication Treatment Act that recommended the decriminalization of public intoxication and the civil treatment of alcoholics as ill people. The Department of Health, Education, and Welfare of the federal government has been working with the states to have them accept the noncriminal definition of the alcoholic and develop treatment programs.[15] As of 1976 twenty-five states had adopted the Uniform Act and another twelve states had adopted some of the basic provisions of the act while three states had legislation pending.[16]

Legal Definitions

Black defines a drunk as one who is so far under the influence of alcohol that his judgment is impaired and his self-control is lost. A drunkard is one who is always getting drunk.[17] An habitual drunkard is an individual who has a fixed habit of frequently getting drunk but has periods of being sober that may last weeks at a time.[18]

Alcoholism is the pathological effect of excessive indulgence in alcoholic beverages.[19] Drunkenness is the condition of an individual whose mind is affected by the immediate use of alcoholic beverages (i.e., the normal mental and physical condition of the person is altered due to intoxication).[20] Habitual drunkenness, intoxication, or intemperance is the custom or habit of getting drunk. These terms do not imply continuous drinking but rather a normal routine for a person which interferes with one's daily routine at home and work and is a source of problems for both the individual and others dealing with him on a continuous basis.[21]

Statutes and Enforcement Policy

At the present time half the states of the United States have decriminalized public intoxication. Several other states have adopted some form of comprehensive treatment legislation but have not decriminalized all forms of public drunkenness.[22] The Uniform Alcoholism and Intoxication Treatment Act states that it is the policy of the state that alcoholics and intoxicated persons may not be subjected to criminal prosecution for their consumption of alcoholic beverages, but should be given a series of treatments in order that they may be able to lead as normal a life as possible so as to be a productive member of the community.[23]

The Uniform Act requires that the states establish programs for the treatment of alcoholics and those who are drunk. Intoxicated individuals and drunkards should be assisted to their residences or to treatment facilities by the police or emergency service personnel (i.e., fire department or ambulance services) in protective custody under civil law. Political subdivisions of each state (i.e., counties and municipalities) are prohibited from adopting any statute making public drunkenness or any related behavior or condition with the exception of drunk driving a criminal offense or the subject of any sanction of any kind.[24]

Last the Uniform Act suggests a treatment program that should be part of the administrative procedure for the state to follow. There should be emergency treatment provided in dealing with the alcoholic or drunkard who is incapacitated and in need of immediate care. There should also be in-patient treatment or institutionalized care for those who need it. Treatment should be a combination of out-patient as well as in-patient services. Last there should be community follow-up services to attempt to re-integrate the former alcoholic back into a normal life style.[25]

The statute dealing with the alcoholic in the District of Columbia states that all public officials shall take cognizance of the fact that public intoxication shall be handled as a public health problem rather than as a criminal offense; that a chronic alcoholic is a sick person who needs, is entitled to, and shall be provided adequate medical, psychiatric, institutional, advisory, and rehabilitative treatment services of the highest caliber for his illness. The statute specifically provides that the intoxicated person will be taken into protective custody by the police and either taken to his home or if in need of medical care or a danger to himself taken to the detoxification center in the District and be held for forty-eight hours for treatment.[26]

The D. C. Code states that a chronic alcoholic who is alleged to be unfit to manage or control his estate properly can be summoned before a court and jury and if found to be unfit to manage or control his estate, a fit person shall be appointed by the court to be committee of the person so declared unfit to manage or control his estate.[27] The committee shall control the estate of the alcoholic, both real and personal, and collect all debts owed and pay all debts in the name of said alcoholic. The committee shall apply part of the income of the estate to the maintenance of the alcoholic and his family.[28]

If an individual is found to be driving while under the influence of alcohol, he is liable for a fine of five hundred dollars, a sentence of up to six months in jail, or both, for the first offense. A second arrest for drunk driving can result in a fine up to one thousand dollars, a jail term of up to one year, or both.[29]

The National Institute on Alcohol Abuse and Alcoholism stated that for the year 1971, thirty-five thousand people were arrested for crimes against the person. Arrest reports show that sixty-four percent of all those arrested for homicide had been drinking, forty-one percent of those arrested for assault, thirty-four percent of all those arrested for forcible rape, and twenty-nine percent of those arrested for other sex crimes.[30] It is estimated that offenders processed through the criminal justice system who committed alcohol related violent crimes cost our society over five hundred million dollars annually (i.e., 308 million cost to the police, 43 million cost to the courts, 71 million to the jails, 76 million to the prisons, and 25 million to alcoholic rehabilitation programs).[31]

In states that have not accepted the Uniform Act in all its provisions or rejected the Act entirely, individuals are arrested for drunkenness, public intoxication, being a habitual or common drunkard, drinking in public, or being drunk and disorderly. In states that have adopted the Uniform Act, police still arrest alcoholics but charge them with such offenses as vagrancy, loitering, driving while intoxicated (DWI), or disorderly conduct.[32]

In 1976, fourteen percent of those arrested by the police were arrested for public drunkenness, eleven percent for driving under the influence, four percent for liquor law violations, seven percent for disorderly conduct, and one-half of one percent for vagrancy. It is impossible to deduce what percentage of those arrested for disorderly conduct and vagrancy were alcoholics.[33] A higher percentage of inner city residents were arrested for drunkenness (i.e., 14% to 10%), disorderly conduct (i.e., 8% to 7%), and vagrancy (i.e., .5% to .2%) than suburban residents. On the other hand a higher percentage of suburbanites were arrested for driving under the influence (i.e., 12% to 9%) and liquor law violations (5% to 4%).[34]

The disposition of those processed through the criminal justice systems of selected jurisdictions in 1976 was as follows: 85% of those arrested for drunkenness plead guilty to the original charge, 1% plead guilty to a lessor charge, 12% were acquitted or had their cases dismissed, and 2% were referred to juvenile court. Seventy-six percent of those arrested for driving under the influence plead guilty to the original charge, 13% plead guilty to a lessor offense, 10% were acquitted or had their cases dismissed, and 1% were referred to juvenile court. Sixty-eight percent of those arrested for liquor law violations plead guilty to the offense charged, 1% plead guilty to a lessor charge, 9% were acquitted or had their case dismissed, and 22% were referred to juvenile court. Seventy percent of those arrested for disorderly conduct accepted the original charge, 1% accepted a lessor charge, 20% were acquitted or had their cases dismissed, and 9% were referred to juvenile court. Sixty-one percent of those arrested for vagrancy plead guilty to the offense charged, 1% accepted a lessor charge, 30% were acquitted or had their cases dismissed, and 9% were referred to juvenile court.[35]

The police have a great deal of discretionary power when dealing with a person who is drunk. They can take the individual home, take him to a public detoxification center or hospital that has a unit dealing with alcoholics, or arrest the individual and take him to the municipal or county jail. Arrests for public intoxication vary from jurisdiction to jurisdiction depending on both the type of statutes and the policy of the police departments toward alcoholics. Police officers often arrest an individual on the basis of age, race, and social class as much as the circumstances under which the person is found to be drunk (i.e., skid row bum, college students at a bar or apartment party, minority group members drinking on the street in public, or an apparently affluent citizen who is making a fool of himself at a hotel function or family celebration like a wedding).[36]

An alcoholic who is placed in a municipal or county jail subsequent to arrest is usually placed in what is euphemistically called a drunk tank (i.e., a large holding cell that can accomodate many individuals). The typical drunk tank has no place to sit or lie down and is usually without proper sanitary facilities and ventilation. Thus a drunk who is not sick when he enters the cell usually becomes sick from the stench of others already ill. Since medical care is minimal or not available at all, many alcoholics are not properly screened for any complications resulting from their intoxication. Sometimes a drunk will die in the cell before anyone realizes he was critically ill. The drunk who can make bail is usually released after he sobers up and the forfeiture of the bail bond is accepted in lieu of a court appearance. This usually applies in cases where the alcoholic is middle class or has a steady job.[37]

Skid row types and other indigent alcoholics usually stay in the drunk tank until enough individuals are together to be taken before a magistrate for their hearing. Most often this is the next morning or at night court, epecially on Friday and Saturday nights in major metropolitan areas. Criminal law procedure and Constitutional guarantees rarely apply in cases of drunkenness. Most offenders are rapidly processed and cither fined and released or sentenced to short term stays in the jail. At any rate most alcoholics find themselves back on the street and if they are chronic sufferers with no job or money will usually be re-arrested in a matter of hours or days (i.e., some chronic alcoholics spend much of their time being arrested and released, re-arrested and re-released on an average of two or more times in a given week which adds up to possibly fifty arrests per year).[38]

Driving while intoxicated is a crime in all jurisdictions in the United States yet relatively few drivers are arrested and charged with this serious offense. Approximately 838,000 individuals were arrested for drunken driving in 1976.[39] This figure is only the tip of the iceberg since most individuals manage to avoid arrest or are allowed to plead guilty to lessor offenses in court. Approximately one half of the 50,000 highway deaths and 750,000 of those seriously injured in traffic accidents yearly are attributable to drunk driving and drunk drivers.[40] The costs of such motor vehicle accidents with resulting loss of life and property damage was estimated to be approximately five billion dollars in 1976.[41]

Most Americans feel that drunk drivers should be severely punished yet most offenders are usually not treated as criminals by members of the community. More suburbanites are arrested for drunk driving than inner city residents, more males than females, and more individuals over twenty-five years of age than under that age. It appears that those who are initially arrested for drunk driving usually repeat the offences within a relatively short period of time although they may not be apprehended the second time. A fatality caused by a drunk driver could result in a criminal charge of negligent manslaughter and a serious injury to another driver or a pedestrian could bring a five year sentence in prison as a felony conviction but most alcoholics who drive do not consider the consequences of their actions behind the wheel.[42]

Description of Specific Deviance

There are approximately ten million problem drinkers in the United States today and the problem appears to be on the increase. Thus alcoholism is the most serious drug problem in the country with an estimated twenty-five billion dollars wasted in economic loss due to this problem.[43] In 1976, over one million individuals were arrested for drunkenness (93% male and 7% female). An additional one and three quarters million people were also arrested on alcohol related charges.[44] Thus close to three million individuals were dealt with by the criminal justice system.

Several studies and surveys show that individuals who have trouble with the police and employers most frequently are those living in metropolitan areas of the East, Midwest, and West; those with either high school or higher education past the bachelor's degree level; those with either low incomes or high incomes; and those having unskilled jobs or professional/managerial positions. Those least likely to have problems with the police and employers are individuals with grade school educations, residents of rural areas, those residing in the South, those with low incomes, and those employed as unskilled workers.[45]

Most of the studies point to the fact that just about any individual from a given subculture in our society (i.e., race, ethnic, religious, regional, urban-rural, and social class) or ascribed status group (i.e., age, sex, and marital status) can be an alcoholic and have problems with the criminal justice system at any given time.[46]

It appears that those who most frequently encounter trouble with the police due to their drinking habits are those in the age cohorts 18-21 and 40-49 while those having the least problem with the law and drinking are over sixty-five years of age (i.e., the latter typically drink in private).[47] More men than women are problem alcoholics in general but more white males than Black have difficulties with the police although more Black women than white are problem drinkers.[48] Married individuals are less often problem drinkers than unmarried, divorced, or widows/widowers.[49] Protestants of unspecified denominations, Catholics, and those with no religious affiliations are more prone to the problem drinkers than Jews, Methodists, and Mormans.[50] The Irish-Americans appear to have more problems concerning intoxication than other ethnic groups while Italian-Americans have the least problems with alcoholism.[51] Chinese-Americans appear to have the lowest rates of public intoxication while Blacks and American Indians have the highest rates of problems with alcohol.[52]

A special class of alcoholics has drawn the wrath of the community and immediate attention and action by the police. This class of drunkards is the skid row or skid road bum (male and female). They usually congregate in slum/transitional areas of the largest cities like the bowery area of New York, South State Street area of Chicago, and other similar areas of Philadelphia, Los Angeles, San Francisco, etc. These "colorful" vagrants constitute less than ten percent of the chronic alcoholics of our population yet they account for more than sixty percent of the arrests (i.e., some arrested for public drunkenness who are skid row bums have been to court as many as twenty or more times in a given year in some jurisdictions).[53]

The typical skid row alcoholic is more a public nuisance than a criminal. He or she is typically an unemployed individual who has serious personal problems and uses drink as an escape from reality. Many of these individuals and the slum areas with the typical bars and flophouses are tourist attractions and part of our American heritage. Often the police leave the skid row individuals alone unless they cannot take care of themselves or are annoying the general public.[54]

Drug Addiction

Legal History

The non-medical use of opium was legal in England as well as the United States in the late eighteenth century and throughout the nineteenth century. Opium was legally imported as well as grown within the United States during this period. In fact opium was legally grown in America until almost mid-twentieth century.[55]

State Laws

San Francisco was the first municipality to pass an ordinance in 1875 prohibiting the smoking of opium in so-called opium dens. The penalty for violation of this statute was a fine, imprisonment, or both.[56] Virginia City, Nevada passed an ordinance in 1876 prohibiting the smoking of opium in smoking houses. This was followed by a tougher state law in Nevada in 1878.[57] Oklahoma was the first state to ban peyote in an 1899 statute but rescinded the law in 1908.[58] The period 1883-1914 in the United States shows a gradual increase in the number of statutes passed by state and municipal governments against opium smoking and other drugs (i.e., twenty-seven laws were passed). Several of these statutes also made it a crime to possess an opium pipe.[59]

Most states since 1914 adopted statutes in line with those of the federal government dealing with the possession, sale, and giving away of such drugs as morphine, heroin, and cocaine.[60] After the enforcement of the Volstead Act (i.e., Prohibition) in 1920, marijuana slowly became a partial substitute for alcohol among many Americans.[61] In 1921 fourteen states had enacted legislation prohibiting cigarettes and bills to the same effect were under consideration in twenty-eight other state legislatures. But by 1927, all states had rescinded their anti-cigarette statutes except for sale to minors.[62] In 1922, several states passed statutes providing that the prosecution did not have to prove that the offender was in illegal possession of drugs since the burden of legality of possession of narcotics rested with the defendant. Some states made it a criminal offense to make an attempt to provide narcotics to a minor (i.e., the intent was an offense). Finally a number of jurisdictions made the buying, possessing, or selling of a hypodermic syringe or needle or other equipment without a prescription an offense.[63]

Louisiana in 1927 passed a statute providing a maximum penalty of five hundred dollars fine or six months jail term for possession or sale of marijuana. The penalties were later increased to thirty years at hard labor or even to the death penalty for sale to youth under twenty-one for the first offense.[64] Colorado passed a similar statute against marijuana in 1929.[65] New Mexico outlawed peyote in 1929 but never enforced the statute and amended it in 1959 to permit ritual use of the substance by the Native American Church of North America.[66] By 1937 forty-six states and the District of Columbia had laws against marijuana. The substance was often designated as a narcotic and penalties were as severe as those applying to the opiates and cocaine.[67] Since 1937 restrictive legislation on marijuana increased in both quantity and severity (i.e., most state statutes stated that penalties should be the same as for heroin). Thus as penalties rose for law violations concerning the opiates, they rose for law violations concerning marijuana. Nineteen states made no distinction as to the quantity of marijuana or opiates sold or in one's possession and giving away the substances was also a crime.[68] Thus the various states between 1914 and the early 1950s passed hundreds of statutes dealing with marijuana, opiates, and cocaine. Maximum penalties were increased from five years in 1914 to ten years in 1922 to twenty, forty, or ninety-nine years by 1953. Minimum sentences were increased over the decades and in most states neither probation nor a suspended sentence were allowed.[69]

By the late 1940s states began passing laws against non-prescription barbiturates.[70] By 1962 some states followed the federal example and passed statutes on the use of amphetamines for non-medical purposes.[71] The same year legislation was initiated in some states against glue-sniffing.[72] New York, California and several other jurisdictions had provisions in the 1960s that made it mandatory for the incarceration not only of drug addicts but also those who were in supposed danger of becoming addicts. This involuntary commitment of pre-addicts became known as civil commitment as initiated in California legislation in 1961 and followed by New York statute in 1963.[73] During the period 1965-1969, several states banned by statute LSD (i.e., New York, Calfornia, and Maryland).[74] By 1977, eight states (California, Colorado, Alaska, Maine, Minnesota, Ohio, Oregon, and South Dakota) passed laws reducing penalties for marijuana possession. The California statute makes possession by an individual of an ounce or less of marijuana a misdemeanor subject to a traffic type citation and a fine of up to one hundred dollars. Possession of more than an ounce or possession for sale are felony offenses. Individuals under age eighteen can be arrested for possession of any amount of marijuana.[75]

Federal Laws

The first federal legislation concerning narcotics was a statute passed in 1887 by Congress that prohibited the importation of a type of opium that was used for smoking. This statute also prohibited the importation of opium by ethnic Chinese living in the United States. Congress in 1890 limited the manufacture of opium for smoking to American citizens.[76] The Pure Food and Drug Act of 1906 required that medicines containing opiates and certain other drugs state the contents on their labels. The Act also stated that the quantity of each drug must be truly noted on the label and every drug must meet official standards of identity and purity.[77] In 1909 Congress enacted a law prohibiting the importation of opium except for medicinal purposes. Violation of the statute could bring a jail sentence as long as two years.[78] The 1909 statute was amended in 1914.[79] Congress passed another statute dealing with opium in 1914 which imposed a prohibitive tax on opium prepared for smoking within the United States.[80]

The Harrison Narcotic Act of 1914 was the first major drug legislation of the twentieth century in America. The Act provided for the registration of, with collectors of internal revenue, and the imposition of a special tax upon, all persons who produce, import, manufacture, compound, deal in, dispense, sell, distribute, or give away opium or coca leaves, their salts, derivatives, or preparations. The Act specifically applied to manufacturers, importers, pharmacists, and doctors who were licensed. The license could be obtained at a moderate cost. Patient-medicine manufacturers were exempted from both licensing and tax provisions provided that their products did not contain more than a specified amount of opium, morphine, cocaine, or heroin. The Act was quite clear that doctors, dentists, and veterinarians could prescribe these drugs if registered in the course of their professional practice only. Punishment for violation of this Act was up to five years imprisonment.[81]

The Jones-Miller Act of 1922 made importation of opiates and other narcotics illegal. The Act also provided that the prosecution need not prove that the defendant is in illegal possession of narcotics as the burden of proof is on the defendant to prove that his possession is legal. Whenever on trial for a violation of this Act, if the offender is shown to have or to have had possession of a narcotic drug, such possession shall be deemed sufficient evidence to authorize conviction unless the defendant explains the possession to the satisfaction of the jury. The punishment for violation of this Act was up to a five thousand dollar fine and a ten year prison term.[82]

Congress passed a statute in 1924 prohibiting the importation of heroin even for medicinal use.[83] The Federal Bureau of Narcotics established the Uniform Narcotic Drug Act of 1932 which was designed to aid the states in creating uniform statutes and law enforcement procedures and practices when dealing with narcotics.[84] The Federal Bureau of Narcotics also lobbied the various states to enact legislation against marijuana. By 1937 forty-six states and the District of Columbia had laws prohibiting marijuana which were as severe as those enacted against morphine, heroin, and cocaine, although, like the latter drug, marijuana was not a narcotic.[85]

The Marijuana Tax Act of 1937 fully recognized the medicinal use of the drug and specified that physicians, dentists, veterinarians, and other licensed persons could continue to prescribe cannabis if they paid a license fee of one dollar per year, that druggists who sold it should pay a license fee of fifteen dollars per year, that growers should pay twenty-five dollars per year, and that importers, manufacturers, and compounders should pay fifty dollars per year. Only the non-medicinal untaxed possession or sale of marijuana was outlawed on the federal level.[86] The Federal Bureau of Narcotics pressured the United States Pharmacopoeia to remove marijuana as an accepted drug in 1942 although it had been listed since 1850.[87] The Opium Poppy Control Act of 1942 prohibited the growth of this poppy in the United States and its territories except under license.[88] By the late 1940's the Food and Drug Administration and Federal Bureau of Narcotics had begun seizing illicit supplies of non-prescription barbiturates and arresting individuals selling and possessing them.[89]

The Boggs Amendment of 1951 was a response to the Kefauver Committee on Crime of the United States Senate which examined the link of organized crime to narcotics and marijuana. This congressional amendment attached mandatory minimum sentences to narcotic violations with no suspended sentence or probation for repeaters.[90] The Narcotics Control Act of 1956 made penalties for possession and sale of narcotics and marijuana more severe and inflexible than the Boggs Amendment, especially sales to juveniles.[91]

In 1962 the Food and Drug Administration began a crackdown on legal sources of amphetamines.[92] By 1965 the Food and Drug Administration passed regulations concerning LSD and Congress passed a law restricting the use of the drug for scientific purposes. The National Institute of Mental Health controlled the distribution of LSD for research.[93] The Community Mental Health Centers Act of 1963 provided federal aid for state and local treatment of mental illness which included drug dependence cases.[94]

The Federal Drug Abuse Control Amendments of 1965 were made to strengthen further the drug laws relating to amphetamines, barbiturates, and other drugs. It allowed the Food and Drug Administration to keep tabs on the manufacturers and wholesalers of these substances. The Amendment made it a crime to possess these substances without a prescription and added severe penalties for sale of these drugs to youth under the age of 21.[95] The Narcotic Addict Rehabilitation Act of 1966 allowed civil commitment of a drug addict in lieu of incarceration. The Act implied that a ninety day mandatory treatment could be imposed if the individual did not volunteer for treatment.[96] The Alcoholic and Narcotic Addict Rehabilitation Amendment of 1968 provided special grants for treatment of addicts. The Federal Bureau of Prisons would provide institutional and community aftercare for certain types of narcotic offenders.[97]

The Comprehensive Drug Abuse Prevention and Control Act of 1970 removed the tax base of control and eliminated the Harrison Act, the Opium Smoking Act, the Marijuana Tax Act, the Narcotics Control Act, and other congressional acts dealing with drugs. The Act defined categories (i.e., schedules) of drugs on the basis of potential abuse and harm. Federal law took jurisdiction over all scheduled drugs and enforcement authority resided in the Department of Justice. Criminal penalties were generally reduced for all opiates, cocaine, marijuana, and other "dangerous" substances.[98] This Act simplified all the fifty-five previous federal drug laws that were passed since 1914 to supplement the Harrison Act. The year 1970 also was noted for an act of Congress allowing federal agents under certain circumstances to enter the homes or apartments of private citizens without knocking in order to secure evidence against drug dealers, manufacturers, or addicts. Thus the Act of 1970 made conviction of drug abusers easier and "No-Knock" laws made arrests easier.[99]

Federal Court Decisions

The Supreme Court ruled in the *Webb* case (1919) that a prescription of drugs for an addict not in the course of professional treatment in the attempted cure of the habit, but issued for the purpose of providing the user of morphine with sufficient drugs to keep him comfortable by maintaining his customary use, was not a prescription within the meaning of the law and was not included within the exemption for the doctor-patient situation.[100] In the *Moy* case (1920), the Supreme Court ruled that possession of smuggled drugs by an addict was a violation of the law. Thus physicians were the only legal source of drugs but the Court ruled that a doctor could not legitimately prescribe drugs to cater to the appetite or satisfy the craving of one addicted to the use of the drug.[101]

In the *Behrman* decision (1922), the Supreme Court ruled that narcotic drug prescriptions were illegal regardless of the purpose the doctor might have had.[102] The Supreme Court ruled in the *Lindner* case (1925), that addiction is a disease and that a physician acting in good faith and according to fair medical standards may give an addict moderate amounts of drugs to relieve withdrawal symptoms without necessarily violating the law.[103]

In examining the decisions of the federal courts in the 1930s, a number of conclusions can be reached (i.e., *Strader, Anthony,* and *Carey* cases). First, the courts have decided when a doctor has acted in "good faith" and have never defined what "good faith" is. Second, a doctor's determination that an addict needs treatment has not been a good defense. Third, reputable doctors have been constantly convicted of violations of federal and state drug laws. Further, medical experts have also been silenced via convictions for their treatment of addicts. Last the courts have rejected their own statement that addiction is an illness, not social deviance.[104]

The Supreme Court ruled in *Rochin* (1952) that the police cannot forcibly pump the contents of a drug peddler's stomach because they suspect that he had swallowed drugs that have not been taxed.[105] The federal courts ruled in the *Blackford* case (1957) that a forcible search of a drug dealer's rectum is legal on the grounds that probable cause existed for believing that drugs were concealed there.[106] In the *Sherman* case (1958) the courts dealt with the problem of police entrapment in drug cases.[107] In the *Robinson* case (1962), the Supreme Court ruled that imprisonment merely for being an addict was prohibited by the Eighth Amendment to the Constitution. This decision did not remove the stigma of criminality from drug addiction since both purchase and possession of narcotics were still punishable offenses. But the case set precedent for the concept of civil commitment as an alternative to incarceration for drug addicts.[108]

Federal Agencies and Commissions

From the early 1900s until 1920, the Narcotics Division of the Treasury Department dealt with enforcement of federal drug laws. The Narcotics Division became part of the Bureau of Prohibition from 1920 until 1930. In 1931 the Bureau of Narcotics was set up in the Treasury Department.[109]

Although the Narcotics Division closed down all privately run narcotic dispensing clinics by 1924, the United States Public Health Service set up the first Public Health Service Hospital in 1935 followed by a second in 1938.[110]

The various federal agencies of the Departments of Treasury and Health, Education, and Welfare responsible for control of narcotics were merged and transferred in 1968 to the Department of Justice as the Bureau of Narcotics and Dangerous Drugs.[111] In 1971 the United States Bureau of Prisons established a Drug Abuse Program in sixteen federal prisons.[112] The same year a Special Action Office of Drug Abuse Prevention was set up in the Executive Office of the President to coordinate the fourteen federal agencies that were engaged in research, prevention, training, treatment, education, and rehabilitation of drug addicts (SAODAP). In 1972 the Treatment and Alternatives to Street Crime (TASC) became the primary federal mechanism for referral of pretrial and post-trial criminal offenders into community based treatment programs financed by the federal government.[113]

The National Institute of Drug Abuse of the Alcohol, Drug Abuse, and Mental Health Administration of the Public Health Service of the U.S. Department of Health, Education, and Welfare was established in 1972. This institute deals with non-law enforcement aspects of drug addiction and abuse, prevention, control, and treatment programs. The institute conducts research on drug addiction and abuse, trains professional and para-professional personnel at state and federal levels, and advises states, counties, and municipalities on training and planning for drug addiction and abuse prevention programs.[114]

The Drug Enforcement Administration of the Department of Justice was established in 1973. The DEA is charged with national and international control of narcotic and dangerous drugs. This Administration has law enforcement as well as non-law enforcement programs to achieve its purpose. It regulates the legal trade in narcotic and dangerous drugs; provides training for state, federal, and foreign law enforcement personnel; and performs law enforcement functions in coordination with state, other federal, and foreign police department personnel dealing with criminals involved in all aspects of the narcotic drug and dangerous substances trade.[115]

The Kefauver Committee (i.e., Senate Special Committee to Investigate Organized Crime in Interstate Commerce) in 1951 turned its attention to the topic of narcotics and marijuana. The McClellan Subcommittee (i.e., Permanent Subcommittee on Investigations of the Senate Committee on Government Operations) during the period 1963-1965 also dealt with narcotics.[116] In 1962, the White House Conference on Narcotic and Drug Abuse was held.[117] The President's Advisory Commission on Narcotic and Drug Abuse was established as an outcome of the White House Conference in 1963.[118] The President's Commission on Law Enforcement and

Administration of Justice set up a task force on narcotic and drug abuse which issued a report and series of recommendations in 1967.[119] The National Commission on Marijuana and Drug Abuse was set up in 1971 and issued reports in 1972 and 1973 that were critical of both traditional law enforcement and correctional facilities.[120]

Non-Governmental National Committees

The Joint Committee on Narcotic Drugs, American Bar Association and American Medical Association (ABA-AMA) issued an interim report in 1958 and a final report in 1959 which was critical of the criminal justice system's way of handling drug addicts and abusers.[121] The American Medical Association and the National Research Council of the National Academy of Sciences (AMA-NRC) issued a report in 1963 dealing with the use of narcotics in medical practice.[122] The first National Conference on Methadone Treatment was held in New York City in 1968.[123]

British Laws and Commissions

The English Parliament in 1920 enacted the Dangerous Drugs Act.[124] The Rolleston Committee in 1924 recommended that physicians freely prescribe morphine and heroin for addicted patients. The Committee after visiting the United States rejected the American model that was based on the crime control model (i.e., Harrison Narcotics Act of 1914).[125] The British Interdepartmental Committee of 1961 did not approve changes in the official policy toward drug addicts (i.e., no compulsory committal of addicts, no compulsory registration of addicts, no specialized treatment facilities for addicts). Thus the treatment of addicts remained on a voluntary basis utilizing a non-criminal justice medical approach to the problem.[126] The Brain Committee of 1966 recommended the establishment of heroin dispensing clinics in place of physician prescriptions. This change of policy applied only in the case of heroin addicts as doctors could still prescribe morphine or methadone. The clinics could prescribe all three drugs to addicts.[127] The Dangerous Drugs Act of 1967 put the Brain Committee recommendations into operation.[128]

International Laws and Commissions

The Hague International Opium Convention of 1912 was held in an attempt to get all nations to pass statutes preventing and controlling the growth, processing, and sale of opiates to drug addicts.[129] The United Nations Commission on Narcotic and Drug Abuse was established in 1950 to gather statistics and provide advice on the international drug problem to member countries. In 1961 the United Nations Single Convention on Narcotic Drugs established international treaty obligations for all participating countries.[130]

Legal Definitions

A drug is defined by Black as any substance (i.e., animal, vegetable, or mineral) used as a medicine.[131] An addict is an individual who has acquired the habit of using alcohol or narcotics to such an extent as to deprive oneself of reasonable self-control.[132] Drug addiction is the voluntary regular use of a drug (i.e., morphine, opium, cocaine, and marijuana) which causes the person to become psychologically dependent on the substance.[133] Addiction is the psychological or physiological dependence of an individual on a drug which is manifested when the person becomes dysfunctional when the supply of the drug is abruptly terminated.[134]

The Expert Committee on Addiction-Producing Drugs of the World Health Organization differentiates between drug addiction and drug habituation. Drug addiction is a state of periodic or chronic intoxication produced by the repeated consumption of a drug. It includes an overpowering desire or need to continue taking the drug and to obtain it by any means; a tendency to increase the dose; both a pyschological and physical dependence on the effects of the drug; and a detrimental effect on the person and on society. Drug habituation on the other hand is a condition resulting from the repeated consumption of a drug. It includes a desire but not a need to continue taking the drug for the sense of improved well-being which it produces; little or no tendency to increase the dose; some degree of psychological dependence on the effect of the drug, but absence of physical dependence and lack of withdrawal symptoms; and detrimental effects are primarily on the individual.[135]

The National Commission on Marihuana and Drug Abuse (1973) believes that the definitions proposed by the World Health Organization are confusing. The Commission proposes to use the term, drug dependence (i.e., actually a dependence continuum). Drug dependence involves most of our American population. The concept should be seen as a continuum starting from a low degree of dependence as measured by minimal individual preoccupation with drug-using behavior and minimal disruptive effects upon interruption of the behavior, and escalating to compulsive dependence as measured by total preoccupation with drug-using behavior and serious behavioral disruption attending deprivation of the drug. Drug dependence exists in many patterns and in all degrees of intensity depending upon the nature of the drug, the route of administration, the dose and frequency of administration, other pharmacological variables, the personality of the user, and the nature of the environment. There is no static model of drug dependence within which finite values are assigned to these various factors (i.e., drug dependence is a dynamic phenomenon).

The primary basis of dependence for all drug use is psychological reinforcement based on reward. Reward is composed of two elements (i.e., conscious and subconscious experiences of the individual and the psychosocial environment which shape the needs that produce drug-seeking behavior and result in drug experiences). When physical dependence is a part of chronic drug administration the threat of adverse withdrawal symptoms serves as a powerful secondary reinforcement for continued drug-using behavior. Drug dependence is not necessarily harmful either to the person or to the community. The social cost of drug dependence is related directly to the intensity of user-preoccupation. The compulsive extreme of drug dependence could lead to disorders or defects of behavior with serious implications for the criminal justice system as well as medical and social service administrations. On the other hand, there are many forms of drug dependence that do not cause negative social consequences for the individual and the community (i.e., widespread chronic use of tobacco and coffee).[136]

The Commission attempts to clarify the confusion concerning the definitions of drug abuse by examining the history of the definitions. The Commission states that a drug can be defined in either a scientific or a social manner. The former definition leads to the concept of drug use while the latter definition leads to the concepts of drug abuse, narcotics (i.e., habit forming, opiates and cocaine), dangerous drugs (i.e., amphetamines, barbiturates, etc.), soft drugs (i.e., marijuana, LSD, etc.), and hard drugs (i.e., opiates, etc.).

The scientific definition of a drug is any substance other than food which by its chemical nature affects the structure or function of a human being.[137] Drug use must be understood in the cultural context of the society in which it occurs. Drugs have effects other than those which are sought (i.e., drug effects vary with amount and frequency of use, the characteristics of the user, and the environment in which they are used). Therefore different cultures have applied different value-attitudes to the presumed consequences of drug use (i.e., beneficial or harmful). Each society has determined which needs are legitimate concerning drug use (i.e., legitimate and valuable with tolerable risks involved). These judgments are based on the normative system concerning specific drugs, their effects, the reasons for using a particular drug, and the type of people who use the drug. Members of society do not continue to use drugs that do not fulfill some imagined or real need. People use drugs because they feel it is useful socially or psychologically despite the fact that the drug may have no real positive effect physically on the individual. Use of specific drugs may determine group membership or status within an institution or the total community. Drugs may function as symbolic representations of rebellion, alienation, independence, or sophistication within society. Drug use cannot be explained pharmacologically (i.e., classifying substances, listing effects, and counting users and non-users) but must be explained in terms of meaning and function to people in society.[138]

Thus drug use has been a common feature of all societies throughout the history of civilization. No society has successfully eliminated drug use altogether, although most have attempted to set limits, and modern societies have tried to contain specific groups that opposed all drug use among their own members (i.e., the Mormons and other fundamentalist religious sects). Drug use can be socially controlled when it is routinized, ritualized, and structured in ways which reduce to a minimum the occurrence of drug-induced behavior which society considers harmful to its members. This is easier to accomplish in traditional (i.e., gemeinschaft) rather than urban-industrial (i.e., gesellschaft) societies. In American society responsibility for control of drug use has passed from the family and church to the school, the mass media, and the state. Thus formal, impersonal institutions have made the task of social control of drug-taking behavior very difficult, especially since the economy produces such a variety of drugs each and every year. Therefore the criminal justice system in cooperation with public legislative bodies has taken an increased role in trying to contain undesirable drug use within supposedly tolerable cultural limits.[139]

The social definition of a drug is anything but a socially neutral concept. Thus one usually thinks of a drug as a social problem or a substance that has been abused. Drug abuse is therefore synonymous with drug use. Drug abuse refers to any type of drug without regard to its pharmacologic actions. The concept creates the impression that all drug-using behavior is either good, safe, beneficial, and without negative social consequences or is bad, harmful, without benefit, and having negative social consequences.[140]

The term narcotic means a habit-forming substance such as the opiates and cocaine. Many identify narcotics with deviant subcultures and conclude that any drug used by these types of individuals is a narcotic. The term has become a symbol of socially disapproved use of drugs whether addicting or not.[141] The term dangerous drugs evolved to define those substances (i.e., hallucinogens, barbiturates, and amphetamines) that were non-narcotic.[142] Finally the terms hard and soft drugs were evolved to differentiate between the opiates and cocaine (i.e., hard) and marijuana, hallucinogens, barbiturates, and the amphetamines.[143]

Statutes and Enforcement Policy

The District of Columbia Code consists of two sections dealing with drug offenses, narcotic drugs (chapter 4) and drugs other than narcotics (chapter 7). Narcotic drugs are defined as coca leaves, opium, cannabis, isonipecaine, and opiate, and every substance not chemically distinguishable from them, and any compound, manufacture, salt, derivative, or preparation of coca leaves, opium, cannabis, isonipecaine, or opiate, whether produced directly or indirectly by extraction from substances of vegetable origin, or independently by means of chemical synthesis, or by a combination of extraction and chemical synthesis. Coca leaves includes cocaine and any compound, manufacture, salt, derivative, mixture, or preparation of coca leaves except derivatives of coca leaves that do not contain cocaine, ecgonine, or substances from which cocaine or ecgonine may be synthesized or made. Opium includes morphine, codeine, and heroin and any compound, manufacture, salt, derivative, mixture, or preparation of opium. Cannabis includes all parts of the plant Cannabis sativa L., whether growing or not; the seeds thereof; the resin extracted from any part of such plant; and every compound, manufacture, salt, derivative, mixture, or preparation of such plant, its seeds, or resin, including specifically the drugs known as American hemp, marijuana, Indian hemp or hashish, as used in cigarettes, or in any other articles, compounds, mixtures, preparations, or products whatsoever, but shall not include the mature stalks of such plants; fiber produced from such stalks; oil or cake made from the seeds of such plant; any compound, manufacture, salt, derivative, mixture, or preparation of such mature stalks (except the resin extracted therefrom); fiber, oil, or cake; or the sterilized seed of such plant which is incapable of germination.[144]

It shall be unlawful for any person to manufacture, possess, have under his control, sell, prescribe, administer, dispense, or compound any narcotic drug except as authorized. Arrests without warrant and searches of the person and seizures pursuant thereto may be made for a violation by police officers upon probable cause that the person arrested is violating such statute at the time of arrest.[145]

A narcotic drug user is any person who takes or otherwise uses narcotic drugs, except a person using such narcotic drug as a result of sickness or accident or injury, and to whom such narcotic drugs are being furnished, prescribed, or administered in good faith by a duly licensed physician in the course of his professional practice. A vagrant shall mean any person who is a narcotic drug user or who has been convicted of a narcotic offense and who has no lawful employment or visible means of support; is found in any place, abode, house, shed, dwelling, building, structure, vehicle, boat in which any illicit narcotic drugs are kept, found, used, or dispensed; or wanders about in public places either alone or in the company with a narcotic drug user or convicted narcotic law violator.[146]

Any police officer with probable cause can arrest such vagrant and submit him to be examined by a physician to determine whether there is evidence of narcotic drug usage. Upon affirmative determination that the person is a narcotic drug user, or if the person has been convicted of a narcotic offense in D.C. or elsewhere, and if such person is also a vagrant, he shall be arraigned and prosecuted under this statute. Any person found guilty shall be fined not more than five hundred dollars or jailed for more than a year, or both. The court in sentencing may in its own discretion impose conditions upon the offender which can include medical and mental examinations and treatment by proper public health and welfare authorities and confinement in a suitable institution.[147]

All narcotic drugs which are not in lawful possession and come into possession of a police officer shall be either disposed of according to regulation or turned over as evidence in any criminal proceeding.[148] No person shall obtain or attempt to obtain a narcotic drug, or procure or attempt to procure the administration of a narcotic drug by fraud, deceit, misrepresentation, or subterfuge; by the forgery or alteration of a prescription or of any written order; or by the concealment of a material fact; or by the use of a false name or the giving of a false address. Information communicated to a physician in an effort unlawfully to procure a narcotic drug, or unlawfully to procure the administration of any such drug shall not be deemed a privileged communication. No person shall willfully make a false statement in any prescription, order, report, or record required by law. No person shall for the purpose of obtaining a narcotic drug falsely assume title of, or represent himself to be a manufacturer, wholesaler, pharmacist, physician, dentist, veterinarian, or other authorized person. No person shall make or utter any false or forged prescription or false or forged written order. No person shall affix any false or forged label to a package or receptacle containing narcotic drugs.[149]

A person violating any statute or regulation for which no specific penalty is otherwise provided shall be fined not less than one hundred dollars nor more than one thousand dollars or imprisoned for not more than one year, or both. A person convicted of an offense who shall have previously been convicted of such offense or who shall have previously been convicted either in D.C. or elsewhere of a violation of the laws of the United States or of a state or subdivision thereof which would have been a violation of this statute shall be fined not less than five hundred dollars nor more than five thousand dollars, or imprisoned for not more than ten years, or both.[150]

The term dangerous drug means amphetamine, desoxyephedrine, or compounds or mixtures thereof, including all derivatives of phenolethylamine or any of the salts thereof which have a stimulating effect on the central nervous system, except preparations intended for use in the nose and unfit for internal use; barbituric acid, also known as malonylurea, and its salts and derivatives, and compounds, preparations, and mixtures thereof; other drugs or compounds, preparations, or mixtures thereof which are habit-forming, excessively stimulating, or to have a dangerously toxic, or hypnotic or somnifacient effect on the body of a human or animal. The term dangerous drug shall not include any drug the manufacture or delivery of which is regulated by federal narcotic drug laws or by the narcotic drug laws of D.C.[151]

The following acts, the failure to act as hereinafter set forth, and the causing of any such act or failure are unlawful: (1) the delivery of any dangerous drug unless such dangerous drug is delivered by a pharmacist upon a prescription and there is affixed to the immediate container of such or in which such drug is delivered a label bearing the name and address of the owner of the establishment from which such drug was delivered, the date on which the prescription for such drug was filled, the number of such prescription as filed in the prescription files of the pharmacist who filled such prescription, the name of the practitioner who prescribed such drug, the name and address of the patient, and directions for the use of the drug as contained in the prescription; or (2) such dangerous drug is delivered to a practitioner by a pharmacist for this professional to use in his practice, in which case the pharmacist may deliver the drug without affixing any additional label to the original package of such drug and must immediately record such sale and delivery by filing a suitable record of such sale and delivery in the prescription file as maintained for prescriptions for such drugs;[152] or, (3) such dangerous drug is delivered by a manufacturer's representative or drug salesman to a practitioner in the course of calling upon the practitioner, in which case the manufacturer's representative or drug salesman shall immediately record in a suitable record book the name and quantity of the drug delivered, the date such drug was delivered, and the name and address of the practitioner to whom the drug was delivered; or, (4) such dangerous drug is delivered by a practitioner in the course of his practice and the immediate container in which such drug is delivered bears a label on which appears the directions for use of such drug, the name and address of such practitioner, and the name and address of the patient;[153] the refilling of any prescription for a dangerous drug except as designated on the prescription or by the consent of the practitioner; (5) the delivery of a dangerous drug upon prescription unless the pharmacist who filled such prescription files and retains it as required; (6) the possession of a dangerous drug by any person, unless such person obtained such drug on the prescription of a practitioner, or in accordance with this statute; (7) the making or uttering by any person of any false or forged prescription or false or forged written order for the purpose of obtaining any dangerous drug; (8) the delivery of any dangerous drug to any person not lawfully entitled to receive such drug; (9) the willful making of or concealment of any material false statement or representation of any prescription, order, report, or record required by law; (10) the refusal to make available and to accord full opportunity to check any record or file as required by law; (11) the failure to keep records as required by law.[154]

Drugs exempted from the statute are such compound, mixture, or preparation of barbituric acid, its salts and derivatives that have or contain no habit-forming properties and do not have a dangerously toxic or hypnotic or somnifacient effect on the human body or of an animal; or such compound, mixture, or preparation of amphetamine, desoxyephedrine, phenolethylamine, or their salts or derivatives that do not have an excessively stimulating effect upon the central nervous system and do not have any habit-forming properties or dangerously toxic effect upon the body of a human or animal.[155]

The statute shall not be applicable to the delivery of dangerous drugs to persons included in any of the classes hereinafter or to agents or employees of such persons, for use in the normal or usual course of their business or practice or in the performance of their official duties, as the case may be, or to the possession of dangerous drugs by such persons or their agents or employees for such use: pharmacists; practitioners; persons who procure dangerous drugs for handling by or under the supervision of pharmacists or practitioners; or for the purpose of lawful research, teaching, or testing and not for resale; hospitals which procure dangerous drugs for lawful administration or use by practitioners; laboratories which procure dangerous drugs for lawful medical and scientific purposes; officers or employees of appropriate enforcement agencies of federal, state, D.C., or local governments, pursuant to their official duties; manufacturers and wholesalers; manufacturers' representatives and drug salesmen; and carriers and warehousemen.[156]

Any person who violates this statute or any regulation shall be punished for the first offense by a fine of not less than one hundred dollars nor more than one thousand dollars or by imprisonment of not more than one year, or both; and for any subsequent offense by a fine of not less than five hundred dollars nor more than five thousand dollars, or by imprisonment not exceeding ten years, or both. The conviction of any person for a violation of this statute involving any dangerous drug shall constitute ground for suspension or revocation or denial of renewal of the professional license of such person.[157] Any dangerous drug seized pursuant to any lawful search or which may have come into the custody of a police officer, the lawful possession of which cannot be established or the title to which cannot be ascertained, shall be forfeited and destroyed in the manner provided for narcotic drugs.[158]

There were approximately 500,000 arrests in the United States in 1976 for narcotic drug law violations.[159] A sample of over seven thousand persons processed through the criminal justice systems of selected jurisdictions shows that 45 percent plead guilty to the offense charged, 4 percent plead guilty to a lessor charge, 24 percent were acquitted or had their cases dismissed, and 27 percent were referred to juvenile court.[160] As Haskell and Yablonsky state the possession of a narcotic or dangerous drug or the equipment associated with such drugs provides the police with a prima facie case against anyone apprehended but there is a great amount of official disagreement on the amount and types of crimes attributable to drug addicts and abusers.[161]

The National Commission on Marihuana and Drug Abuse stated clearly that the relationship between drugs and criminal behavior is difficult to comprehend despite public opinion showing that most drug addicts supposedly resort to crime to support their habits.[162] The perpetuation of this dope fiend myth goes back to the nineteenth century and in its present form attributes all forms of violent crime to not only those addicted to the opiates but also users of marijuana and abusers of amphetamines, barbiturates, and the hallucinogens.[163]

The Commission states that marijuana use is neither a cause nor directly associated with crime (i.e., violent or non-violent). The only crimes which can be directly attributed to marijuana-using behavior are those resulting from the use, possession, or transfer of an illegal substance.[164] Barbiturates have a similar effect on people to alcohol and various studies on the relationship between the use of alcohol and the commission of violent crimes (i.e., murder, assault, etc.) show that alcohol was used by at least half of the offenders just before the crime took place. Thus a high level of barbiturate use may also be linked to violent crime.[165] Studies of amphetamine users shows that they were disproportionately involved in criminal activities (i.e., assaults, robberies).[166]

The various studies show that most opiate addicts (i.e., usually heroin) are individuals who have had long histories of delinquent or criminal behavior prior to their being identified as drug addicts. It has also been shown that opiate use becomes a further expression of deviant tendencies and most heroin addicts continue to be arrested subsequent to release from prison, hospital, or rehabilitation programs. It appears that opiate addicts tend to escalate the seriousness of their offenses and to experience more arrests after identification as addicts than before becoming addicted. Most of the crimes committed by addicts are crimes against property and/or non-violent crimes against the person in order to obtain money or goods easily converted to cash. The research shows that opiate addicts are less likely to commit homicide, rape, and assault than users of amphetamines and barbiturates.[167] Users of cocaine suffer from the same reactions as amphetamine abusers (i.e., paranoia, hostility, impulsiveness) but data indicates they commit more crimes against property than against the person.[168]

Users of hallucinogens, non-barbiturate sedative-hypnotics, glue and similar volatile inhalants are not inclined toward violent criminal behavior except in cases where there is drug-induced panic or toxic reactions. Some of the non-barbiturate sedatives (i.e., methaqualone) and the hydrocarbon solvents have a potential for inducing violent behavior although crime statistics are lacking.[169]

A thorough review of the literature by the Commission and others shows that it is difficult to establish a direct relationship between crime and the use of various drugs. But it is possible to show that drug use in combination with a number of physiological, psychological, and sociological factors may assume an important role in the causation of deviant behavior of a delinquent or criminal nature.[170]

The costs to society from criminal activity associated with all types of drugs from opiates to hallucinogens is in the billions of dollars. Most of the research has concentrated on heroin addicts and findings indicate that suppliers and users spend and earn close to one billion dollars per year.[171] If one adds to this cost, the money spent in selling and buying marijuana, cocaine, amphetamines, barbiturates, and the hallucinogens, the costs could go as high as fifteen billion dollars a year. This estimate is based on a comparison with costs of alcoholic consumption.[172] Costs to the criminal justice system can only be roughly estimated. If we assume that all 500,000 persons arrested went to jail for one twenty-four hour period at twenty dollars per person per day, the cost would be ten million dollars. If one attempts to estimate the cost of police investigation and arrest, trial, sentencing, treatment and rehabilitation in addition to incarceration, the costs must easily be somewhere in the area of one billion dollars or more (i.e., making the comparison to alcohol related criminal justice costs).[173]

The legal policy of American society towards the use of all types of drugs, whether opiates, marijuana, or the prescription drugs that are abused has been quite punitive-oriented since 1914. Thus as with alcoholic beverages during prohibition the official policy of federal, state, and local jurisdictions has been preventing people from abusing drugs and controlling individuals who are currently misusing drugs. This has left the hard and soft drug market wide open to organized crime which has found ways of always supplying and catering to the needs of Americans, poor and affluent, white and nonwhite, who want to use drugs.[174]

The Bureau of Customs, Drug Enforcement Administration, F.B.I., and the U.S. Border Patrol all work at the federal level to deal with both international and interstate problems concerning the drug market. All federal agencies are supposed to cooperate with state, county, and municipal police department divisions dealing with narcotics and dangerous drugs. The smuggling of narcotics into the United States has proven to be an impossible phenomenon to prevent since there are as many ways to smuggle as there are smugglers. Organized crime as well as amateurs have been successful at smuggling the opiates. Such drugs as marijuana are grown almost everywhere so enforcement is quite difficult. Hallucinogens can be made quite easily and transported in a variety of ways that defy detection. The drug industry cannot keep control over all the legal amphetamines and barbiturates manufactured, stored, shipped, and delivered to pharmacies and hospitals — let alone deal with those clandestine laboratories that manufacture the same substances.[175]

Local and state police are not equipped to deal with the millions of people who may be violating the criminal code statutes on drugs of any given jurisdiction. Thus most police departments have traditionally concentrated crime prevention and control efforts on the opiates and cocaine. Since the early 1960s more effort has been directed in dealing with marijuana and the other soft drugs (i.e., hallucinogens, amphetamines, and barbiturates). The drug problem is no longer one that takes the time of only metropolitan police officers since much of the soft drug and cocaine problems tend to be increasingly prevelant in the suburbs.[176]

Law enforcement practices dealing with importers and wholesalers are usually left to federal officials. Street traffic deals with the pusher and the addict or drug abuser depending on whether one is dealing with hard or soft drugs. Effective enforcement of narcotic and dangerous drug statutes is rather difficult since all aspects of a drug transaction are illegal and carried out as covertly and rapidly as possible. Police must utilize covert operations and resort to utilizing addict-informers, pro-stitutes, and other social deviants who are paid to give information on the drug trade in a given jurisdiction. Informers are either paid for their information, supplied with drugs, or let off from arrest for an offense for their cooperation with the police. The officers assigned to narcotics operations must use informant information to learn what is happening on the street and then spend time and money on the street as part of the drug subculture in order to gather evidence. This may take from several months to a year at considerable time and cost. Police may use entrapment to obtain evidence and naturally officers, prosecutors, and judges do not like these procedures since they are either unconstitutional or border on it. Further undercover officers may be exposed and either become part of the drug operation as bribed onlookers or be targets of organized crime or pushers to be shot or beaten up. Usually a discovered detective is left alone and the drug traffic moves to a different location.[177]

Description of Specific Deviance

In 1970 over 200 million legal prescriptions for drugs (i.e., stimulants, sedatives, tranquilizers, and depressants) were filled for Americans who had consulted their doctors. Barbiturates and barbiturate substitutes accounted for twenty-nine percent of these prescriptions, minor tran-quilizers accounted for thirty-nine percent, stimulants made up thirteen percent, anti-psychotics accounted for ten percent, and anti-depressants made up the rest of the total. Americans also obtained large quantities of non-prescription drugs such as sleeping agents, tranquilizing agents, and caffeine stimulants. Thus a substantial percentage of the American population of all ages, both sexes, and all types of socio-economic backgrounds use drugs legally. This does not count the millions of Americans who smoke cigarettes and use alcoholic beverages.[178]

Concerning illicit drug use in American society, all we have are estimates of the problem. It has been estimated that over one million people abuse barbiturates, almost the same number abuse amphetamines, and over one million regularly smoke marijuana. It is estimated that there are sixty thousand drug addicts in society, most of whom are dependent on heroin. This estimate is based on arrest records. Estimates of heroin users who have not been arrested are approximately 500,000 individuals. The National Commission of Marihuana and Drug Abuse survey of almost 2500 individuals concludes that six percent of the sample abused over the counter sedatives, tranquilizers, and stimulants; three percent abused prescription sedatives; four percent abused prescription tranquilizers and stimulants; fifteen percent smoked marijuana; five percent used hallucenogens; four percent abused inhalants; two percent used cocaine; and only one percent used heroin.[179]

Most of the data gathered by researchers has been on drug addicts (mainly heroin) since these people come in contact with the criminal justice system and rehabilitation programs sooner or later. Most heroin addicts are young (i.e., under age thirty). Most state they started abusing drugs by age sixteen and became addicted to heroin by age nineteen or twenty. Once addicted these individuals soon turned to crimes against property and eventually crimes against the person to secure money for their habit. Most had been arrested within five years of initiating their dependence on heroin. Few heroin addicts completed high school and while in school most were labeled as delinquent despite normal intelligence and achievement potential. Without educational and occupational skills most addicts were employed at unskilled or at best semi-skilled jobs. Many state that their heroin habit keeps them from working since they either are out looking for new supplies or more money. Thus many addicts are on welfare, being supported by friends, pimping, or prostituting themselves to take care of their habit. Consequently most addicts are poor job and vocational training risks even after being in such programs in prison or community treatment centers since their recidivism rate is high.[180]

Heroin addicts are generally inner city or older suburban area residents. Their environment is typically characterized by economic instability and family problems. Drinking and other forms of social deviance are common among immediate family members and close friends. Marital instability with high desertion and divorce rates characterizes both the addict's parents and his or her own marital situation. The addict's preoccupation with drug use is a major contributing factor in his or her social isolation and prevents him from attempting to make proper adjustments to adult roles in both the family and the community. The heroin addict has been characterized as immature, resentful of authority, passive-aggressive, sexually inadequate, anxiety-ridden, rebellious, withdrawn, socially isolated, depressed, and suicidal. The typical addict tends to repress aggressive and hostile feelings, to require immediate gratification, to be easily frustrated, and to lack self-respect.[181]

There is one special type of drug addict that does not fit this description. This is the junkie physician, nurse, dentist, and pharmacist. These individuals have access to prescription narcotics and most are able to carefully control their habit and are able to afford to maintain it. Thus these respectable members of the community rarely come in contact with the criminal justice system yet are responsible for the health and welfare of others. It is estimated that approximately ten percent of those in the medical and paramedical professions are drug addicts although few are addicted to heroin.[182]

Notes

[1]Marshall Clinard, *Sociology of Deviant Behavior,* New York: Holt, Rinehart and Winston, 1974, p. 428; President's Commission on Law Enforcement and Administration of Justice, *Task Force Report: Drunkenness,* Washington, D.C.: US Government Printing Office, 1967: US Department of Health, Education, and Welfare, *First Special Report to the US Congress on Alcohol and Health,* Washington, D.C.: US Government Printing Office, 1972: Robert Bell, *Social Deviance,* Homewood, Illinois: The Dorsey Press, 1971, p. 171; "Alcoholism, Public Intoxication, and the Law," *Columbia Journal of Law and Social Problems,* 2 (1966), pp 109-132; Robert Merton and Robert Nisbet (eds.), *Contemporary Social Problems,* New York: Harcourt, Brace and World, 1966; Paul Horton and Gerald Leslie, *The Sociology of Social Problems,* New Jersey: Prentice-Hall, 1974, p. 539.

[2]42, 43 Victoria, c. 19.

[3]*Ibid.*

[4]James Timberlake, *Prohibition and the Progressive Movement, 1900-1920,* Cambridge, Massachusetts: Harvard University Press, 1970; *First Special Report to the US Congress on Alcohol and Health, op. cit.;* Merton and Nisbet, *op. cit.;* Horton and Leslie, *op. cit.;* John Krout, *United States Since 1865,* New York: Barnes and Noble, 1955, p. 182.

[5]Krout, *op. cit.,* pp. 182-183.

[6]*First Special Report to the US Congress on Alcohol and Health, op. cit.,* pp. 85-86.

[7]*Easter v. District of Columbia,* 361 F. 2d (D.C. Cir. 1966); Clinard, *op. cit.,* p. 485; Herbert Bloch and Gilbert Geis, *Man, Crime and Society,* New York: Random House, 1970; Robert Pursley, *Introduction to Criminal Justice,* Encino, California: Glencoe Press, 1977.

[8]*Driver v. Hinnant,* 356 F. 2nd 761 (4th Cir. 1966); Bloch and Geis, *op. cit.,* pp. 327-328; Pursley, *op. cit.,* p. 105.

[9]District of Columbia Register, *D.C. Rules and Regulations,* Washington, D.C.: US Government Printing Office, 1971, title 3, section 5.1, pp. 16-17; Clinard, *op. cit.,* p. 485.

[10]*Task Force Report: Drunkenness, op. cit.*

[11]*Powell v. Texas,* 392 U.S. 514-516 (1968); Bloch and Geis, *op. cit.,* p. 328; Pursley, *op. cit.,* p. 105.

[12]National Institute of Mental Health, *National Institute on Alcohol Abuse and Alcoholism,* Washington, D.C.: US Government Printing Office, 1971.

[13]Horton and Leslie, *op. cit.,* p. 541.

[14]*First Special Report to the US Congress on Alcohol and Health, op. cit.,* p. 92.

[15]National Institute of Mental Health, *Alcoholism and the Law,* Washington, D.C.: US Government Printing Office, 1973, p. 14; Horton and Leslie, *op. cit.,* p. 541.

[16]Alcoholic Topics in Brief, *Decriminalization of Public Intoxication — Is It Working?* January 31, 1977.

[17]Henry Black, *Black's Law Dictionary,* St. Paul, Minnesota: West Publishing Company, 1968, p. 587.

[18]*Ibid.,* p. 839.

[19]*Ibid.,* p. 93; Henry Fairchild (ed.), *Dictionary of Sociology,* Paterson, New Jersey: Littlefield, Adams and Company, 1962, p. 8.

[20]Black, *op. cit.,* p. 587.

[21]*Ibid.,* p. 839.

[22]Alcoholic Topics in Brief, *op. cit.*

[23]Alcoholism and the Law, *op.cit.,* p. 14; *First Special Report to the US Congress on Alcohol and Health, op. cit.,* pp. 92-93; Department of Health, Education, and Welfare, *The Legal Status of Intoxication and Alcoholism,* Washington, D.C.: US Governmen Printing Office, 1976.

[24]*Ibid.*

[25]*Ibid.*

[26]District of Columbia Register, *op. cit.*

[27]*District of Columbia Code,* Annotated, Washington, D.C.: US Government Printing Office, 1973, 2, 21-1301, 1326.

[28]*Ibid,* 21-1302, 1326.

[29]*Ibid.,* 11-501, 11-921.

[30]National Institute on Alcohol Abuse and Alcoholism, *Alcohol and Health,* Washington, D.C.: US Government Printing Office, 1974, p. 42; R.E. Berry et al., *Further Analysis of the Economic Costs of Alcohol Abuse and Alcoholism,* National Institute on Alcohol Abuse and Alcoholism, Washington, D.C.: US Government Printing Office, 1977; Julian Roebuck and Ronald Johnson, "The Negro Drinker and Assaulter as a Criminal Type," *Crime and Delinquency,* 3 (1962), p. 21-33; Marvin Wolfgang, *Patterns in Criminal Homicide,* Philadelphia: University of Pennsylvania Press, 1958, p. 166; Austin MacCormick, "Correctional Views on Alcohol, Alcoholism, and Crime," *Crime and Delinquency,* 9 (1963), pp. 24-25; Division of Alcoholic Rehabilitation, *Criminal Offenders and Drinking Involvement,* Sacramento, California: California State Department of Public Health, 1964; Lloyd Shupe, "Alcohol and Crime," *Journal of Criminal Law and Criminology,* 44 (1954), pp. 661-664; Paul Haberman and Michael Baden, "Alcoholism and Violent Death," *Quarterly Journal of Studies on Alcohol,* 35 (1974), pp. 221-231.

[31]*Ibid.,* p. 42.

[32]*First Special Report to the US Congress on Alcohol and Health, op. cit.*; Department of Health, Education, and Welfare, *Second Special Report to the US Congress on Alcohol and Health,* Washington, D.C.: US Government Printing Office, 1975.

[33]Uniform Crime Reports of the F.B.I., *Crime In the United States—1976,* Washington, D.C.: US Government Printing Office, 1977, p. 184.

[34]*Ibid.,* pp. 192-201.

[35]*Ibid.,* p. 217.

[36]*Task Force Report: Drunkenness, op. cit.*; Frank Grad, *Legal Aspects of Alcoholism,* New York: Academic Press, 1973; Raymond Nimmer, "The Public Drunk: Formalizing the Police Role as a Social Help Agency," *The Georgetown Law Journal,* 58 (1970); Nimmer, *Two Million Unnecessary Arrests: Removing a Social Service Concern From the Criminal Justice System,* Chicago: American Bar Foundation, 1971; Wayne LaFave, *Arrest: The Decision to Take a Suspect into Custody,* Boston: Little, Brown and Company, 1965, pp. 108-110; John Murtagh, "Arrests for Public Intoxication," *Fordham Law Review,* 35 (1967), pp. 1-14; Melvin Selzer, "Alcoholism and the Law," *Michigan Law Review,* 56 (1957), pp. 237-248; Martin Haskell and Lewis Yablonsky, *Criminology: Crime and Criminality,* Chicago: Rand McNally, 1978, pp. 337-338; Lloyd Shupe, *op. cit.*

[37]*Ibid.*

[38]David Pittman (ed.), *Alcoholism,* New York: Harper and Row, 1967; Pittman and Wayne Gordon, *Revolving Door: A Story of the Chronic Police Case Inebriate,* New York: Free Press, 1958; Earl Rubington, "The Chronic Drunkenness Offender," *The Annals,* 315 (1958), pp. 65-72; *Task Force Report: Drunkenness, op. cit.,* pp. 2, 9; James Spradley, *You Owe Yourself a Drink: An Ethnography of Urban Nomads,* Boston: Little, Brown and Company, 1970; Spradley, "The Moral Career of a Bum, *Transaction,* 7 (1970), pp. 17-29; Nimmer,

op. cit., pp. 1-2; Keith Lovald and Holger Stub, "The Revolving Door: Reactions of Chronic Drunkenness Offenders to Court Sanctions," *Journal of Criminal Law and Criminology,* 59 (1968), pp. 525-530.

[39]Uniform Crime Reports, *op. cit.*, p. 184.

[40]Seldon Bacon, "Traffic Accidents Involving Alcohol in the USA: Second Stage Aspects of a Social Problem," *Quarterly Journal of Studies on Alcohol,* Supplement number 4 (1968); Wolf Middendorff, *The Effectiveness of Punishment: Especially in Relation to Traffic Offenses,* South Hackensack, New Jersey: Fred Rothman and Company, 1968; A. Dale (ed.), *The Drinking Driver in Traffic Accidents,* Bloomington, Indiana: Indiana University Press, 1964; Wolfgang Schmidt and Reginald Smart, "Alcoholics, Drinking, and Traffic Accidents," *Quarterly Journal of Studies on Alcohol,* 20 (1959), pp. 631-644; George Beitel, "Probability of Arrest While Driving Under the Influence of Alcohol," *Quarterly Journal of Studies on Alcohol,* 36 (1975), pp. 109-116; R.D. Yoder, "Prearrest Behavior of Persons Convicted of Driving While Intoxicated," *Quarterly Journal of Studies on Alcohol,* 36 (1975), pp. 117-125.

[41]Berry et al., *op. cit.*

[42]Bloch and Geis, *op. cit.*, pp. 332-335; Middendorff, *op. cit.*, p. 20; Clinard, *op. cit.*, pp. 442-444; Merton Hyman, "The Social Characteristics of Persons Arrested for Driving While Intoxicated," *Quarterly Journal of Studies on Alcohol,* 29 (1968), pp. 138-177; Harvey Marshall and Ross Purdy, "Hidden Deviance and the Labelling Approach: The Case for Drinking and Driving," *Social Problems,* 19 (1972), pp. 541-553.

[43]Second Report to the National Commission on Marihuana and Drug Abuse, *Drug Use In America: Problem in Perspective.* Washington, D.C.: US Government Printing Office, 1973, p. 143: *Second Special Report to the US Congress on Alcohol and Health, op. cit.*, pp. 49-59; Vera Efron et al., *Statistics on Consumption of Alcohol and on Alcoholism,* New Brunswick, New Jersey: Rutgers Center of Alcohol Studies, 1974.

[44]Uniform Crime Reports, *op. cit.*, p. 184.

[45]Harold Mulford, "Drinking and Deviant Behavior, USA," *Quarterly Journal of Studies on Alcohol,* 25 (1964), pp. 634-650; Don Cahalan et al., *American Drinking Practices: A National Study of Drinking Behavior and Attitudes,* New Brunswick, New Jersey: Rutgers Center of Alcohol Studies, 1969; Margaret Bailey et al., "The Epidemiology of Alcoholism in an Urban Residential Area," *Quarterly Journal of Studies on Alcohol,* 26 (1965), pp. 19-40; Harrison Trice and Paul Roman, *Spirits and Demons at Work: Alcohol and Other Drugs on the Job,* Ithaca, New York: Industrial and Labor Relations Paperback, Cornell University Press, 1972; Thomas Plaut, *Alcohol Problems: A Report to the Nation by the Cooperative Commission on the Studies of Alcoholism,* New York: Oxford University Press, 1967; *Task Force Report: Drunkenness, op. cit.*, Erich Goode, *Deviant Behavior: An Interactionist Approach,* New Jersey: Prentice-Hall, 1978, pp. 284-286; Merton and Nisbet, *op. cit.*, p. 189.

[46]David Pittman and Charles Snyder (eds.), *Alcohol, Culture, and Drinking Patterns,* New York: John Wiley, 1962; Pittman, *op. cit.*; Harrison Trice,

Alcoholism in America, New York: McGraw-Hill, 1966; Genevieve Knupfer and Robin Room, "Age, Sex, and Social Class as Factors in Amount of Drinking in a Metropolitan Community," *Social Problems,* (Fall, 1964), pp. 224-240.

[47]Mulford, *op. cit.;* Nisbet and Merton, *op. cit.,* pp. 203-206; George Maddox (ed.), *The Domesticated Drug: Drinking Among Collegians,* New Haven: College and University Press, 1970; Peter Park, "Dimensions of Drinking Among Male College Students," *Social Problems,* 14 (1967), pp. 473-482; Kaye Fillmore, "Drinking and Problem Drinking in Early Adulthood and Middle Age," *Quarterly Journal of Studies on Alcohol,* 35 (1974), pp. 819-840; Muriel Sterne et al., "Teenagers, Drinking, and the Law: A Study of Arrest Trends for Alcohol Related Offenses," in Pittman (ed.), *op. cit.,* p. 57.

[48]Don Cahalan and Robin Room, *Problem Drinking Among American Men,* New Brunswick, New Jersey: Rutgers Center of Alcohol Studies, 1974; Mulford, *op. cit.;* Cahalan et al., *op. cit.;* Margaret Bailey et al., *op. cit.*

[49]*Ibid.*

[50]Charles Snyder, *Alcohol and the Jews,* New York: Free Press, 1958; Jerome Skolnick, "Religious Affiliation and Drinking Behavior," *Quarterly Journal of Studies on Alcohol,* 19 (1958), pp. 452-270; John Riley and Charles Marden, "The Social Pattern of Alcoholic Drinking," *Quarterly Journal of Studies on Alcohol,* 8 (1947), pp. 265-273; Robert Bales, "Cultural Differences in Rates of Alcoholism," *Quarterly Journal of Studies on Alcohol,* 6 (1946), pp. 480-500; Genevieve Knupfer and Robin Room, "Drinking Patterns and Attitudes of Irish, Jewish, and White Protestant American Men," *Quarterly Journal of Studies on Alcohol,* 28 (1967), pp. 676-699; Charles Snyder, "Culture and Jewish Sobriety: the Ingroup-Outgroup Factor," in Pittman and Snyder (eds.), *op. cit.,* pp. 188-225; D.D. Glad, "Attitudes and Experiences of American-Jewish and American-Irish Male Youth as Related to Differences in Adult Rates of Inebriety," *Quarterly Journal of Studies on Alcohol,* 8 (1947), p. 452.

[51]Bales, *op. cit.;* Giorgio Lolli et al., *Alcohol in Italian Culture,* New York: Free Press, 1958; William and Joan McCord, "Some Current Theories of Alcoholism: A Longitudinal Evaluation," *Quarterly Journal of Studies on Alcohol,* 20 (1959), p. 746; Knupfer and Room, *op. cit.*

[52]George Chu, "Drinking Patterns and Attitudes of Rooming-House Chinese in San Francisco," *Quarterly Journal of Studies on Alcohol,* (May, 1972), pp. 58-68; Milton Barnett, "Alcoholism in the Cantonese of New York City: An Anthropological Study," in Diethelm (ed.), *Etiology of Chronic Alcoholism,* Springfield Illinois: Charles C. Thomas, Publisher, 1955, pp. 179-227; Omer Stewart, "Questions Regarding American Indian Criminality," *Human Organization,* 23 (1964), pp. 61-66; Edward Dozier, "Problem Drinking Among American Indians: The Role of Socio-Cultural Deprivation," *Quarterly Journal of Studies on Alcohol,* 27 (1966), pp. 72-87; Donald Weast, "Patterns of Drinking Among Indian Youth: The Significance of Amonia and Differential Association," *The Wisconsin Sociologist,* 9 (1972), pp. 12-28; Muriel Sterne, "Drinking Patterns and Alcoholism Among American Negroes," in Pittman (ed.), *op. cit.,* pp. 74-98; Roebuck and Johnson, *op. cit.,* pp. 21-23; Robert Strayer, "A Study of the Negro Alcoholic," *Quarterly Journal of Studies on Alcohol,* 22 (1961), pp. 111-123.

[53]The President's Commission on Law Enforcement and Administration of

Justice, *The Challenge of Crime in a Free Society,* Washington, D.C.: US Government Printing Office, 1967, pp. 233-235.

[54]Don Gibbons, *Society, Crime, and Criminal Careers,* New Jersey: Prentice-Hall, 1973, pp. 437-441; Spradley, *op. cit.*; Joan Jackson and Ralph Conner, "The Skid Row Alcoholic," *Quarterly Journal of Studies on Alcohol,* 14 (1953), pp. 468-486; Donald Bogue, *Skid Rows in American Cities,* Chicago: Community and Family Study Center of University of Chicago, 1963, pp. 272-304; Earl Rubington, "The Bottle Gang," *Quarterly Journal of Studies on Alcohol,* 29 (1968), pp. 943-955; Jacqueline Wiseman, *Stations of the Lost: The Treatment of Skid Row Alcoholics,* New Jersey: Prentice-Hall, 1970; Pittman and Gordon, *op. cit.*, pp. 16-93, 109-124; Samuel Wallace, *Skid Row as a Way of Life,* Totowa, New Jersey: Bedminster Press, 1965; Francis Feeney et al., "The Challenge of the Skid Row Alcoholic," *Quarterly Journal of Studies on Alcohol,* 16 (1955), pp. 647-667; Jack Peterson and Milton Maxwell, "The Skid Row Wino," *Social Problems,* 5 (1958), pp. 308-316; Sara Harris, *Skid Row,* New York: Doubleday, 1956.

[55]A. Gordon, "The Relation of Legislative Acts to the Problem of Drug Addiction," *Journal of Criminal Law and Criminology,* 8 (1971), pp. 211-215; Gilman Udell, *Opium and Narcotic Laws,* Washington, DC: US Government Printing Office, 1968, pp. ii-iv; Edward Brecher et al., *Licit and Illicit Drugs,* Boston: Little Brown and Company, 1972; Charles Terry and Mildred Pellens, *The Opium Problem,* New York: Committee on Drug Addictions, Bureau of Social Hygiene Inc., 1928; Alfred Lindesmith, *Opiate Addiction,* Evanston, Illinois: Principia Press, 1947; *The Addict and the Law,* Bloomington, Indiana: Indiana University Press, 1965; Lawrence Kolb and A.G. DuMez, *The Prevalence and Trend of Drug Addiction in the United States and Factors Influencing It,* Treasury Department, Washington, DC: US Government Printing Office, 1924; The President's Commission on Law Enforcement and Administration of Justice, *Task Force Report: Narcotic and Drug Abuse,* Washington, DC: US Government Printing Office, 1967; William Eldridge, *Narcotics and the Law,* Chicago: University of Chicago Press, 1967; John O'Donnell and John Ball (eds.), *Narcotic Addiction,* New York: Harper and Row, 1966; Ball, "Two Patterns of Narcotic Drug Addiction in the United States," *Journal of Criminal Law,* 56 (1965), pp. 203-211; David Maurer and Victor Vogel, *Narcotics and Narcotic Addiction,* Springfield, Illinois: Charles C. Thomas, 1967; Troy Duster, *The Legislation of Morality: Laws, Drugs, and Moral Judgement,* New York: Free Press, 1970; David Musto, *The American Disease: Origins of Narcotic Control,* New Haven: Yale University Press, 1973; Gilbert Geis, *Not the Law's Business,* Washington, DC: US Government Printing Office, NIMH, 1972; David Cantor, "The Criminal Law and the Narcotics Problem," *Journal of Criminal Law and Criminology,* 51 (1961), pp. 512-527.

[56]Brecher, *op. cit.*, pp. 42-43.

[57]*Ibid.*, pp. 43-44.

[58]*Ibid.*, p. 339.

[59]*Ibid.*, p. 44.

[60]*Ibid.*, p. 276.

[61]*Ibid.,* p. 410.

[62]*Ibid.,* p. 231.

[63]*Ibid.,* p. 59.

[64]Robert Walton, Marijuana: *America's New Drug Problem,* Philadelphia: JB Lippincott, 1938, pp. 29-33.

[65]*Ibid.,* p. 37.

[66]Brecher, *op. cit.,* p. 329.

[67]Bureau of Narcotics, U.S. Treasury Department, *Traffic in Opium and Other Dangerous Drugs for the Year Ending December 31, 1935,* Washington, DC: US Government Printing Office, 1936, p. 30; David Solomon (ed.), *The Marijuana Papers,* New York: Bobbs-Merrill, 1966, p. xv.

[68]Brecher, *op. cit.,* pp. 419-420.

[69]Udell, *op. cit.,* pp. ii-iv; Brecher, *op. cit.,* p. 56.

[70]Brecher, *op. cit.,* pp. 254-255.

[71]*Ibid.* pp. 282-283.

[72]*Ibid.,* pp. 328-329.

[73]*Ibid.,* p. 73.

[74]*Ibid.,* pp. 370-372.

[75]Martin Haskell and Lewis Yablonsky, *Criminology: Crime and Criminality,* Chicago: Rand McNally, 1978, p. 313.

[76]Terry and Pellens, *op. cit.,* p. 747.

[77]Brecher, *op. cit.,* p. 47.

[78]Public Law Number 221, 60th Congress.

[79]Public Law Number 46, 63rd Congress.

[80]Public Law Number 47, 63rd Congress.

[81]Public Law Number 233, 63rd Congress; Brecher, *op. cit.,* pp. 48-55.

[82]Brecher, *op. cit.,* p. 59.

[83]*Ibid.,* p. 51.

[84]*Ibid.,* p. 413.

[85]Solomon, *op. cit.,* p. xv.

[86]Public Law Number 238, 75th Congress; Brecher, *op.cit.,* pp. 415-416.

[87]Brecher, *op. cit.,* p. 405.

[88]Public Law Number 400, 78th Congress.

[89]Brecher, *op. cit.,* pp. 254-255.

[90]21 U.S.C., Sec. 174 (65 Stat., 767); Charles Reasons, "The Addict as a Criminal: Perpetuation of a Legend," *Crime and Delinquency,* 21 (1975), pp. 22-23.

[91]Public Law Number 78-728, 84th Congress; Brecher, *op. cit.,* p. 420; Eldridge, *op. cit.,* pp. 177-231; Reasons, *op. cit.,* p. 23.

[92]Brecher, *op. cit.,* pp. 282-283.

[93]*Ibid.,* pp. 366-372.

[94]The President's Commission on Law Enforcement and Administration of Justice, *The Challenge of Crime in a Free Society,* Washington, DC: US Government Printing Office, pp. 228-229.

[95]Brecher, *op. cit.,* p. 283.

[96]Narcotic Addict Rehabilitation Act of 1966, Public Law Number 793, Title II, The Narcotic Addict Rehabilitation Act of 1966, Public Health Service, U.S. Department of Health, Education, and Welfare, Washington, DC: US Government Printing Office, 1969.

[97]*Ibid.,* pp. 2-3.

[98]Brecher, *op. cit.,* p. 420; Reasons, *op. cit.,* p. 25.

[99]*Ibid.,* p. 60.

[100]*Webb v. United States,* 249 U.S. 96 (1919); Alfred Lindesmith, "Federal Law and Drug Addiction," in Chambliss (ed.), *Crime and the Legal Process,* New York: McGraw-Hill, 1969, p. 64.

[101]*Jin Fuey Moy v. United States,* 254 U.S. 189 (1920); Lindesmith, *op. cit.,* p. 64.

[102]*United States v. Behrman,* 258 U.S. 280 (1922); Lindesmith, *op. cit.,* pp. 64-65.

[103]*Linder v. United States,* 268 U.S. 5 (1925); Lindesmith, *op. cit.,* pp. 66-67.

[104]*Strader v. United States,* 72 F. 2nd 589 (10th Cir., 1934); United States v. Anthony, 15 F. Supp. 533 (1936); *Carey v. United States,* 86 F. 2nd 461 (9th Cir., 1936); Lindesmith, *op. cit.,* p. 69.

[105]*Rochin v. California,* 342 U.S. 165 (1952); Lindesmith, *op. cit.,* p. 71.

[106]*Blackford v. United States,* 247 F. 2nd 745 (9th Cir., 1957); Lindesmith, *op. cit.,* p. 71.

[107]*Sherman v. United States*, 356 U.S. 369 (1958); Edwin Schur, *Crimes Without Victims: Deviant Behavior and Public Policy*, New Jersey: Prentice-Hall, 1965, p. 136.

[108]*Robinson v. California*, 370 U.S. 660 (1962); Brecher, *op. cit.*, pp. 59-60; Herbert Bloch and Gilbert Geis, *Man, Crime, and Society*, New York: Random House, 1970, p. 339.

[109]Brecher, *op. cit.*; *Task Force Report: Narcotic and Drug Abuse, op. cit.*; *The Challenge of Crime in a Free Society, op. cit.*; Reasons, *op. cit.*

[110]*Ibid.*

[111]*Ibid.*

[112]Brecher, *op. cit.*, p. 78.

[113]Marshall Clinard, *Sociology of Deviant Behavior*, New York: Holt, Rinehart and Winston, 1974, p. 384.

[114]*1977/78 U.S. Government Manual*, Washington, DC: US Government Printing Office, 1977, pp. 261-262.

[115]*Ibid.*, pp. 350-351.

[116]President's Commission on Law Enforcement and Administration of Justice, *Task Force Report: Organized Crime*, Washington, DC: US Government Printing Office, 1967, pp. 1-2.

[117]*Proceedings*, White House Conference on Narcotic and Drug Abuse, Washington, DC: US Government Printing Office, 1962.

[118]*Final Report*, President's Advisory Commission on Narcotic and Drug Abuse, Washington, DC: US Government Printing Office, 1963.

[119]*Task Force Report: Narcotic and Drug Abuse, op. cit.*

[120]National Commission on Marihuana and Drug Abuse, *Marihuana: A Signal of Misunderstanding*, Washington, DC: US Government Printing Office, 1972; Technical papers, volumes 1-2; National Commission on Marihuana and Drug Abuse, *Drug Use in America: Problem in Perspective*, Washington, DC: US Government Printing Office, 1973, Technical papers, volumes 1-4.

[121]American Bar Association and American Medical Association, Joint Committee on Narcotic Drugs, *Drug Addiction: Crime or Disease*? Bloomington, Indiana: Indiana University Press, 1961.

[122]*The Challenge of Crime in a Free Society*, op. cit., pp. 230-231.

[123]Health Research Council of New York City, New York State Narcotic Addiction Control Commission, and National Association for the Prevention of Addiction, *Proceedings of the First National Conference on Methadone Treatment*, New York, 1968.

[124]Brecher, *op. cit.,* p. 120; Shur, *op. cit.,* pp. 153-154; Schur, *Narcotic Addiction in Britain and America: The Impact of Public Policy,* Bloomington, Indiana: Indiana University Press, 1962; Schur, "British Narcotics Policies," *Journal of Criminal Law and Criminology,* 51 (1961), pp. 619-624; Schur, "Drug Addiction Under British Policy," *Social Problems,* 9 (1961), pp. 156-166; Alfred Lindesmith, "The British System of Narcotics Control," *Law and Contemporary Problems,* 22 (1957), pp. 138-154.

[125]Brecher, *op. cit.,* p. 121.

[126]Ministry of Health, Interdepartmental Committee on Drug Addiction, *Report,* London: Her Majesty's Stationery Office, 1961.

[127]Brecher, *op. cit.,* p. 125.

[128]Robert Pursley, *Introduction to Criminal Justice,* Encino, California: Glencoe Press, 1978, p. 106.

[129]Brecher, *op. cit.,* p. 48.

[130]*Ibid.,* pp. 22, 468.

[131]Henry Black, *Black's Law Dictionary,* St. Paul, Minnesota: West Publishing Company, 1968, p. 587.

[132]*Ibid.,* p. 59.

[133]Henry Fairchild (ed.), *Dictionary of Sociology,* Paterson, New Jersey: Littlefield, Adams and Company, 1962, p. 99.

[134]The Dushkin Publishing Group, *Encyclopedia of Sociology,* Guilford, Connecticut: Dushkin Inc., 1974, pp. 85-86.

[135]Expert Committee on Addiction-Producing Drugs, *Seventh Report,* World Health Organization Technical Report Series, Geneva, Switzerland: W.H.O. of the United Nations, 1957, in *Drug Use in America, op. cit.,* p. 124.

[136]*Drug Use in America, op. cit.,* pp. 136-140.

[137]*Ibid.,* p. 9.

[138]*Ibid.,* p. 28.

[139]*Ibid.,* pp. 37-38.

[140]*Ibid.,* pp. 9, 11, 13.

[141]*Ibid.,* pp. 16-17.

[142]*Ibid.,* p. 18.

[143]*Ibid.,* p. 19.

[144]*District of Columbia Code,* Annotated, Washington, DC: US Government Printing Office, 2, 1973, 33-401, 2158.

[145]*Ibid.,* 33-402, 2159.

[146]*Ibid.,* 33-416a, 2171.

[147]*Ibid.*

[148]*Ibid.,* 33-417, 2175.

[149]*Ibid.,* 33-420, 2175.

[150]*Ibid.,* 33-423, 2176.

[151]*Ibid.,* 33-701, 2177.

[152]*Ibid.,* 33-702, 2178-2179.

[153]*Ibid.*

[154]*Ibid.*

[155]*Ibid.,* 33-703, 2179-2180.

[156]*Ibid.,* 33-704, 2180.

[157]*Ibid.,* 33-708, 2181.

[158]*Ibid.,* 33-711, 2182.

[159]Uniform Crime Reports of the F.B.I., *Crime in the United States—1976,* Washington, DC: US Government Printing Office, 1977, p. 184.

[160]*Ibid.,* p. 217.

[161]Haskell and Yablonsky, *op. cit.,* p. 319.

[162]*Drug Use in America, op. cit.,* pp. 154-155.

[163]Schur, *Crimes Without Victims,* op. cit., pp. 120-122; Isidor Chein et al., *The Road to H: Narcotics, Delinquency and Social Policy,* New York: Basic Books, 1964; David Musto, *op. cit.;* Geis, *op. cit.;* Cantor, *op. cit.;* Duster, *op. cit.;* Terry and Pellens, *op. cit.;* Eldridge, *op. cit.;* Lindesmith, *op. cit.;* Lindesmith, "Dopefiend Mythology," *Journal of Criminal Law and Criminology,* 31 (1940), pp. 199-208; Lindesmith, "The Drug Addict as a Psychopath," *American Sociological Review,* 5 (1940), pp. 914-920; Reasons, *op. cit.;* Reasons, "Images of Crime and the Criminal: The Dope Fiend Mythology," *Journal of Research in Crime and Delinquency,* (1976), pp. 133-144.

[164]*Marihuana: A Signal of Misunderstanding, op. cit.,* pp. 424-477.

[165]*Drug Use in America, op. cit.,* pp. 157-160.

[166]*Ibid.*, pp. 160-161.

[167]*Ibid.*, pp. 161-163.

[168]*Ibid.*, p. 163.

[169]*Ibid.*, p. 165.

[170]*Ibid.*, p. 156; Clinard, *op. cit.*, pp. 422-423; Schur, *Crimes Without Victims, op. cit.*, pp. 138-141; Haskell and Yablonsky, *op. cit.*, pp. 319-322; Don Gibbons, *Society, Crime and Criminal Careers*, New Jersey: Prentice-Hall, 1973, pp. 426-430.

[171]Clinard, *op. cit.*, p. 401; Kolb and DuMez, *op. cit.*; *Task Force Report: Narcotic and Drug Abuse, op. cit.*; *Drug Use in America, op. cit.*, pp. 174-175; Arthur D. Little Inc., *Drug Abuse and Law Enforcement*, A Report to the President's Commission on Law Enforcement and Administration of Justice, *op. cit.*; Edward Preble and John Casey, "Taking Care of Business—The Heroin User's Life on the Street," *International Journal of the Addictions*, 4 (1969), pp. 1-24; Brecher, *op. cit.*, pp. 90-100.

[172]Clinard, *op. cit.*, p. 463; *Drug Use in America, op. cit.*, pp. 174-175.

[173]*Drug Use in America, op. cit.*, pp. 175-176; Brecher, *op. cit.*, pp. 475-481.

[174]Brecher, *op. cit.*, pp. 90-100; Donald Cressey, *Theft of the Nation: The Structure and Operations of Organized Crime in America*, New York: Harper and Row, 1969, pp. 91-95, 161, 278, 287; *Task Force Report: Organized Crime, op. cit.*, pp. 3-4.

[175]*The Challenge of Crime in a Free Society, op. cit.*, pp. 216-221; Brecher, *op. cit.*, pp. 90-100.

[176]Brecher, *op. cit.*, pp. 473-498; Robert Bell, *Social Deviance*, Homewood, Illinois: Dorsey Press, 1971, pp. 219-224; Erich Goode, *The Marijuana Smokers*, New York: Basic Books, 1970; *Marihuana: A Signal of Misunderstanding, op. cit.*; *Drug Use in America, op. cit.*; Lester Grinspoon and James Bakalar, *Cocaine: A Drug and Its Social Evolution*, New York: Basic Books, 1976; Grinspoon and Peter Hedblom, *The Speed Culture*, Cambridge, Massachusetts: Harvard University Press, 1975.

[177]Schur, *Crimes Without Victims, op. cit.*, pp. 134-138; Brecher, *op. cit.*, pp. 304-305; Interview with Captain Donald Randall, Special Investigations Branch, Metropolitan Police Department of the District of Columbia, 1977.

[178]Clinard, *op. cit.*, pp. 388-392; *Drug Use in America, op. cit.*, pp. 42-43; Herbert Abelson and Ronald Atkinson, *Public Experience with Psychoactive Substances*, Princeton, New Jersey: Response Analysis Corp., 1975; Abelson and Patricia Fishburne, *Nonmedical Use of Psychoactive Substances*, Princeton, New Jersey: Response Analysis Corp., 1976.

[179]Clinard, *op. cit.*, pp. 388-392, 400-404; *Drug Use in America, op. cit.*, pp. 63-69.

[180] *Drug Use in America, op. cit.,* pp. 167-170; Gibbons, *op. cit.,* pp. 430-435; Clinard, *op. cit.,* pp. 404-408.

[181] *Ibid.*

[182] Clinard, *op. cit.,* pp. 406-407; Ricjard Hessler, "Junkies in White: Drug Addiction Among Physicians," in Bryand (ed.), *Deviant Behavior,* Chicago: Rand McNally, 1974, pp. 146-153; Charles Winick, "Physician Narcotic Addicts," *Social Problems,* 9 (1961), pp. 174-186; J.D. Fox, "Narcotic Addiction Among Physicians," *Journal of Michigan Medical Society,* 56 (1957), pp. 214-217; Charles Jones, Narcotic Addiction of Physicians, *Journal of the Medical Association of the State of Alabama,* 37 (1968), pp. 816-827; Solomon Garb, "Drug Addiction in Physicians" *Anasthesia and Analgesia—Current Researches,* 48 (1969), pp. 129-133; William Quinn, "Narcotic Addiction: Medical and Legal Problems with Physicians," *California Medicine,* 94 (1961), pp. 214-217.

Conclusion

English Precedents

There is a clear and decisive linkage between the rulings of English courts and governmental commissions and subsequent American legal policy in the area of criminal law. It would appear almost as if both American legislative bodies and courts are waiting for the English to prove or disprove that certain types of societal social deviance should be criminalized or decriminalized. Once the decision has been made to deal with a certain type of deviance in the English courts or Parliament, it is only a matter of time before an American state legislature or court decides to evaluate the precedent being set in England. Thus American debate on specific types of criminality or proposed criminalization of social deviance inevitably utilizes both the English Common Law tradition and contemporary social engineering before making decisions affecting American criminal law.

Obscenity

In the area of pornography and obscenity, the Curl case of 1797 set the Common Law crime in England that was subsequently accepted in the early part of the nineteenth century by most American states. Although England has clearly dealt with this area of deviance since the early 1960s, the Supreme Court of the United States has been quite indecisive on this issue despite the English example of increased tolerance for adults on this matter.[1]

Prostitution

The English Common Law did not deal with prostitution as a social problem until after 1640 and apparently cases of solicitation were not handled as crimes until approximately 1707.[2] The Wolfenden Committee favored a partial decriminalization of prostitution statutes in England in 1957. Only the state of Nevada legalized prostitution in 1970 although there is still much debate on the issue in America.[3]

Heterosexual Deviance

Most forms of heterosexual deviance were not considered as crimes but as torts at the Common Law (i.e., adultery, bigamy, seduction, illicit cohabitation, fornication). Sodomy, indecent public exposure, and notorious lewdness were crimes at the Common Law.[4] Until very recently most forms of heterosexual deviance (i.e., premarital, comarital, and extramarital) have been criminal offences in America whereas England has held that heterosexual deviance in general is a private matter between two consenting adults.[5]

Homosexuality

The Common Law made homosexuality a crime that was punishable by death by act of Parliament in 1553. It was not until 1861 that Parliament modified the law to allow life imprisonment for homosexuals. The Wolfenden Committee recommended repeal of the criminal sanction for homosexuality in 1957.[6] Parliament decriminalized homosexual acts between consenting adults in 1961 but it was not until 1967 that a number of states have decriminalized homosexuality.[7] A federal government task force study (i.e., Department of Health, Education, and Welfare) in 1967 recommended that all state and federal codes follow the English example.[8]

Venereal Diseases

There was a double standard applied to those who contracted venereal diseases in English society. Prostitutes who contracted a disease were considered as bad as criminals while their male clients were considered as deviant. Although the Common Law did not deal with communicable diseases, Parliament in 1864 tried to control the spread of venereal diseases by ordering examinations for prostitutes. A number of royal commissions and parliamentary acts since 1870 have dealt more and more openly with the problem of venereal disease prevention and control.[9] The United States accepted common English practices concerning the prevention and control of venereal diseases until 1873 when Congress banned both the mailing of literature concerning birth control and birth control devices (i.e., the condom which prevented contraction of venereal diseases). It was not until the last decade that American federal courts allowed juveniles and adults free access to diagnosis, treatment, and education concerning venereal diseases.[10]

Family Conflicts

According to the Common Law, all acts of deviance in connection with the institution of the family were not considered crimes. Until 1857 England had no satisfactory solution to domestic problems except for the rare divorce (i.e., usually granted only to the very wealthy). The Common Law did not give a wife a legal standing outside of the marital context. Such family problems as desertion, adultery, bigamy, incest, and illegitimacy were civil matters.[11] Some states after 1776 liberalized their laws regarding divorce, desertion, and illegitimacy while making crimes of such deviant acts as adultery, bigamy, and incest.[12] Thus the United States has been more liberal and tolerant than England in this area of the law.

Abortion

The Common Law does not deal with abortion as a crime. It was not until 1803 that Parliament declared all abortions criminal. This law was challenged in 1938 although Parliament did not pass a liberal act dealing with abortions until 1967.[13] Two states (California and Colorado) made their laws coincide with the English Act. Up until 1967, individual states followed a variety of laws dealing with the abortion issue. It was not until 1973 that the United States Supreme Court followed the English example, thus making all states conform to one policy.[14]

Euthanasia

Parliament failed to enact legislation dealing with euthanasia in both 1901 and 1931. Thus it was in the United States that attempts have been made to legally separate euthanasia from so-called mercy killing (i.e., criminal homicide). Neither England nor any state in America have accepted the euthanasia issue. Thus legal precedent has not been determined on this matter.[15]

Suicide

Suicide is a crime at Common Law in England as was attempted suicide until 1961. The American states followed the English example until the late nineteenth century when a number of states abolished their statutes concerning suicide. It was not until recently that all states rescinded their statutes concerning attempted suicide as a crime.[16]

Mental Disorders

The Common Law dealt specifically with the mental capabilities of different age groups in society who commit crimes. It was not until 1536 that the Crown allowed some public assistance for the poor insane. The first legal test dealing with criminal insanity was determined in 1843 in an English case. By and large the United States followed the English example although states such as Iowa, New Hampshire, and New York attempted to improve upon English precedent in the late nineteenth century. It was not until the last decade that both the federal executive and judicial branches of American government began modernizing social policy concerning the criminally insane.[17]

Gambling

Public supported gambling (i.e., lottery) was established in England in 1569 in order to raise funds for public works projects. The various states as well as the federal government supported lotteries until about 1840. By the turn of the century in the United States, gambling was a major social problem that spread to epidemic proportions. By the 1950s, Congressional hearings and legislation showed that gambling was beyond effective control. Parliament legalized various forms of gambling in 1960. By 1975 several states were again operating lotteries in addition to many other forms of gambling in order to raise new tax revenues.[18]

Alcoholism

The Common Law does not define an alcoholic as a criminal although in 1606 Parliament made public drunkenness a crime. The various states enacted legislation dealing with alcoholics as well as the manufacture, sale, and distribution of alcoholic beverages early in our national history. Between 1830 and 1933, all types of state and federal legislation was passed in an attempt to deal with alcohol and the alcoholic in the United States.[19] An act of Parliament in 1879 is the modern basis for dealing with alcoholics and their problems but it was not until the last ten years that Congress, the executive branch, the federal courts, and the American Medical Association have accepted the English governmental policy toward alcoholics.[20]

Drug Addiction

The use of opiates was legal in both England and the United States throughout the eighteenth and nineteenth centuries. Between 1883 and 1914, a growing number of municipalities and states began enacting anti-drug legislation. Between 1914 and 1929, the American federal government enacted legislation against most known addicting substances and marijuana. The federal courts also became very active with drug cases after 1919. Finally various federal commissions, agencies, and congressional hearings came into being after 1920.[21]

The English Parliament enacted legislation in 1920 patterned after American legislation but began questioning the effectiveness of the American model in the 1920s. By the 1960s the English government was handling both drug addiction and abuse problems via the medical model while in the United States the crime control model approach was causing more problems than it could alleviate in an effective manner. All Presidential Commissions, White House Conferences, and federal agencies (i.e., Drug Enforcement Administration and its predecessors) could not cope with the increasing problems of drug addiction, abuse, and misuse in the 1960s. Thus despite all the decades of time and huge amounts of money spent on this issue, the United States still has not followed the English approach to resolving the drug issue.[22]

Overcriminalization Problem

Kadish refers to the term overcriminalization to explain the huge number of criminal code statutes that deal with victimless crimes in the United States on the federal, state, county, and municipal levels. He feels that the creation of these crimes in the area of morality creates more problems for the criminal justice system than the statutes are worth. Kadish feels that the criminal law is overcriminalized in the areas of: (1) public morality (i.e., in the declaration or enforcement of community standards on private value-attitudes), (2) provision of social services (i.e., where other social agencies fail or refuse to deal with the deviant behavior), and (3) using the criminal law in extralegal fashion by the police (i.e., in the name of protective custody of the deviant).[23]

The overcriminalization problem is most obvious in the area of enforcement of morals. Here one finds all the statutes dealing with sex offences (i.e., homosexuality, heterosexuality, venereal diseases, sex education, birth control, pornography and obscenity). There have been and are presently in the United States more statutes dealing with sexual behavior than in any country. The United States Code and the state criminal codes contain statutes dealing with sodomy (i.e., bestiality or intercourse between a human and an animal; buggery or intercourse by a male with another male or with a woman by the anus; and deviant sex acts such as oral stimulation of sexual organs). Sodomy statutes are sometimes referred to as crimes against nature.[24]

Prostitution (i.e., sexual intercourse for money or other tangible favors) statutes are found in all states with the exception of certain counties in Nevada. Other related statutes deal with solicitation of prostitutes, keeping a house of prostitution, earning an income from prostitutes (i.e., pimps and madams), and patronizing prostitutes. Almost all statutes deal with females and not males. Another aspect of sexual behavior dealt with by statute is lewd and lascivious behavior (i.e., openly cohabiting and associating with an individual known not to be one's spouse under circumstances implying sexual intercourse). A third common statute deals with seduction (i.e., a man who seduces a previously chaste woman to engage in sexual intercourse under the promise of marriage).[25]

Other crimes dealing with sexuality are bigamy, adultery, and incest. Bigamy is going through the form or ceremony of marriage by one having another living spouse. Adultery is illicit sexual intercourse between individuals either of whom is married to another person. Incest is sexual intercourse between individuals who are defined by the jurisdiction as so clearly related to each other that a marriage between them would be a crime. Incest also includes sexual intercourse between parent and child (i.e., mother-son or father-daughter).[26]

Finally until recently in the United States it was a criminal act to teach about sexual behavior and birth control in the public schools, write, lecture, or send through the mails material (i.e., pamphlets, books, articles) on birth control, or advertise, sell, and purchase birth control devices or supplies. These so-called criminal acts go back to the federal Comstock Law and subsequent state laws (i.e., Connecticut) which were only recently ruled unconstitutional by the United States Supreme Court.[27] These same Comstock type laws at the state level governed the definition of what constituted pornographic and obscene materials. Indirectly these laws also hampered the effective prevention and control of venereal diseases among both juveniles and adults.[28]

The overcriminalization problem is evident in the area of social services misuse. Here we find criminal statutes dealing with alcoholics, drug abusers and addicts, individuals who create family conflicts (i.e., child and spouse abusers, deserters, and divorced individuals under certain circumstances), and individuals having mental disorders or potential suicides. According to Kadish the criminal law has been utilized to provide social services to certain types of social deviants in society. The criminal law is not meant to deal with the rehabilitation function nor are the police trained to deal with the types of social deviants forced upon law enforcement personnel and facilities.[29]

As the President's Commission on Law Enforcement and Administration of Justice states, alcoholism (i.e., drunkenness) should not be a crime.[30] From a practical point of view, public health or social service facilities should handle this problem. If a public drunk is of no threat to anyone or to himself, it is really dysfunctional for the police to place the individual in jail. Unfortunately in some police departments as many as half of the misdemeanor arrests are for public drunkenness. This means that time and money are diverted from better purposes and the drunk will be out on the street the next day and back to the same routine in most cases (i.e., most chronic alcoholics usually are arrested on a regular basis, especially if they are lower class).[31]

In dealing with drug abuse and drug addiction, the problem of whether these areas can be dealt with effectively by social services, medical services, or the police is a very complicated question to resolve. The criminal justice system at both the federal and state levels have tried to deal with both abuse and addiction in the same manner through a policy of enforcing the criminal statutes and then dealing with the offender on the basis of type of drug abused, first offence or chronic offender, dealer or user, and any other criminal offences committed in connection with the misuse of drugs. The laws are much stricter concerning habit forming substances (i.e., opiates) than with so-called soft drugs (i.e., barbiturates, amphetamines) although the various state statutes are confused in dealing with the hallucinogens, marijuana, and cocaine.[32]

The area of domestic relations deals with a variety of family conflicts such as child and spouse abuse, desertion, and divorce problems (i.e., refusal to pay child support and/or alimony). This whole area of domestic relations is a very difficult one for the police since they are not trained to deal with social work practices, yet the criminal code and departmental operating procedures make it mandatory for law enforcement personnel to deal with a variety of situations that are basically torts but could escalate into criminal acts. The welfare department should handle such problems but often the police are called to resolve the problem since many times the family conflict could lead to violence. Thus the police are used as an instrument of force in an attempt to force a husband to stop abusing members of his family or pay the money that the court has ordered him to give to his ex-wife and/or children (i.e., the police are called in as a last resort to reason with the family member before he is arrested and jailed for failure to comply with a civil court order).[33]

The last social service provision allocated to the police by the criminal code is in dealing with people suffering from mental disorders or potential suicides. These laws of the criminal code are aimed at the self-protection of the individual. Again as in the case of alcoholics and drug abuser/addicts, the police neither have the training, the facilities, nor the time to deal with such individuals in light of more serious problems brought to their attention. In the case of people suffering from serious mental problems, all the police can do is either take them to the nearest mental hospital or general hospital or place them in a holding cell until some social welfare authority takes over the case. The police are not trained for such work and if a mentally ill person becomes violent have a hard time properly handling the case. People who attempt suicide pose a problem since they are usually suffering great mental stress and can endanger the lives of fire or police personnel who may try to convince them not to commit suicide. This would be especially true if the person is trying to jump off a building or bridge. There is also the case of suicide pacts between two parties where the end result turns into a case of one party committing suicide and the other party not being successful or changing his mind. The police are then dealing with a possible murder situation and the unsuccessful suicide may attempt to complete the act after being taken into custody. Thus the criminal law does not consider the social service aspect when it comes to the implementation of the statutes by the police.[34]

The last area of overcriminalization deals with such minor crimes as disorderly conduct and vagrancy. This is an area of the criminal law that allows the police to use their discretionary powers to deal with borderline cases of social deviance. Disorderly conduct statutes differ from state to state and are usually enforced when an individual's deviant behavior does not match that behavior described in existing statutes. Thus an individual who is allegedly swearing in public, engaged in a family argument, and acting in a strange or sexually unusual manner could be charged under this statute (i.e., it is used to cover new crimes or crimes that cannot be easily classified or defined.) The vagrancy statutes are even more vague than the disorderly conduct statutes. They have been used to arrest and detain all sorts of social deviants who have not committed even an act that could be classified as disorderly. Thus the visibly unemployed, people roaming the streets or shopping centers, loiterers, prostitutes, drunks, gamblers, and youth who are not wanted in a particular location or place of business are all dealt with by the police using this statute.[35]

Decriminalization Debate

Decriminalization is a social process that does not automatically lead to legitimization of social deviance. There are arguments both for the retention of victimless crimes as well as for the decriminalization of such deviant acts. Most of the arguments for the retention of victimless crimes revolve around the morality issue with some concern about the harm done to the individual both physically and psychologically.[36] On the other hand the decriminalization arguments state that some acts of deviance are really normal behavior (i.e., prostitution, premarital and extramarital sex, homosexuality, abortion, euthanasia, family conflicts, gambling, and soft drug use). Some people do not accept that all victimless crimes are or should be considered normal behavior. These adherents of decriminalization want tolerance for those who practice their deviance in private with other adults who are willing to indulge in such activities (i.e., pornography, premarital and extramarital sex, homosexuality, and other behavior dealing with sexuality). Finally there are those who feel that the victimless crime is deviant and evil but not worth the time and cost to the criminal justice system to catch and punish the offender (i.e., prostitution, homosexuality, pornography, gambling, drug addiction, and alcoholism). There is obviously no consensus as to what victimless crimes should be dealt with in which of the three suggested ways of decriminalization.[37]

According to Sagarin the decriminalization process goes through several stages: (1) simple obsolescence, (2) new judicial interpretations, and (3) social conflict and movements to rescind legislation.[38] Enforcement of statutes against morality in a community may become out of date because the mores of the population have changed significantly since the statute was originally passed. This is true of inner cities and their cosmopolitan suburbs where "X" rated movies and adult bookstores are tolerated, laws dealing with heterosexual behavior, divorce, massage parlors, prostitution, gambling, public drunkenness, and certain types of mental disorders are accepted by the public and police alike. State supreme courts and the federal courts have made new judicial interpretations of various victimless crimes. This is especially true in the area of abortion, pornography and obscenity, family conflicts, gambling, and alcoholism. To a lesser extent the courts have been reviewing the issues of euthanasia, drug addiction, mental disorders, and homosexuality. In the cases of abortion, pornography, alcoholism, and drug abuse the courts have been somewhat contradictory as one Supreme Court ruling will be definitive and other rulings will return the same issue back to the states for their re-interpretation of community standards. There is much conflict of law between federal and state courts as well as within county courts in the same state on many victimless crime issues.[39]

Finally social conflict and social movements have been quite influential in dealing with both the criminalization and decriminalization issues. Sagarin feels that conflict will result when public morality weakens on a victimless crime or when individuals feel that the deviance has not diminished and/or has caused an increase of secondary crime that is getting beyond control. This has often happened when the criminalization process was fostered by a well-organized minority who really did not represent the majority view on public deviance. The Comstock laws on pornography and obscenity, the abortion issue, venereal disease issue, prohibition issue, marijuana and drug abuse problems, and sexual psychopath issue are all examples of problems that have been created by a zealous minority who had political power. Eventually these minority statutes lead to social movements that are aired via the mass media, public demonstrations, and political lobbying and campaigns to replace conservative politicians. This has been the case with homosexuality, abortion, and to a lesser extent with the issues of prostitution, heterosexual behavior, pornography, gambling, and alcoholism.[40]

Pornography and Obscenity

The President's Commission concluded that the majority of American adults want to read or see any erotic materials they wish to examine. There is agreement among adults that children and juveniles should not be permitted to see such erotic materials but most felt that it would be virtually impossible to enforce the statutes against obscene material.[41] For example Fairfax County, Virginia (suburban area of D.C.) requires that such magazines as *Playboy, Penthouse,* and *Hustler* be placed behind the counter or in back of hardboard covers so youth cannot see such material. Ordinances have been passed in several Northern Virginia jurisdictions keeping adult bookstores a certain distance from schools, churches, and residential areas.

The Commission recommended in 1970 the repeal of all federal, state, and local legislation prohibiting the commercial distribution, exhibition, and sale of erotic materials to consenting adults. The Commission also recommended special legislation prohibiting the same material's sale, display, or distribution to children or adolescents. The Commission thus advocated the decriminalization of the possession, sale, and display of erotic materials among adults and pointed to the need for free discussion of sexual behavior in American society. Thus the Commission recommended an open sex education program built in the public schools.

Much of the problem regarding materials which depict explicit sexual activity stems from the inability or reluctance of people in our society to be open and direct in dealing with sexual matters. This often manifests itself in the inhibition of talking openly and directly about sex. Professionals use highly technical language when they discuss sex; others escape by using euphemisms or by not talking about sex at all. Direct and open conversation about sex between parent and child is too rare in our society. Failure to talk openly and directly about sex has several consequences. It overemphasizes sex, gives it a magical, nonnatural quality, making it more attractive and fascinating. It diverts the expression of sexual interest out of more legitimate channels. Such failure makes teaching children and adolescents to become fully and adequately functioning sexual adults a more difficult task. And it clogs legitimate channels for transmitting sexual information and forces people to use clandestine and unreliable sources.[42]

Justice Douglas in his dissenting opinion in *Miller v. California* states that the sovereign states in their criminal codes and the Supreme Court in *Miller* are interfering with the Constitution in its guarantees as stated in both First and Fourteenth amendments. Thus society's attempts to legislate for adults in the area of obscenity have not been successful. Present laws prohibiting the consensual sale or distribution of explicit sexual materials to adults are extremely unsatisfactory in their application. The Constitution permits material to be deemed obscene for adults only if as a whole it appeals to the prurient interest of the average person, is patently offensive in light of community standards, and lacks redeeming social value. These vague and highly subjective aesthetic, psychological and moral tests do not provide meaningful guidance for law enforcement officials, juries or courts. As a result law is inconsistently and sometimes erroneously applied and the distinctions made by courts between prohibited and permissible materials often appear indefensible. Errors in the application of the law and uncertainty about its scope also cause interference with the communication of constitutionally protected materials.[43]

Unfortunately President Nixon totally rejected the recommendations of his own Commission and one of his appointees to the Supreme Court, Justice Rehnquist, in *California v. LaRue* stated that indecent exposure and sexual assaults result from adult males viewing nude female ladies and certain sexual acts in California bars.[44] Thus both the executive and judicial branches of the federal government have not accepted the social policy formulated by the Commission on Pornography and Obscenity and all the research done to support its recommendations.

Those who are opposed to the decriminalization of pornography and obscenity are those who tend to be against freedom of expression (i.e., those who campaigned against the TV program "Soap" even before it went on the ABC network and those who feel that sex education is a communist plot). Those opposing decriminalization tend to be female, older, less educated, more religious, and less open to social change in society.[45] Thus the so-called anti-pornographic or public decency crusades that go back to the time of Comstock and the YMCA in New York state are likely to get their support from rural and suburban areas of the country rather than the inner cities. These groups are fundamentalist in religious outlook, politically conservative, and usually lower middle class. The leadership for such groups come from the ranks of those who have already been active in religious or patriotic voluntary organization. These people often have the support of wealthy members of the community. They use the obscenity issue as a way to attempt to stop change in other aspects of our daily lives. These people do not want to lose their way of life but attempt to stop others from freely changing their way of life.[46]

Prostitution

Decriminalization of prostitution in the United States has been a topic of discussion for many years. With the exception of the state of Nevada which decriminalized prostitution in 1971 and claims that it has been able to control this activity and related secondary crimes state wide, the debate on the legislation of prostitution persists today.

The major points in favor of decriminalization contend that the state should not impose its morality upon consenting adults who wish to endulge in sexual relations as a business transaction. There are many women who are prosecuted for solicitation who have been entrapped by the police. Proponents of decriminalization feel that it is virtually impossible to arrest a prostitute without first entraping her because the average prostitute usually does not openly solicit her clients. Decriminalization of prostitution would allow the police to deal with more important matters rather than having detectives pose as prostitutes and pimps to catch both street-walker and client. The prostitute who is convicted for solicitation and institutionalized does not benefit from her incarceration since recidivism rates are almost one hundred percent and the costs of maintaining separate facilities for women are not justified. Many experts feel that prostitutes are not mentally ill so being placed in a mental institution does not serve any useful purpose.[47]

Decriminalization of prostitution would help lower the number of sex crimes (i.e., rape, incest, procuring, and pandering) in society. There would also be less interest in organized crime in providing this service. Venereal disease control would be easier since medical authorities would know where prostitutes and their customers were located. Legalization would also allow houses of prostitution to be located in areas of the community that would not be offensive to adults in general. Finally decriminalization of prostitution would allow local, state, and federal governments to benefit from the tax revenues and license fees collected from clients, prostitutes, and the managers of houses of prostitution rather than the funds going to organized crime, corrupt police officers, and public officials.[48]

The opponents of decriminalization state that prostitution leads to all sorts of secondary crime (i.e., drug addiction and abuse, assaults, robberies, blackmail, and even murder). Decriminalization would not eliminate the need for pimps but would encourage more males to become pimps. Thus such crimes as seduction, procuring, and pandering would lead to more violent crimes among pimps and prostitutes would compete with each other to maximize their profits. Prostitution leads to the spread of venereal disease, corrupts the morals of youth, and involves the police in degrading and compromising situations that may lead to taking bribes or even setting up their own vice operations from the knowledge gained in dealing with prostitutes. Some adherents to strict enforcement of prostitution statutes feel that the police can use prostitutes as informants on robbery, drug, and gambling problems in the community in return for not arresting girls who cooperate. Last many people feel that the decriminalization or legalization of prostitution will lead to the decline of societal norms and encourage people not to marry, to engage in acts of sexual deviance, and lead young girls and women into this way of life as a career rather than engage in legitimate occupations and roles better suited to women.[49]

Heterosexual Deviance

Proponents of decriminalization of the sex laws feel that these statutes go too far and only those sexual behaviors that use or threaten to use force or are applied to juveniles should retain their criminal status. There is also agreement that sex acts performed in public places should not be decriminalized. Thus the criminal laws affecting voluntary sexual relations between consenting adults should be rescinded from the state criminal codes.[50]

Packer feels that the existence of statutes governing heterosexual deviance creates more deviance (i.e., subcultures); creates a disregard for the criminal law since most of these statutes are not enforced; no harm results from heterosexual deviance if between consenting adults; the fear of detection and arrest can allow for the growth of secondary crimes such as blackmail or police bribery; most members of the community tend to be accepting of most types of heterosexual deviance; and the criminal sanction serves no useful purpose since no harm has been done by consenting adults.[51]

Those opposed to decriminalization feel that heterosexual sex crimes should not be decriminalized since they are against the normative system of society; against basic religious tenets; are a negative influence upon the next generation; and are a destructive force upon the socio-psychological functioning of the family. The author agrees that such crimes as incest, bigamy, and such behaviors as sadism and masochism should be controlled by the criminal justice system. One also must exclude such behavior from the youth of society. This is a most difficult task to accomplish since sexual behavior is becoming more public (i.e., mass media) with the coming of each new generation.

Homosexual Deviance

The debate in favor of decriminalization of the criminal laws against homosexual practices of consenting adults began in 1957 with the results of the Wolfenden Committee in Great Britain. The committee report concluded that adult consensual homosexual practices do not threaten the family, church, or even the stability of the society; that adult homosexuality does not lower community standards of decency nor does it create a law enforcement problem; and finally that this adult example of private sexual deviance does not interfere with the normal socialization process concerning heterosexuality of the next generation of youth in society.[52]

Since 1952 the American Law Institute, based on its view that homosexuality should not be a crime per se, has advocated the repeal of state criminal statutes. The Model Penal Code accepted the decriminalization concept based on the British example but it was the Task Force on Homosexuality of the National Institute of Mental Health that recommended that all criminal statutes dealing with adult consensual homosexual practices be rescinded.[53]

The Task Force on Homosexuality concluded in particular that special training for all police officers who deal with morals issues be provided. Although many members of society still regard homosexuality with negativism, there is evidence that public attitudes are changing, especially in the large metropolitan areas. Discreet homosexual practices are recognized by many heterosexuals to be a private matter that should not be regulated by statute. The Task Force also noted that criminal sanctions are not effective in preventing or reducing homosexual practices between consenting adults who conduct their activities in private. The mental health of adult homosexuals would improve and decriminalization would encourage them to be more positive and open about their lifestyle.[54]

The main arguments for decriminalization state that: (1) the police are indiscriminate in dealing with lesbian behavior but discriminate against private gay activities; (2) law enforcement policies lead to suicides, blackmail, and increased public deviancy as acts of defiance of the law; (3) homosexuals would make better adjustments to living in the community; (4) the criminal justice system makes it difficult for those who are stigmatized by an incident involving homosexuality to become heterosexuals if they wish to make that decision; and (5) there should be clear distinctions between what constitutes public and private homosexual behavior for consenting adults.[55]

Those who favor the continued enforcement of the criminal statutes against adult consensual homosexual private practices state that the criminal law keeps homosexual behavior in the closet where it belongs. Overt actions of various gay liberation groups only encourage teenagers to consider experimenting with homosexual lifestyles. The openness of homosexuality in large metropolitan areas encourages homosexual prostitution and the gay/lesbian bar that caters to all sorts of sexual deviance. Homosexuality leads to the moral decay of the family, church, and school which will ultimately destroy the very fabric of society. Finally homosexuals are in need of psychiatric treatment and the continuance of the sexual psychopath laws are a necessity to protect the lives of decent members of society.[56]

Venereal Diseases

As Bell states, venereal diseases are usually a covert aspect of some form of social deviance which may be a crime (i.e., fornication, sodomy, homosexuality adultery, incest, and prostitution). As long as society considers the individual who has venereal disease to be immoral, there will be a problem in dealing with the topic in a direct manner. Thus one who contracts venereal disease is a violator of the sexual mores of society and should be punished. This makes the person suffering from the disease hide his or her medical problem so that he or she will not be ostracized by the community. This is difficult enough for the single person but worse for the husband or wife who infects an innocent spouse.[57]

As long as states like Virginia treat individuals who contract venereal diseases as criminals, it is most unlikely that these diseases will be controlled. The U.S. Public Health Service cannot ever hope to gather accurate statistics on this social problem when most people do not want to mention these diseases since they originate in behavior that is taboo (i.e., the Old Testament makes numerous references to what appears to be both gonorrhea and syphilis — Book of Leviticus, Book of Numbers, Thirty-Eighth Psalm).[58]

It is obvious that both state and federal governments must deal properly with this issue as has been done in the District of Columbia Code (i.e., find, treat, and cure those affected with venereal disease) rather than punish individuals for having a contagious disease. Proper sex education would be a real benefit to all members of the community. The opening of more treatment clinics that are free or charging a nominal fee would also help. Finally hotlines that answer questions concerning venereal diseases and tell individuals where they can seek medical and psychological advice are needed. In our society only the military take a proper approach to the venereal disease problem through both preventative and control methods. The United States should follow the proven methods utilized in Great Britain since World War II concerning venereal disease.

Family Conflicts

Family conflicts are a diverse problem for the legislatures and law enforcement agencies to handle. Some problems are not presently dealt with through the criminal court but by domestic relations, family, and/or juvenile courts in the United States. These are problems such as adultery, desertion, divorce, and battered wives and children. Some jurisdictions like the District of Columbia have criminalized social deviance that deals with child abuse, both physical and sexual but most leave the problems to be handled by the local jurisdictions through actions taken by departments of social welfare. The police are only called in when an emergency situation occurs (i.e., someone's life is being threatened or seriously endangered).

Bigamy and incest are crimes in most jurisdictions of the United States but most victims do not report the offences because of the negative publicity they would receive in the press and in the community in general. Thus most cases of bigamy and incest go unknown and unreported to the police or when known to the police are left unprosecuted since the public prosecutor does not want to follow through on such negative cases unless other crimes are also involved. Many times a criminal or juvenile court feels it is in the best interest of the offender to have the individual seek out voluntary psychiatric treatment as an alternative to incarceration.

Research has pointed out that those who commit family related crimes are usually immature, frustrated, sociopathic or psychopathic, or suffering from the pathological effects of alcohol, drugs, or other physiological problems.[59] Adultery is very rarely seen on the arrest records of police departments since it is so common and divorces granted on this ground rarely result in the guilty party being turned over to the proper authorities for criminal prosecution. Divorce is not a crime but many of the grounds for same could be easily prosecuted by the public prosecutor who usually never sees such a source for his caseload. The increasing number of divorced fathers who fail to pay child support has prompted some jurisdictions to criminalize this behavior as a potent threat to force reluctant ex-husbands to pay for the support of their children so that local social welfare authorities do not have to pay for these children.[60]

Thus in the case of family conflict problems, one can see that crimes stemming from deviant behavior of family members has often been criminalized but lack of public interest and/or the commonality of such behavior leads the criminal justice authorities to overlook most of the offenses. Yet in the cases of child and spouse abuse there is a growing feeling that these forms of deviance should be criminalized and specialized staff recruited and trained to handle such victims and rehabilitate their offenders.

Abortion

Since abortion is currently not a criminal issue, it does not belong under the topic of victimless crimes. But the debate continues in and out of the courts, state legislatures, and Congress on the topic of abortion. Obviously some people feel very strongly that abortion and for that matter birth control are forms of social deviance that should be criminalized. This appears to be a religious and ethical, not a criminal justice issue at this time in our national history. The Roman Catholic Church along with some fundamentalist Protestant and Orthodox Jewish leaders are opposed to abortion and spearhead the controversy in the United States.[61]

The current debate is not concerned with the decriminalization of abortion but the decriminalization of nontherapeutic and in some cases even therapeutic abortions. The abortion issue is further confused by opposition of these groups to the Equal Rights Amendment for women, sex education in the public schools, and the availability of contraceptive devices and information to all age groups at commercial shopping centers and public health and welfare offices.[62]

The abortion debate should not center around whether abortions should remain legal or not. The issue should be one of freedom of access to all forms of family planning which comes through a thorough understanding of the part sexual behavior plays in the everyday life of the average person in society. Since it has been shown that the family does not properly prepare the children of the next generation in the area of sex education, then the church and school should take over this public responsibility. If these two institutions cannot assume this responsibility, then only the state can provide leadership. It is very inconsistent for the United States government in its foreign policy to push programs of birth control on other countries while denying a national policy for our own population. It appears that only the military institution is concerned about sex education, birth control, and family planning for its membership in our society.[63]

Our Constitution gurarantees that every citizen has the right to freedom of speech. Thus one is not proposing that there should not be disagreements concerning ethical and religious issues in society. But there is also the guarantee in this country of separation of church and state and this means that no religious group should be able to force any other group or person in society to follow its particular dictates. The abortion issue is one where the adherents of the church are attempting to interfere with the rights of the citizen in a secular state. Let the individual citizen decide for or against the practice of abortion in the privacy of his or her home, not in the public courts or legislatures where it constitutionally has no place in our society.

Euthanasia

Proponents of the euthanasia movement are asking for legislation, not seeking decriminalization. The right-to-die laws and the use of the "living will" have enabled people to control their destiny without creating problems for physicians and the hospitals in which they are treated.[64] Many opponents to euthanasia are misinformed about the topic and react emotionally without examining the actual facts and looking at the state laws where euthanasia is allowed (i.e., California Natural Death Act of 1977). Some of the most valid arguments against euthanasia involve the fear of its abuse concerning individuals other than the terminally ill. There is also the basic religious arguments that taking another person's life is immoral as well as illegal. Finally, physicians and other medical personnel are not quite sure what their legal and moral status and obligations are concerning euthanasia.[65]

The controversy over euthanasia will continue for as long as medical technology keeps prolonging life. The basic question should be whether life should be preserved at all costs if the patient is technically dead or incapable of functioning normally or be allowed to painlessly die with dignity. In a society that is concerned with overpopulation, disappearing natural resources, and a deteriorating quality of life, the euthanasia issue should be carefully examined before being rejected by any state legislature.

Suicide

Since it is not a crime to commit suicide in the United States, little can be said concerning the decriminalization of this practice. The practice of suicide is still considered by many as immoral and reprehensible. Thus most of the concern with this form of social deviance is with suicide prevention.

Those who attempt suicide can endanger others by the method utilized (i.e., using a vehicle as a means of killing oneself, attempting suicide via use of gas, jumping off high places, and lying down on railroad or subway tracks). There are also those individuals who try to involve others consciously or subconsciously in the act of suicide (i.e., force another person to deliberately kill them or murder someone else in order to be forced into the act of self-destruction). Our present criminal statutes dealing with homicide supposedly deal with murder-suicide cases and suicide pacts, but are somewhat confusing as to how to deal with the particular circumstances of suicide cases.[66]

Thus the criminal justice system must develop some way of dealing with suicide prevention cases other than processing these individuals as offenders except in the cases of murder-suicide attempts. There should be better coordination of police with mental health personnel. General orders should be developed to aid law enforcement personnel to deal with the variety of types of potential suicides. Finally since a high percentage of police officers are themselves potential suicides, there should be specialized personnel in each department (i.e., psychologist or psychiatrist) to counsel officers who appear to be in need of help.

The federal government which already operates The Center For Studies of Suicide Prevention should actively work with both professional and volunteer groups on the county and municipal levels to educate the public on this social problem. The stigma attached to the individual who attempts suicide should be handled in a similar manner to that of Alcoholics Anonymous so that the individual will not be forced into another attempt that may succeed in his or her self-destruction. Thus the mass media should be involved along with various educational and social service institutions in an effort to prevent suicide and suicide-homicides in our society.[67]

Mental Disorders

As Halleck notes, there is a problem in the diagnosing of mental illness by psychiatrists. Yet these medical experts are utilized by the criminal court to determine whether the offender meets the legal test of insanity or not. Psychiatrists are also used to determine whether the offender should be committed before trial or even if he should have a trial at all. Thus the criminal justice system allows the psychiatrist and his knowledge of medical jurisprudence to determine whether the criminal offender goes to trial at all; whether he is legally sane or insane (i.e., psychiatric testimony usually determines which way the jury votes in most instances); whether the offender should be diverted to a court clinic, or hospital for the criminally insane; operate programs for sexual psychopaths, diagnostic reception centers, alcoholic rehabilitation centers, and narcotics hospitals; operate programs for juvenile delinquents in training schools; and serve as part-time staff at state prisons for the general inmate population.[68] It must be apparent to the average person who comes in contact with anyone dealing with mental health or the criminal justice system that the word of the psychiatrist is almost law (i.e., the so-called medical model which has been proposed by psychiatrists has been accepted by state legislatures in creating statutes dealing with the mentally ill, the mentally defective or deficient, the criminally insane, and sexual psychopaths). Thus we live in the age of the therapeutic state where medical science and social science team up to create a new type of social control over our daily existence which can be used to benefit the average person as well as take away his constitutional rights in the name of psychiatric therapy.[69]

As already mentioned, the criminally insane and the mentally ill are not the only individuals who are involuntarily committed to a mental hospital or special institution for the insane criminal. There are special institutions for juvenile delinquents who are known as "defective delinquents" like the Patuxent Institution in Maryland, the narcotics hospital like the federal institutions in Kentucky and Texas, the institutions that deal with alcoholics, and the state and county hospitals that care for the mentally defective and deficient.

All states have statutes governing the individual who seeks voluntary commitment to a mental hospital. The major problem deals with the laws that govern the involuntary commitment of all kinds of people who may or may not be in need of psychiatric assistance. Some states have judicial commitment procedures while others have nonjudicial proceedings (i.e., administrative or medical certification).[70]

Forty-two states have involuntary commitment procedures that are considered judicial in nature (i.e., before a judge and jury). Notice must be given to the person who is alleged to be mentally ill in twenty-six of these states. In most states a mandatory hearing is provided but only eleven require that the defendant be present. All forty-two states provide that the alleged ill person has the right to be represented by an attorney but only twenty-four states provide for the appointment of a lawyer if the mentally ill person cannot afford one.[71]

Nonjudicial proceedings are either administrative or medical certification. Ten states allow administrative commitment where a board determines whether the alleged mentally ill person should undergo treatment. Some of these administrative hearings do not even allow the patient the opportunity to be heard. Involuntary commitment by medical certification is accomplished on the basis of one or more psychiatric reports being filed with the court. Thus the psychiatrist decides the fate of an individual without his ability to properly defend his past or present behavior in a court of law. Thirty-one states provide medical certification proceedings for the mentally ill and allow judicial review of the medical certification and allow for the patient's release within a designated time if he gives formal notice to the court that he wants to be re-examined in order to obtain release from the mental hospital.[72]

What one finds is the indefinite involuntary commitment of approximately forty percent of all alleged mental patients in the United States today. Once the procedures for commitment are initiated, most individuals usually are placed in an institution or are labeled as social deviants who must seek treatment at an outpatient clinic under court order and thus lose their constitutional safeguards or have limited freedoms due to the impact of the therapeutic state (i.e., psychiatrist's control of the individual adjudicated as mentally ill).[73]

Finally we must deal with those committed to special institutions for the criminally insane (i.e., sexual psychopaths, sociopaths, and those criminals who are innocent of their crimes by reason of insanity). At one time twenty-eight states and the District of Columbia had sexual psychopath laws. These statutes are vague and open to misinterpretation and many states have rescinded their laws dealing with this type of social deviance. Unfortunately for individuals labelled as psychopaths, psychiatrists do not in general know how to deal with this category of mental illness so rehabilitation is difficult. The term sociopath is synonomous with psychopath but some jurisdictions make a legal differentiation between the two concepts. At any rate, an offender who is committed to an institution for the criminally insane will probably spend more time in jail than a criminal who commits the same offence and accepts a jail sentence at the state penitentiary. Thus the criminally insane are given indeterminate sentences and allowed to deteriorate mentally even further while the same type of offender who serves his time as a normal criminal will be out in society to cause the same problem again and not be stigmatized as much as the criminally insane individual by society.[74]

Gambling

Those who favor the legalization of all forms of gambling state that most people are going to gamble anyway so one might as well decriminalize this form of supposed social deviance. Economically decriminalization of gambling is the only politically feasible way to raise new public revenue for municipal, county, state, and the federal governments. Currently only Nevada and New Jersey benefit from almost all forms of legalized gambling in terms of gained revenues. A gambling tax is not regressive and is voluntary since only those who gamble are taxed. Gambling does not compete with the business community as it actually attracts more potential business for an area that may be economically depressed.[75]

Decriminalization of gambling would aid in the destruction of secondary crimes associated with gambling. Loan sharking (i.e., lending money at usurious interest rates) which is operated by organized crime lends money to compulsive gamblers in order to pay their debts (i.e., interest rates may vary from one to one hundred-fifty percent per week depending on the circumstances of the loan and the characteristics of the person in debt). The loan shark makes an average of twenty percent per client and makes more money on the interest so usually encourages continued gambling as long as the gambler keeps up his payments on the debt. Associated with loan sharking is another type of secondary crime, extortion. This is the threat of force or use of brutal force if the gambling debt is not quickly paid. Thus the gambler is intimidated into promptly paying any interest rate charged, is afraid of going to the police, and does not protest very much about his treatment since the loan shark's customer may be severely beaten, members of his family threatened, or even be killed if he does not pay promptly and quietly.[76]

Thus legalization of gambling would deny organized crime its largest single source of revenue (i.e., gambling and loan sharking that goes with indebtedness due to gambling). Organized crime would then be denied the use of ready funds that are utilized for paying graft to police, politicians, and members of the business community. Further the criminal justice system has not been able to effectively prosecute members of organized crime involved in either gambling or loan sharking, let alone the average person who gambles since most individuals desire to gamble. The criminal justice system can best utilize its personnel and monitary resources elsewhere.[77]

There is no conclusive evidence that freedom to gamble legally will cause a great increase in compulsive gamblers. Gambling may be a positive social force that will allow people to escape the tensions and frustrations of everyday life and is a legitimate form of recreation. Thus it is highly improbable that the legalization of gambling will cause a breakdown of the family, work ethic, and one's responsibility toward local government and the community in general. Research has pointed out that gambling allows the poor and minorities the opportunity to achieve success through winning at gambling. The numbers game supposedly allows Blacks the hope that if they win the "big one" they will be able to escape the ghetto. Some research even points to the fact that gambling provides members of the ghetto community with jobs that they would not otherwise have.[78]

The National Gambling Commission concludes that the states should have the primary responsibility for determining what forms of gambling may be allowed. The federal government should prevent interference by one state with the gambling policies of another. Specifically the Commission states that winnings derived from legal gambling should not be part of one's gross income but be part of the taxpayer's responsibility to report all sources; that states refrain from legalizing single-event sports wagering under the present structure of federal taxation; that on-track takeout in paramutual racing be reduced in order to increase revenues; that racing commissioners be prohibited from holding financial interests in racetracks within their jurisdictions and public disclosure of all financial interests be made of all racing operations; that states fully inform the public of the odds of winning in all types of lotteries; that states legalize all forms of public gambling; and that statutes dealing with gamblers who are associated with organized crime and gambling establishments that are fronts for organized crime be stringently enforced.[79]

Those who are opposed to the decriminalization of gambling feel that the existing statutes should be thoroughly enforced and corrupt police and public officials be severely punished. Legalization of gambling would lead to more crime since more people would gamble. Easy access to gambling would produce more compulsive gamblers and the family and community would suffer a breakdown of moral ties and become anomic. The poor and minorities would be hurt since they would not try to improve themselves socio-economically but rely on winning it big through gambling. The taxation of gambling would be regressive since the poor who can least afford more taxes are the most frequent bettors. Legalized gambling would increase law enforcement costs and also cause more people to be forced on welfare since the breadwinner would gamble away money that is for food and rent. Legalized gambling will not create new jobs and will hurt the legitimate businesses in any community in which it is located. Gambling revenues are unreliable and each state would compete for the gambling population that would ultimately force more federal regulation of state and local community tax sources. Taxation of gambling is not a cure for public fiscal problems.[80]

Drug Abuse

The criminal justice system has been a failure in its efforts to prevent and control alcoholics and public drunkenness. The President's Commission noted this fact in 1967 and it is even more true in 1978.[81] Public drunkenness and related crimes place an undue burden on the law enforcement system since the individual police officers make arbitrary decisions on the basis of the appearance of the drunk whether to arrest the individual, refer him to a social services organization, or take him home. Those who are most often arrested and booked are usually the skid row types whose Constitutional safeguards are often violated as they are the most familiar inhabitants of the municipal or county jail (i.e., officers have dealt with these recidivists so often that they take for granted that the drunk knows his rights and waives his phone call to a lawyer since he does not want one anyway).

The criminal courts are not any better concerning the processing of public drunkards. Since a defense attorney is rarely present, judges and magistrates take the opinion of the arresting officer that the defendant is intoxicated without applying the various medical tests to determine if in fact that the person is drunk (i.e., coordination, breath, or blood tests). Most court caseloads are overwhelmed with intoxication in public and related cases. Thus most judges are forced to dispose of these cases in bulk with as many as 25-50 alcoholics being dealt with at the same time. These cases represent a drain on the time and money of the court since most often the judge must deal with serious felony and misdemeanor situations. The arresting officer usually is the expert and complaining witness and must be off the street at a time when his services could be put to better utilization.[82]

The alcoholic who is sent to the municipal or county jail cannot be properly provided for and takes up space that should be utilized for those who are in need of incarceration. Often as many as half or more of the jail population is composed of those convicted of public drunkenness and related charges. The jail provides the public with the service of removing temporarily the skid row bum from the streets but all the personnel can do is dry him out, provide food, clothing, shelter, and the most limited sort of medical treatment.[83]

The President's Commission stated that public drunkenness should be decriminalized. They did not advocate decriminalization for alcohol related crimes like driving under the influence, liquor law violations, and crimes such as disorderly conduct and vagrancy.[84] Since the Commission's report, the American Medical Association has defined alcoholism as a sickness and other prestigious national organizations have lobbied for the decriminalization of public drunkenness (i.e., as noted elsewhere in this chapter). The Commission report did request the expansion of detoxification centers around the country as well as aftercare programs for patients who have successfully been "dried out".

The detoxification center in Washington, D.C. is federally funded and the police as well as social service personnel bring alcoholics to the center. The inhabitants of the center are dealt with physically and medically in order to dry them out (i.e., proper diet with vitamin supplements and medication are administered). Alcoholics Anonymous members are allowed to counsel inhabitants in addition to social work staff. Unfortunately once an alcoholic is deemed healthy, he cannot be held any further in the center and if he has committed a crime has to be returned to the custody of the police and processed through the criminal justice system.[85]

A number of programs have been initiated to deal with aftercare services for the chronic alcoholic. The Salvation Army, Alcoholics Anonymous, public hospitals and their outpatient clinics, mental health associations, and psychologists and psychiatrists all deal with the problem drinker. Halfway houses have been utilized to deal with former alcoholics and are operated by a combination of professional staff and former alcoholics. The new resident is expected to get a job in order to pay for his room and board and take part in all facets of the rehabilitation process.[86]

A tremendous amount of work has been done by Alcoholics Anonymous to deal with former drunkards both within and outside of prisons, mental hospitals, and other total institutions. Alcoholics Anonymous has been utilized as an alternative and as a supplement to traditional approaches to treatment of alcoholics. This organization deals with those convicted of public drunkenness, related crimes such as driving under the influence, and felons and misdemeants who admit that their crimes were related to their abuse of alcohol.[87]

It appears that there is no active organized movement to retain the public drunkenness statutes in the United States today. Many who support the decriminalization of this minor offense also support the continued enforcement of statutes related to alcoholism. A major criticism of those convicted of these alcohol related crimes is the lack of consistency of the criminal justice system in dealing with offenders and the lack of success in rehabilitating them. This is especially true in the cases of driving while intoxicated where injuries and deaths result.[88]

The treatment of drug addicts (i.e., opiates) by physicians actually preceded the criminalization of drug addiction in the United States. From 1870 to 1900 most drug addicts did not receive any special treatment since clinics were mostly private. Thus the addict either was treated by a doctor or utilized patent remedies, most of which were opium-based. During the years 1900-1915 many private clinics for alcoholics and drug addicts were opened. The first narcotic dispensing clinics were established in Florida and Tennessee in 1912 and 1913. A medical model was developed to deal with drug addicts.[89]

After the passage of the Harrison Act, the Treasury Department began to discourage doctors from prescribing opiates to addicts and a number of court cases resulted in most physicians losing interest in a medical cure for addiction. The Treasury Department did encourage the establishment of temporary clinics for the maintenance of drug addicts after doctors stopped prescribing opiates in 1919. By 1921 there were forty-four such clinics in the United States. These clinics were to treat addicts and cure them but in reality were opiate maintenance centers. Some clinics were careless about the distribution of narcotics and by 1925 the Treasury Department closed all clinics. Thus the therapeutic model was a failure and gave way to the punitive model of dealing with drug addicts.[90]

Congress authorized the establishment of two drug treatment hospitals in 1929 but the facility at Lexington, Kentucky was not established until 1935 and the second at Fort Worth, Texas in 1938. These facilities were designed to deal with federal drug law offenders but accepted voluntary patients as well. Studies showed that ninety percent of the patients relapsed into drug addiction after release.[91] These two federal facilities remained the only drug addict treatment programs in America until 1952 when Riverside Hospital in New York City was opened to deal with juvenile addicts. Under the state law the patients were kept in custody for three years and then released. The program was closed in 1963 since ninety-five percent of the patients returned to drug addiction after release.[92] In 1956 New York state set up a special narcotic parole project that lasted until 1959.[93] Between 1930 and 1960 the laws of thirty-four states allowed drug addicts to receive treatment in state mental hospitals although only California and New York for the most part did send addicts to such facilities.[94]

The failure of the criminal justice system to deal with prevention and control of drug addicts became increasingly apparent by the early 1960s. In 1961 California set up statewide treatment programs for addicts followed by New York in 1962. These programs were to place addicts in mandatory programs that were indeterminate in nature so that the individual could be truly physically and mentally rehabilitated. Many addicts chose to go to prison rather than enter treatment since the period of incarceration was shorter.[95] In 1966 the federal Narcotic Addict Rehabilitation Act was passed by Congress and was modeled after the California and New York state programs which were based on the civil commitment procedure. Forty-eight community based treatment facilities were in operation financed by the federal government by 1971 under this Act.[96]

A number of private organizations also became active in the 1960s concerning rehabilitation of addicts. Synanon was founded in 1959 to deal with addicts based on the Alcoholics Anonymous model.[97] A methadone maintenance program was set up in New York City in 1964 which was successful and led to the annual conferences on methadone treatment (first national conference held in 1968).[98] Liberty Park Village was established in 1969 in New Jersey and Daytop Lodge in New York City.[99]

Those who are opposed to decriminalization of drug addiction and abuse (i.e., opiates, marijuana, and cocaine) state that any legal provision of addicting or harmful drugs to people would constitute the condoning of such social deviance in society. Secondly legalization would cause more harm than benefits to society since more people would become addicted and abuse drugs. The critics of decriminalization have mixed into one class of social deviants all drug addicts, drug abusers, and drug users (both over the counter and prescription purchasers). The critics of the decriminalization concept have made their argument difficult to defend since they are dealing with all types of drugs (i.e., barbiturates, amphetamines, hallucinogens, cocaine, opiates, and marijuana) not just the opiates.

It is obvious that there must be different solutions to the personal and social problems created by using and abusing different kinds of drugs. It would appear from the continuous attempts to deal with the medical management of drugs that a medical solution (both physiological and psychological) would be more appropriate than a simple criminal justice approach. Federal as well as local officials have for too long felt that both the drug addict and abuser are criminals, not people in need of medical and psychiatric attention.[100]

Those who favor decriminalization are quite selective in how best to deal with what types of drugs. Obviously drug addicts have different problems than drug abusers. The latter group is composed of individuals who use cocaine, marijuana, hallucinogens, amphetamines, and barbiturates. Each one of these substances has its own particular properties and potential for abuse. Thus one must approach each substance from the point of view that there will be different types of people utilizing these substances for a variety of reasons. Some people will abuse several substances, others will be quite selective in their use or abuse of these drugs. It is well known that many individuals combine one or more of these drugs with alcohol, tobacco, or coffee. These latter drugs can be dangerous in and of themselves in large quantities so the problem is more difficult to deal with when combinations of legal drugs are utilized along with illicit drugs.[101]

Those who favor decriminalization believe that the legal suppression of all types of drugs has made it impossible for law enforcement personnel to control the traffic in drugs. This is due to the fact that organized crime has a willing and interested class of people wanting to experiment, defy the law, and just plain enjoy the effects of certain types of drugs. The drug addict (i.e., heroin user) is the least of our problems today since that population appears to have been approximately 58,000 known addicts since the 1920s.[102] All drug abusers become criminals under our current drug laws and are stigmatized by society by their arrest records which makes rehabilitation difficult and makes a career as a drug deviant more easy.[103]

Many individuals and prestigious groups have advocated that drug addiction and abuse be considered primarily as a medical problem. Thus the Joint Committee of the American Bar Association and the American Medical Association on Narcotic Drugs, The National Commission on Marihuana and Drug Abuse, The President's Commission on Law Enforcement and Administration of Justice, as well as Lindesmith, Schur, Geis, Reasons, and others have been pushing for alternatives to incarceration for drug addicts and abusers and the decriminalization of certain types of criminal statutes.[104]

Brecher succinctly sums up the most probable solution to America's drug problem with six caveats: (1) stop emphasizing measures designed to keep drugs away from people; (2) stop publicizing the horrors of the so-called drug menace; (3) stop increasing the damage done by drugs; (4) stop misclassifying drugs; (5) stop viewing the drug problem as primarily a national problem that can only be solved on a national basis; and (6) stop trying to wipe out illicit drug use.[105] One more point should be added to Brecher's caveats: start paying attention to all the national commissions dealing with analysis and potential solutions to our drug problems rather than the misdirected and sometimes damaging statements of some of our politicians.[106]

Costs To American Society

Organized Crime

The criminalization of goods (i.e., drugs, alcohol, pornographic materials) or services (i.e., prostitution, gambling, abortion) makes access to these goods or services difficult and forces the prices up. Since it is a crime to sell such items or services as well as purchase such items or services, those offering these items or services are taking high risks. Thus organized crime which has access to funds, can provide its employees with protection, and has means to both pay off police and use force to collect debts, enters and expands the black market for such goods and services. The fact that people want such goods and services and are willing to pay for such attracts individuals into the subterranean network of manufac-turers, wholesalers, and retailers of such products since transactions are in cash with no reporting of earnings to public authorities. Thus amateurs as well as professionals enter the victimless crime field for profit.[107]

The most common reason for secondary crime is the constant need for the services or products that are offered on the black market which continually go up in price since the risks also become greater the more people know about the problem (i.e., mass media exposure, church and political activism to "clean up" the problem). Thus compulsive gamblers may borrow money from loan sharks and then steal or embezzle funds from work to cover these debts. Hard drug addicts may steal and/or resort to prostitution (male and female) in order to pay for their daily habit. Prostitutes may decide to steal from clients rather than service them since all they want is money to pay their pimps and/or the police. Some addicts may turn dealer in order to obtain more money and thus expose themselves to trouble with other drug suppliers and addicts who will try to steal from them. Thus this individual will have to arm himself and expose himself to greater risks than those of an addict.[108]

Blackmail is a secondary crime that is usually associated with homosexuality, adultery, prostitution (i.e., call girls), gambling operations, abortion, and euthanasia. On the other hand individuals are rarely blackmailed for being an alcoholic, being sexually active outside of marriage (i.e., premarital relationships), or taking drugs with the exception of hard drugs (i.e., heroin, morphine, etc.). Of course the blackmailer is also open to criminal prosecution so he usually is associated with organized crime and uses his victim for other purposes than obtaining money. It is becoming more common for runaway children and women to get involved in victimless crimes and then become open to blackmail by those with whom they associate in their activities.[109]

Loss of Credibility of Criminal Justice System

Pursley estimates that from one-third to one-half of all arrests made by the police fall into the crimes without victims category. This is estimated to cost the taxpayer billions of dollars in terms of processing these millions of people through the criminal justice system in any given year. The cost is assuming that most of those arrested will not get past the police-magistrate level and many will not even be jailed except for short periods of time. A larger cost to the taxpayer is impossible to even estimate in tax dollars. This is the area of organized crime since the black market for goods and services would not exist if the victimless crime statutes did not exist. Organized crime is able to make billions of dollars per year in the areas of gambling, narcotics, prostitution, and loan sharking because the public demands these goods and services and the statutes that criminalize such goods and services give organized crime a monopoly. Thus tax dollars are lost since the goods and services are not taxed, the police and other sectors of the criminal justice system are clogged with victimless crime cases that bring in little money by way of fines as compared to criminal justice system costs, and the police often accept bribes which are estimated to run over two billion dollars a year.[110]

The offender also suffers in a number of ways due to the existence of victimless crimes statutes. There is obvious loss of self-respect and status in the community due to being arrested for such crimes. The offender may lose his job, cause his family to suffer and be labeled as deviant, and cause the children to be viewed with suspicion (i.e., potential delinquents) by classmates and teachers. This labeling process could end up with the offender and/or members of his family committing other deviant acts (i.e., drinking, drugs, or becoming delinquent/criminal) and thus causing more problems for the community and the taxpayer. The offender might also be forced to seek out and associate with other known deviants and develop a deviant subculture. This has happened frequently with alcoholics, drug addicts, and homosexuals. This is also the most likely way in which a juvenile becomes associated with a street gang. Thus the ostracism of the offender can trigger the self-fulfilling prophecy cycle that will not only degrade the deviant but involve family and friends, lead to unemployment, and possibly be causal in the start of a delinquent or criminal career. All these negative results are a tremendous cost to the individual and the taxpayer.[111]

The criminal justice system has been placed in a negative light due to the victimless crime problem. First of all, task forces have to be created to deal with the enforcement of the statutes (i.e., morals or vice divisions) and officers trained. Second, organized crime units have to be created to deal with the suppliers of goods and services. Last, internal security units have to be created to check on the police because of the constant possibility of bribes by both offenders and organized crime. Thus the costs in training and manpower taken away from enforcement of statutes dealing with crimes against the person and property is beyond belief. Usually there is a point reached by public administrators in terms of costs where it is more beneficial to the taxpayer to ignore the victimless crime in terms of law enforcement and criminal justice processing and concentrate tax dollars and manpower on serious crimes. Politicians usually see this reality during election year when asked to account for increased costs for enforcement policies that do not work and are unpopular with many in the community.[112]

The police have utilized both vagrancy and disorderly-conduct type statutes in addition to the existing statutes dealing with specific forms of deviance to arrest, search, question, or detain individuals who appear to be undesirables in a given community. Thus the victimless crime and related catch-all statutes have been used in many inner city and suburban jurisdictions as a harassment tactic by the police. Some jurisdictions such as New York, the District of Columbia, and Ohio have instituted so-called stop and frisk laws that allow the police more discretion in dealing with deviants.[113]

In dealing with victimless crimes the police are often forced to resort to the use of electronic surveillance devices and the use of undercover officers in order to entrap the offender. This is especially true in drug, gambling, and sexual deviance (i.e., prostitution, homosexuality, pornography) cases. These activities can be dangerous to the undercover officer, are degrading and demoralizing, and can and do lead to corruption of some officers by offenders and organized crime personnel. Thus the courts have become clogged with entrapment cases.[114]

The United States Supreme Court has handled numerous decisions dealing with the extralegal methods of the police in dealing with victimless crimes. *Mapp v. Ohio* (1961) dealt with pornography and obscenity (i.e., illegal search and seizure). Entrapment decisions were reached in the areas of gambling and narcotics cases (i.e., *Sorrels v. US* (1932) and *Sherman v. US* (1958)). Admissibility of evidence as a result of illegal arrests have come from gambling, alcohol, and drug cases (i.e., *Beck v. Ohio* (1964); *Benanti v. US* (1957); *Johnson v. US* (1958); and *Draper v. US* (1959). Unlawful search and seizure cases dealing with alcohol and drugs have been *Carrol v. US* (1925), *Agnello v. US* (1925), *Marron v. US* (1927), *Go-Bart Company v. US* (1931), *Lefkowitz v. US* (1932), *Johnson v. US* (1948), *Rochin v. California* (1952), *Jones v. US* (1960), *Wong Sun v. US* (1963), and *Ker v. California* (1963). There have also been several cases involving the illegal use of wire-tapping, bugging, and other forms of electronic eavesdropping in victimless crime cases (i.e., *Olmstead v. US* (1928); *Nardone v. US* (1938); *Lee v. US* (1952); *Irvine v. California* (1954); *Benanti v. US* (1957); *Silverman v. US* (1961)).[115]

All the problems concerning the processing of offenders for commiting victimless crimes results in a general disrespect for the law on the part of the offenders, many of the public, and some members of the criminal justice system — especially the police. There is usually the differential enforcement of statutes for crimes without victims against the lower class and nonwhite segments of the population, the young, and inner city residents rather than suburbanites. Homosexuals are more often arrested than lesbians, street walkers than call girls, inner city gamblers and alcoholics than suburban gamblers and drinkers, and hard drug users than soft drug abusers. There is also differential imposition of sentences based on social class, race, age, and place of residence for offenders. Thus an adolescent may receive a longer sentence for possession of marijuana in Virginia than for commission of armed robbery as a first offender.[116]

Rehabilitation of Offenders

The traditional response to criminal behavior has been incarceration. In general this approach has been a dismal failure in the case of offenders convicted of commiting victimless crimes. Increasingly probation, fines, and community-based facilities are replacing the jail sentence. To a great extent in the past and often in the present certain categories of victimless crime offenders have gone to prison or another total institution such as a mental hospital or public general hospital. Drug addicts and abusers have gone to prison or in some cases the United States Public Health Service Hospitals in either Lexington, Kentucky or Fort Worth, Texas. Some drug addicts and abusers as well as alcoholics have gone to state public or mental hospitals. Often alcoholics go to a county jail for a short stay. The mentally ill have gone to public hospitals, mental institutions, and even to prison on occasion, especially in the case of psychopaths and psychotics. There are even institutions for the criminally insane in some jurisdictions. Homosexuals are rarely incarcerated or placed in mental institutions today although the practice was more common in the past. Prostitutes are sometimes placed in county institutions or state facilities for women. Spouse abusers and those guilty of nonsupport of wife and/or family are sometimes placed in county correctional facilities.[117]

Deviants who are involuntarily committed to total institutions (i.e., prison, mental hospital, or public hospital dealing with alcoholics and addicts) are offered a variety of treatment programs which vary according to the quality and case load of the staff. Such methods as reality therapy, transactional analysis, therapeutic community, guided group interaction, and behavior modification are used with limited success.[118]

There is a growing number of community based treatment and rehabilitation programs in the United States on both federal and state levels. There are guided group interaction projects, foster and group homes, halfway houses, intensive community treatment, medical aftercare programs, and self-help programs (i.e, voluntary associations) that deal with social deviants. Most of these community based programs have been developed in response to the President's Commission of 1967. Community based programs also utilize the various methods of therapy already noted.

The medical aftercare programs are of special interest since they were specifically designed to deal with drug addicts and abusers, alcoholics, the mentally ill, and potential suicides. The federal government has set up detoxification centers to deal with chronic alcoholics on a short term basis. The methadone maintenance program has also been set up by the federal government. Both programs are controversial and appear to lack support by state governments and local authorities in general.[119]

The self-help (i.e., voluntary associations) programs take a great variety of forms and deal with most types of victimless crimes. Alcoholics Anonymous deals with alcoholics and their families. Synanon, Daytop Lodge, and Narcotics Anonymous deal with drug addicts and abusers. Recovery Inc. helps ex-mental patients. Gamblers Anonymous deals with compulsive gamblers. The Mattachine Society, Daughters of Bilitis, and Gay Activist League is concerned with the problems of homosexuals and lesbians. Suicide Prevention Centers and Suicides Anonymous deal with potential suicides. The National Abortion Rights Action League and Pro Life deal with the problems of abortion. The Euthanasia Education Council is concerned with the right of the person to die with dignity. Various community free clinics deal with the control and treatment of venereal diseases, birth control, and abortion information. There are also programs for battered wives and children who run away from home.[120]

Notes

[1]The President's Commission on Pornography and Obscenity, *Report of Commission on Pornography and Obscenity,* New York: New York Times Book by Bantam Books, 1970.

[2]Wayland Young, *Eros Denied: Sex in Western Society*, New York: Grove Press, 1966; Fernando Henriques, *Prostitution and Society*, New York: Grove Press, 1962; Harry Benjamin and R.E.L. Masters, *Prostitution and Morality*, New York: The Julian Press, 1964; Norman St. John-Stevas, *Law and Morals*, London: Burns and Oastes, 1964.

[3]*Report of the Committee on Homosexual Offenses and Prostitution* (Wolfenden Report), London: Her Majesty's Stationery Office, Cmnd, 247, 1957; Robert Bell, *Social Deviance*, Homewood, Illinois: The Dorsey Press, 1971, p. 229.

[4]Morris Ploscowe, *Sex and the Law*, New Jersey: Prentice-Hall, 1951.

[5]Bell, *op. cit.*, p. 45.

[6]Roger Mitchell, *The Homosexual and the Law*, New York: Arco Publishing, 1969; H.M. Hyde, *The Love that Dare not Speak its Name: A Candid History of Homosexuality in Britain*, Boston: Little, Brown, 1970; Wolfenden Report, *op. cit.*

[7]Wolfenden Report, *op. cit.*, pp. 25-26.

[8]John Livingood, (ed.), *National Institute of Mental Health Task Force on Homosexuality: Final Report and Background Papers*, Rockville, Maryland: National Institute of Mental Health, 1972.

[9]R.S. Morton, *Venereal Diseases*, Baltimore: Penquin Books, 1966.

[10]Bell, *op. cit.*, pp. 93-94, 261-262; Edwin Schur (ed.), *The Family and the Sexual Revolution*, Bloomington, Indiana: Indiana University Press, 1964, pp. 337-338.

[11]Ploscowe, *op. cit.*

[12]Lawrence Friedman, *A History of American Law*, New York: Simon and Schuster, 1973, pp. 179-191.

[13]Simon Dinitz et. al. (eds.), *Deviance: Studies in Definitions, Management, and Treatment*, New York: Oxford University Press, 1975, pp. 319-321; David Granfield, *The Abortion Decision*, Garden City, New York: Doubleday, 1969, pp. 73-76; Edwin Schur, *Crimes Without Victims: Deviant Behavior and Social Policy*, New Jersey: Prentice-Hall, 1965.

[14]Schur, *op. cit.; Roe v. Wade*, 410 U.S. 113 (1973); *Doe v. Bolton*, 410 U.S. 179 (1973).

[15]Glanville Williams, *The Sanctity of Life and the Criminal Law*, New York: Alfred A. Knopf, 1957; O.R. Russell, *Freedom to Die: Moral and Legal Aspects of Euthanasia*, New York: Human Sciences Press, 1975; Charles and Diane Triche, *The Euthanasia Controversy: 1812-1974*, Troy, New York: Whetson Publishing Company, 1975.

[16]St. John-Stevas, *op. cit.; Williams, op. cit.;* Erwin Stengel, *Suicide and Attempted Suicide*, Middlesex, England: Pelican Books, 1969.

[17]Michael Foucault, *Madness and Civilization: A History of Insanity in the Age of Reason*, New York: Random House, 1973; Albert Deutsch, *The Mentally Ill in America*, New York: Columbia University Press, 1949; Friedman, *op cit.*, pp. 514-515; Alan Stone, *Mental Health and the Law*, National Institute of Mental Health Crime and Delinquency Issues, Washington, D.C.: US Government Printing Office, 1976.

[18]John Ashton, *A History of English Lotteries*, London: Leadenhall Press, 1893; Commission on the Review of the National Policy Toward Gambling, *Gambling in America*, Washington, D.C.: US Government Printing Office, 1976.

[19]President's Commission on Law Enforcement and Administration of Justice, *Task Force Report: Drunkenness*, Washington, D.C.: US Government Printing Office, 1967; U.S. Department of Health, Education, and Welfare, *First and Second Reports to the U.S. Congress on Alcohol and Health*, Washington, D.C.: US Government Printing Office, 1972, 1975; National Institute of Mental Health, *Alcoholism and the Law*, Washington, D.C.: U.S. Government Printing Office, 1973.

[20]*Ibid.*

[21]Gilman Udell, *Opium and Narcotic Laws*, Washington, D.C.: US. Government Printing Office, 1963; Edward Brecher, *Licit and Illicit Drugs*, Boston: Little, Brown, 1972; Alfred Lindesmith, *The Addict and the Law*, Bloomington, Indiana: Indiana University Press, 1965; William Eldridge, *Narcotics and the Law*, Chicago: University of Chicago Press, 1967; Troy Duster, *The Legislation of Morality: Laws, Drugs, and Moral Judgement*, New York: Free Press, 1970; The President's Commission on Law Enforcement and Administration of Justice, *Task Force Report: Narcotic and Drug Abuse*, Washington, D.C.: U.S. Government Printing Office, 1967; National Commission on Marijuana and Drug Abuse, *Marijuana: A Signal of Misunderstanding*, and *Drug Use in America: Problems in Perspective*, Washington, D.C.: US Government Printing Office, 1972, 1973.

[22]Edwin Schur, *Narcotic Addiction in Britain and America: The Impact of Public Policy*, Bloomington, Indiana: Indiana University Press, 1962; Schur, *Crimes Without Victims, op. cit.*, pp. 153-154; Schur, "Drug Addiction Under British Policy," *Social Problems*, 9 (1961), pp. 154-166; Alfred Lindesmith, "The British System of Narcotics Control," *Law and Contemporary Problems*, 22 (1957), pp. 138-154.

[23]Sanford Kadish, "Overcriminalization," in Radzinowicz and Wolfgang (eds.), *Crime and Justice: The Criminal in Society*, New York: Basic Books, 1971, p. 57; Hart, *op. cit.*; Schur, *Crimes Without Victims, op. cit.*; Norval Morris and Gordon Hawkins, *The Honest Politicians Guide to Crime Control*, Chicago: University of Chicago Press, 1969; Norval Morris, "Crimes Without Victims: The Law is a Busybody," *New York Times Magazine*, 1 (April, 1973), p. 10; Troy Duster, *The Legislation of Morality*, New York: Free Press, 1970; Herbert Packer, *The Limits of the Criminal Sanction*, Stanford, California: Stanford University Press, 1968.

[24]Reid, *op. cit.*, p. 35.

[25]*Ibid.,* pp. 36-38.

[26]Henry Black, *Black's Law Dictionary,* St. Paul, Minnesota: West Publishing Company, 1968, pp. 71-72, 206, 904.

[27]Robert Bell, *Social Deviance,* Homewood, Illinois: The Dorsey Press, 1976, pp. 93-94, 123-126.

[28]*Ibid.,* pp. 261-262.

[29]Kadish, *op. cit.,* p. 64.

[30]President's Commission on Law Enforcement and Administration of Justice, *Challenge of Crime in a Free Society,* Washington, D.C.: U.S. Government Printing Office, 1967, pp. 235-237.

[31]Kadish, *op. cit.,* p. 64; Reid, *op. cit.,* pp. 38-39.

[32]Kadish, *op. cit.,* pp. 61-63; Reid, *op. cit.,* pp. 39-40.

[33]Kadish, *op. cit.,* p. 65.

[34]Reid, *op. cit.,* p. 40.

[35]Kadish, *op. cit.,* pp. 66-68.

[36]Pursley, *op. cit.,* pp. 97-98.

[37]Sagarin, *op. cit.,* pp. 383-384; Pursley, *op. cit.,* pp. 98-99.

[38]Sagarin, *op. cit.,* pp. 385-388.

[39]*Ibid.*

[40]*Ibid.,* pp. 387-388.

[41]The President's Commission, *op. cit.,* p. 49.

[42]*Ibid.,* p. 53.

[43]*Miller v. California,* dissenting opinion of Justice Douglas, *op. cit.;* The President's Commission, *op. cit.,* 59; Harry Clor, *Obscenity and Public Morality,* Chicago: University of Chicago Press, 1969; John Gagnon and William Simon, "Pornography — Raging Menace or Paper Tiger?," *Trans-Action,* (July, 1967), pp. 41-48; Arthur Knight and Hollis Alpert, "The History of Sex in Cinema: The Stag Film," *Playboy* (November, 1967); David Loth, *The Erotic in Literature,* New York: Julian Messner, 1961; Ned Polsky, *Hustlers, Beats, and Others,* Chicago: Aldine Publishing Company, 1967; Polsky, Pornography, in Sagarin and MacNamera, *Problems of Sex Behavior,* New York: Thomas Y. Crowell, 1968, pp. 268-284.

[44]409 U.S. 109 (1972).

[45]The President's Commission, *op. cit.,* p. 49.

⁴⁶L. Zurcher, G. Kirkpatrick, R. Cushing, and C. Bowman, "The Anti-Pornography Campaign: A Symbolic Crusade," *Social Problems,* 19 (Fall, 1971), pp. 217-238; John Gagnon and William Simon, *The Sexual Scene,* Chicago: Aldine Publishing Company, 1970, pp. 149-150.

⁴⁷Robert Pursley, *Introduction to Criminal Justice,* Encino, California: Glencoe Press, 1977, pp. 113-115; Edwin Schur and Hugo Bedau, *op. cit.;* "Prostitution: A Non-Victim Crime?" *Issues in Criminology,* 8 (1973); Robert Boruchowitz, "Victimless Crimes: A Proposal for the Courts," *Judicature,* 1973, pp. 69-78; Alexander Smith and Harriet Pollack, "Crimes Without Victims," *Saturday Review,* December 4, 1971, pp. 27-29; Edward Davis, "Victimless Crimes — The Case for Continued Enforcement," *Journal of Police Science and Administration,* Gaithersburg, Maryland: ICAP, 1976

⁴⁸*Ibid.*

⁴⁹*Ibid.*

⁵⁰Clinard, *op. cit.,* pp. 536-538; Gagnon and Simon, *op. cit.;* Morris and Hawkins, *op. cit.*

⁵¹Packer, *op. cit.,* p. 304.

⁵²Wolfenden Report, *op. cit.,* p. 40; Schur, *Crimes Without Victims, op. cit.,* pp. 107-110; Edwin Schur and Hugo Bedau, *Crimes Without Victims,* New Jersey: Prentice-Hall, 1975, p. 83.

⁵³Livingood, *op. cit.,* pp. 5-6.

⁵⁴*Ibid.*

⁵⁵Schofield, *op. cit.,* p. 193; R.O.D. Benson, *In Defense of Homosexuality: Male and Female,* New York: Julian Press, 1965; Schur, *Crimes Without Victims, op. cit.,* pp. 110-113.

⁵⁶Bloch and Geis, *op. cit.,* p. 268; Schur, *Crimes Without Victims, op. cit.,* pp. 110-111.

⁵⁷Bell, *op. cit.,* pp. 252-254.

⁵⁸Stiller, *op. cit.,* pp. 17-18.

⁵⁹J.H. Fitch, "Men Convicted of Sex Offences Against Children: A Follow-Up Study," *British Journal of Sociology,* 13 (1962), pp. 18-37; Bagley, *op. cit.;* Don Gibbons, *An Introduction to Criminology,* New Jersey: Prentice-Hall, 1973, pp. 375-405.

⁶⁰Kenneth Eckhardt, "Deviance, Visibility, and Legal Action: The Duty of Support," *Social Problems,* 15 (1968), pp. 470-477.

⁶¹Schur, *op. cit.,* pp. 51-55; Bell, *op. cit.,* pp. 130-132; Harold Rosen (ed.), *Therapeutic Abortion,* New York: Julian Press, 1954, pp. 153-165, 155-174; Williams, *op. cit.,* pp. 192-206; Joseph Fletcher, *Morals and Medicine,* Boston:

Beacon Press, 1960; Norman St. John-Stevas, *Life, Death and the Law*, Blooming-ton, Indiana: Indiana University Press, 1962.

[62]Daniel Callahan, *Abortion: Law, Choice and Morality*, New York: MacMillan, 1970; Thomas Diennes, *Law, Politics and Birth Control*, Urbana, Illinois: University of Illinois Press, 1972; Henry Rudel et al., *Birth Control, Contraception and Abortion*, New York: MacMillan, 1973; Betty Sarvis and Hyman Rodman, *The Abortion Controversy*, New York: Columbia University Press, 1973; St. John-Stevas, *Life, Death, and the Law, op. cit.*

[63]*Ibid.;* Edwin Schur and Hugo Bedau, *Crimes Without Victims*, New Jersey: Prentice-Hall, 1975.

[64]Euthanasia News, *op. cit.,* pp. 2-4.

[65]Russell, *op. cit.;* Jacobovits *op. cit.;* McFadden, *op. cit.;* Ramsey, *op. cit.,* Maguire, Williams, *op. cit.*

[66]*District of Columbia Code,* Annotated, Washington, D.C.: U.S. Govern-ment Printing Office, 2, 1973, 22-2401 to 22-2405, 1463-1488.

[67]Norman Farberow and Edwin Schneidman, *The Cry for Help,* New York: McGraw-Hill, 1961; Schneidman and Farberow, *op. cit.;* Stengel, *op. cit.;* Donald McCormick, *The Unseen Killer: A Study of Suicide, its History, Causes and Cures,* London: Chapman and Hall, 1955; Jack Douglas, *op. cit.;* Albert Cain, *Survivors of Suicide,* Springfield, Illinois: Charles C. Thomas, 1972; David Lester, *Why People Kill Themselves: A Summary of Research Findings on Suicidal Behavior,* Springfield: Charles C. Thomas, 1972; Jack Zusman and David Davidson, *Organizing the Community to Prevent Suicide,* Springfield: Charles C. Thomas, 1972.

[68]Seymour Halleck, *Psychiatry and the Dilemmas of Crime: A Study of Causes, Punishment, and Treatment,* New York: Harper and Row, 1967, pp. 205-318; Karl Menninger, *The Crime of Punishment,* New York: Viking Press, 1968; Kittrie, *op. cit.;* Thomas Szasz, *The Myth of Mental Illness: Foundations of Theory of Personal Conduct,* New York: Harper and Row, 1961.

[69]*Ibid.;* Charles McCaghy, *Deviant Behavior: Crime, Conflict, and Interest Groups,* New York: Macmillan Publishing Company, 1976, pp. 330-340; Thomas Szasz, *Law, Liberty and Psychiatry: An Inquiry into the Social Uses of Mental Health Practices,* New York: Macmillan, 1963; Szasz, *Ideology and Insanity: Essays on the Psychiatric Dehumanization of Man,* Garden City, New York: Doubleday, 1970; Thomas Scheff, *Being Mentally Ill: A Sociological Theory,* Chicago: Aldine, 1966; Seymour Halleck, *The Politics of Therapy,* New York: Science House, 1971.

[70]Clinard, *op. cit.,* pp. 608-611; Brackel and Rock, *op. cit.,* pp. 37, 53-59; McCaghy, *op. cit.,* pp. 333-337.

[71]Brackel and Rock, *op. cit.,* pp. 53-59.

[72]*Ibid.*

[73]Thomas Scheff, "The Societal Reaction to Deviance: Ascriptive Elements

in the Psychiatric Screening of Mental Patients in a Midwestern State," *Social Problems,* 11 (1964), pp. 401-413; Scheff, "Social Conditions for Rationality: How Urban and Rural Courts Deal with the Mentally Ill," *American Behavioral Scientist,* 8 (1964), pp. 21-24; Dorothy Miller and Michael Schwartz, "County Lunacy Commission Hearings: Some Observations of Commitments to a State Mental Hospital," *Social Problems,* 14 (1966), pp. 26-35; L. Kutner, "The Illusion of Due Process in Commitment Proceedings," *Northwestern University Law Review,* 57 (1962), pp. 383-399; Sara Fein and Kent Miller, "Legal Processes and Adjudication in Mental Incompetency Proceedings,"*Social Problems,* 20 (1972), pp. 57-64; James Greenley, "Alternative Views of the Psychiatrist's Role,' *Social Problems,* 20 (1972), pp. 252-262; Henry Steadman, "The Psychiatrist as a Conservative Agent of Social Control," *Social Problems,* 20 (1972), pp. 263-271; "The Administration of Psychiatric Justice: Theory and Practice in Arizona," *Arizona Law Review,* 13 (1971); D.L. Rosenhan, "On Being Sane in Insane Places," *Science,* 179 (1973), pp. 250-258; Judith Rabkin, "Public Attitudes Toward Mental Illness: A Review of the Literature," *Schizophrenia Bulletin,* 10 (1974), pp. 9-33; Bruce Ennis, *Prisoners of Psychiatry: Mental Patients, Psychiatrists, and the Law,* New York: Harcourt, Brace Jovanovich, 1972.

[74]Haskell and Yablonsky, *op. cit.,* pp. 373-380, 381-401; McCaghy, *op. cit.,* pp. 337-340; Sutherland, *op. cit.;* Alan Swanson, "Sexual Psychopath Statutes: Summary and Analysis," *Journal of Criminal law and Criminology,* 51 (1970), pp. 215-218; Ralph Brancale, "Psychiatric and Psychological Investigation of Convicted Sex Offenders, "*American Journal of Psychiatry,* 109 (1952), pp. 17-21; Halleck, *op. cit.;* Kittrie, *op. cit.;* William and Joan McCord, *The Psychopath,* New York: Van Nostrand Company, 1964; Harvey Cleckley, *The Mask of Sanity,* St. Louis: C.V. Mosby, 1941; Gordon Trasler, *The Explanation of Criminality,* London: Routledge and Kegan Paul, 1962; Harrison Gough, "A Sociological Theory of Psychopathy," *American Journal of Sociology,* 53 (1948), pp. 365; Albert Rabin, "Psychopathic (Sociopathic Personality)," in Toch (ed.), *Legal and Criminal Psychology,* New York: Holt, Rinehart and Winston, 1961; Harry Allen et al., "Hostile and Simple Sociopaths: An Empirical Typology," *Criminology,* 9 (1971), pp. 27-47.

[75]*Gambling in America, op. cit.*

[76]*Task Force Report: Organized Crime, op. cit.,* p. 3; New York Commission of Investigation, *The Loan Shark Report,* 17 (1965); Pursley, *op. cit.,* p. 100.

[77]*Ibid.*

[78]*Task Force Report: Organized Crime, op. cit.;* Zola, *op. cit.,* p. 360; Thomas Johnson, "Numbers Called Harlem's Balm," *The New York Times,* March 1, 1971; St. Clair Drake and Horace Clayton, *Black Metropolis: A Study of Negro Life in a Northern City,* New York: Harcourt Brace, 1945, pp. 470-494; McCall, *op. cit.;* William Furlong, "Out of the Bleachers, where the Action Is," *Harpers,* 233 (1966), pp. 49-53; Julian Roebuck, "The Negro Numbers Man as a Criminal Type: The Construction and Application of a Typology," *Journal of Criminal Law and Criminology,* 54 (1963), pp. 48-60.

[79]*Gambling in America, op. cit.*

[80]Pursley, *op. cit.,* p. 100; Edwin Schur and Hugo Bedau, *Victimless Crimes: Two Sides of a Controversy,* New Jersey: Prentice-Hall, 1974.

[81] *The Challenge of Crime in a Free Society, op. cit.,* p. 235.

[82] *Ibid.;* Pursley, *op. cit.,* p. 103.

[83] *Ibid.;* Pursley, *op. cit.,* p. 103.

[84] *Ibid.,* p. 235.

[85] Pursley, *op. cit.,* pp. 105-106; Peter Kratcoski, "Some Alternatives to Criminal Prosecution for the Victimless Crimes of Drunkenness Offenders," *Journal of Alcohol and Drug Addiction,* 18 (Spring, 1973); Rupert Wilkinson, *The Prevention of Drinking Problems: Alcohol Control and Cultural Influences,* New York: Oxford University Press, 1970; Trice and Roman, *op. cit.;* Nimmer, *Two Million Unnecessary Arrests, op. cit.*

[86] *Ibid.;* Clinard, *op. cit.,* p. 485-486.

[87] Harrison Trice, "Alcoholics Anonymous," in Gold and Scarpitti (eds.), *Combatting Social Problems: Techniques of Intervention,* New York: Holt, Rinehart and Winston, 1967, pp. 503-511; Joseph Cook and Gilbert Geis, "Forum Anonymous: The Techniques of Alcoholics Anonymous Applied to Prison Therapy," *Journal of Social Therapy,* 3 (1957), pp. 9-13; Harrison Trice and Paul Roman, "Sociopsychological Predictions of Successful Affiliation with Alcoholics Anonymous," *Social Psychiatry,* 5 (1970), pp. 51-59; Trice and Roman, "Delabeling, Relabeling, and Alcoholics Anonymous,"*Social Problems,* 17 (1970), p. 538; Clinard, *op. cit.,* pp. 486-492.

[88] Pursley, *op. cit.; The Challenge of Crime in a Free Society, op. cit.;* Middendorff, *op. cit.*

[89] *Drug Use in America, op. cit.,* pp. 305-306.

[90] *Ibid.,* pp. 308-309.

[91] *Ibid.,* pp. 309-310; Brecher, *op. cit.,* pp. 69-71; John O'Donnell, *Narcotic Addicts in Kentucky,* Washington, D.C.: U.S. Government Printing Office, U.S. Public Health Service, NIMH, 1969; *The Challenge of Crime in a Free Society, op cit.,* pp. 225-226.

[92] *Drug Use in America, op. cit.,* p. 310; Brecher, *op. cit.,* pp. 72-75.

[93] Brecher, *op. cit.,* pp. 72-77; *The Challenge of Crime in a Free Society, op. cit.,* p. 228.

[94] *Drug Use in America, op. cit.,* p. 310.

[95] *Ibid.,* p. 311; Brecher, *op. cit.,* pp. 71-72, 77-78; *The Challenge of Crime in a Free Society, op. cit.,* pp. 226-227.

[96] *The Challenge of Crime in a Free Society, op. cit.,* pp. 228-229; Brecher, *op. cit.,* p. 78; *Drug Use in Society, op. cit.,* pp. 312-314.

[97] *The Challenge of Crime in a Free Society, op. cit.,* p. 227; Brecher, *op. cit.,*

pp. 78-79; *Drug Use in America, op. cit.,* p. 311; Lewis Yablonsky, *Synanon: The Tunnel Back,* New York: Macmillan, 1965.

[98]Brecher, *op. cit.,* pp. 135-182; *The Challenge of Crime in a Free Society, op. cit.,* p. 227; *Drug Use in America, op. cit.,* pp. 311-312.

[99]Brecher, *op. cit.,* pp. 79-81.

[100]Schur, *Crimes Without Victims, op. cit.,* pp. 159-163; Harry Anslinger and W. Tompkins, *The Traffic in Narcotics,* New York: Funk and Wagnalls, 1953; Anslinger and Will Oursler, *The Murderers,* New York: Farrar, Straus and Company, 1961.

[101]*Drug Use in America, op. cit.;* Brecher, *op. cit.*

[102]Brecher, *op. cit.,* pp. 56-89.

[103]Clinard, *op. cit.,* pp. 430-432.

[104]Lindesmith, *op. cit.;* Reasons, *op. cit.;* Geis, *op. cit.;* Schur, *op. cit.;* President's Commission, *op. cit.,* National Commission, *op. cit.,* Joint Committee of AMA-ABA on Narcotic Drugs, *op. cit.;* Pursley, *op. cit.,* pp. 107-110.

[105]Brecher, *op. cit.,* pp. 521-527.

[106]Anslinger, *op. cit.;* Clinard, *op. cit.,* p. 434 (concerning President Nixon); James Eastland, Chairman, *Marihuana-Hashish Epidemic and its Impact on United States Security,* U.S. Senate, Washington, D.C.: U.S. Government Printing Office, 1974; Kefauver Committee, *op. cit.;* McClellan Subcommittee, *op. cit.;* Carl Chambers et al., "Toward Understanding and Managing Nonnarcotic Drug Abusers," *Federal Probation,* 36 (1972); Richard Schroeder, "The Politics of Drugs," Washington, D.C.: *Congressional Quarterly,* 1975; Philip Baridon, *Addiction, Crime and Social Policy,* Lexington, Massachusetts: D.C. Heath and Company, 1976; Lindesmith, *The Addict and the Law, op. cit.;* Duster, *op. cit.;* Schur, *Narcotic Addiction in Britain and America, op. cit.*

[107]Schur, *Crimes Without Victims, op. cit.,* pp. 174-175; Sagarin, *op. cit.,* pp. 388-389.

[108]*Ibid.*

[109]*Ibid.*

[110]Reid, *op. cit.,* pp. 43-44; Robert Pursley, *Introduction to Criminal Justice,* Encino, California; Glencoe Press, 1977, pp. 95-98; Kadish, *op. cit.,* pp. 67-68.

[111]Reid, *op. cit.,* pp. 43-44.

[112]Reid, *op. cit.,* pp. 44-45; Kadish, *op. cit.,* pp. 66-68; Pursley, *op. cit.,* pp. 95-97.

[113]Kadish, *op. cit.,* pp. 44-45; Robert Rich, *Essays on the Theory and*

Practice of Criminal Justice, Washington, D.C.: University Press of America, 1977, pp. 41-74.

[114]Reid, *op. cit.,* pp. 44-45; Kadish, *op. cit.,* pp. 62-63.

[115]Kadish, *op. cit.,* pp. 62-63.

[116]Reid, *op. cit.,* p. 44; Pursley, *op. cit.,* p. 97.

[117]S. Dinitz, R. Dynes, and A. Clarke (eds.), *Deviance: Studies in Definition, Management and Treatment,* New York: Oxford University Press, 1975, pp. 407-588; President's Commission on Law Enforcement and Administration of Justice, *Task Force Report: Corrections,* Washington, D.C.: U.S. Government Printing Office, 1967, pp. 51-53; Vernon Fox, *Introduction to Corrections,* New Jersey: Prentice-Hall, 1972, pp. 239-250; Harry Allen and Clifford Simonsen, *Corrections in America: An Introduction,* Beverly Hills, California: Glencoe Press, 1975, pp. 342-352.

[118]Robert Wicks, *Correctional Psychology: Themes and Problems in Correcting the Offender,* San Francisco: Canfield Press, 1974, pp. 13-73; Reid, *op. cit.,* pp. 550-561.

[119]Reid, *op. cit.,* pp. 469-662; Wicks, *op. cit.,* pp. 13-73; Task Force Report: Corrections, *op. cit.,* pp. 38-42; Dinitz, Dynes, and Clarke, *op. cit.,* Fox, *op. cit.,* Allen and Simonsen, *op. cit.*

[120]*Ibid.*

Index